THE

Common Core

Teaching K–5 Students to Meet the Reading Standards

Maureen McLaughlin
Brenda J. Overturf

INTERNATIONAL
Reading Association
800 BARKSDALE ROAD, PO BOX 8139
NEWARK, DE 19714-8139, USA
www.reading.org

The International Reading Association attempts, through its publications, to provide a forum for a wide spectrum of opinions on reading. This policy permits divergent viewpoints without implying the endorsement of the Association.

Executive Editor, Publications   Shannon Fortner
Acquisitions Manager   Tori Mello Bachman
Managing Editors   Christina M. Terranova and Susanne Viscarra
Editorial Associate   Wendy Logan
Design and Composition Manager   Anette Schuetz
Design and Composition Associate   Lisa Kochel

Art   Cover Design, Lise Holliker Dykes; Cover and Interior Photography, Maureen McLaughlin; Cover Graphic, antishock and 578foot at Shutterstock

The publisher would appreciate notification where errors occur so that they may be corrected in subsequent printings and/or editions.

Library of Congress Cataloging-in-Publication Data
McLaughlin, Maureen.
  The common core : teaching K-5 students to meet the reading standards / Maureen McLaughlin & Brenda J. Overturf.
    pages cm
  Includes bibliographical references and index.
  ISBN 978-0-87207-815-4
1. Language arts (Elementary)--United States. 2. Language arts (Elementary)--Standards--United States. 3. Language arts--Correlation with content subjects--United States. I. Overturf, Brenda J. II. Title.
  LB1576.M29 2012
  372.6--dc23
                        2012036537

Suggested APA Reference
McLaughlin, M., & Overturf, B.J. (2013). *The Common Core: Teaching K–5 students to meet the Reading Standards*. Newark, DE: International Reading Association.

To Connor and Emma Watkins and Ryan, Olivia, and Julianna Brake—
students in the age of the Common Core
—MM

To Jim, Drew, and Whitney, for your belief, support, and patience
—BJO

Contents

PART II   75
Teaching the Common Core State Standards for Reading

About the Authors

Maureen McLaughlin is a professor of reading education at East Stroudsburg University of Pennsylvania in East Stroudsburg, Pennsylvania, USA. She earned her doctorate at Boston University in reading and language development. Prior to her tenure at East Stroudsburg University, Maureen spent 15 years as a classroom teacher, reading specialist, and department chair in a public school system.

Maureen was a member of the Board of Directors of the International Reading Association from 2005 to 2008, and she will serve as the IRA president in 2013–2014. She was the recipient of IRA's Jerry Johns Outstanding Teacher Educator in Reading Award in 2010. The author of numerous publications about the teaching of reading, reading comprehension, content area literacies, and the Common Core State Standards, Maureen recently published the second editions of *Guided Comprehension in the Primary Grades* and *Guided Comprehension in Grades 3–8* (coauthored with Mary Beth Allen), and in spring 2012, she published *Guided Comprehension for English Learners*. She also wrote *Content Area Reading: Teaching and Learning in an Age of Multiple Literacies* (Allyn & Bacon, 2010). Maureen is currently working on multiple Common Core publications. A frequent speaker at international, national, and state conferences, Maureen is a consultant to schools and universities throughout the world.

Brenda J. Overturf served as a 2009–2012 member of the International Reading Association Board of Directors. While on the Association's board, she chaired a Common Core State Standards Task Force, and she continues as chair of the IRA Common Core Standards Committee.

Brenda began her career as a classroom teacher, teaching 18 years at the elementary and middle school levels. She then served as the Jefferson County Public Schools (Louisville, Kentucky, USA) district reading coordinator for six years, where she led professional development, program design, standards implementation, curriculum alignment, and assessment systems for K–12 districtwide literacy development. In 2005, she entered a partnership with the University of Louisville to head the graduate program in reading education, where she designed and taught K–12 literacy courses, chaired committees, provided leadership for literacy grants and programs, and worked on state literacy task forces and initiatives. Brenda was the director of the University of Louisville Kentucky Reading Project site for K–5 teachers, as well as a partner in a Kentucky Striving Readers grant for adolescent literacy development. She is also past president of the Kentucky Reading Association.

Brenda earned her doctorate with a specialty in literacy education from the University of Louisville. She is a consultant to schools and universities and a conference speaker focused on student literacy achievement. Brenda has numerous publications in press, including *Word Nerds: Teaching All Students to Learn and Love Vocabulary* (Stenhouse). She is currently working on additional publications about the Common Core Standards.

Preface

As literacy professionals, we find ourselves in the midst of the Common Core revolution. This transformation has occurred in what might be described as a whirlwind. As a result, we find ourselves wondering, How do the College and Career Readiness (CCR) Anchor Standards for Reading differ from the Common Core State Standards for Reading? How are the Standards structured? What do the Standards mean? What do various grade levels require? and How can we teach to help our students achieve the Standards? In this book, we respond to these queries and more as we explore the Common Core from its inception to its implementation.

The Common Core: Teaching K–5 Students to Meet the Reading Standards is designed to provide essential knowledge not only about the Standards but also about the literacy practices needed to achieve them. The book is divided into two sections. Part I provides information ranging from the inception of the Standards to their assessment, implementation, and effects on curriculum. Chapter 1 details how to effectively use the Standards, and Chapter 2 focuses on both formative assessment and the instruments being developed by the Common Core assessment consortia. Implementing the Standards is delineated in Chapter 3, and the needs of special populations of students (beginning readers, English learners, students with disabilities, and gifted and talented learners) are addressed in Chapters 4 and 5. The curricular implications of the Standards are explored in Chapter 6.

The College and Career Readiness Anchor Standards for Reading are the foundation of Part II, which contains Chapters 7–16. Each chapter is dedicated to one of the CCR Anchor Standards. The structure of these chapters focuses on these essential questions:

- What does the anchor standard mean?
- How do the Common Core Standards build to the CCR Reading Anchor Standards?
- What literacy skills and strategies support the Reading Standards?
- How can we teach the Reading Standards to ensure that our students achieve?
- How do we connect technology to the Standards?
- How can we integrate other ELA Standards with the Reading Standards?
- What does the teaching of the CCR Anchor Standards look like in today's classrooms?

The book concludes with a hopeful glance at future directions, as the Common Core reaches full implementation. Classroom examples permeate Chapters 7–16. Teachers names used throughout the book are pseudonyms.

The Common Core: Teaching K–5 Students to Meet the Reading Standards is designed to be a focused and easily accessed comprehensive resource for classroom teachers, staff developers, reading specialists, curriculum coordinators, school administrators, and teacher educators. It contains everything necessary to successfully teach the Common Core from kindergarten through grade 5.

Acknowledgments

As always, there are many people to thank for making this book possible. We express our appreciation to all who contributed to the manuscript's development as well as all who enhanced the quality of our lives during the research and writing process. We thank them for their insight, their understanding, and their support.

We are particularly grateful to the following people:

- All the teachers who contributed to this book, especially Andronikki Faneromenity-Andrews, Angela Britton, Ashley Heller, and Francesca McCutchan
- Dayle Henry, Rebecca Norman, and Casey Paone
- Connor Watkins, Juliana Brake, and Olivia Brake
- Stroudsburg Area School District, Pennsylvania
- Our colleagues and our students
- Our families and friends
- Shannon Fortner, Executive Editor of Publications, International Reading Association
- Tori Bachman, Acquisitions Manager, International Reading Association

Finally, we thank you, our readers, for joining us in our quest to discover meaningful ways to successfully teach our students to achieve the Common Core State Standards.

—MM and BJO

PART I

The Evolution of the Common Core State Standards

The mischievous schoolboy who narrates Bob Shea (2008) and Lane Smith's picture book *Big Plans* at one point announces, "Listen up, states! I got big plans! Big plans, I say!" (n.p.). Although the story is about an impish youngster who is in trouble in school and daydreams about all the outrageous things that he plans to accomplish once he is free, the young student might well be commenting on the Common Core State Standards Initiative (www.corestandards.org). Adoption of the Common Core State Standards (CCSS) is, indeed, one of the most ambitious big plans ever to be implemented in the United States.

Carrying out the big plans is a challenge faced by every educator in every state that has adopted the CCSS. Questions abound. Answers are often elusive. In this volume, we respond to queries ranging from how the Standards emerged to exactly what each standard means and the multifaceted nature of effective professional development, implementation, and assessment.

We begin in this Part I introduction by posing and responding to six key questions about the development of the CCSS:

1. How did the Common Core State Standards emerge?

2. What is the goal of the Common Core State Standards Initiative?

3. What are the ELA College and Career Readiness Anchor Standards?

4. What are the Common Core State Standards?

5. How can the Appendixes in the Common Core State Standards document serve as resources?

6. How are the Common Core K–12 English Language Arts Standards organized?

How Did the Common Core State Standards Emerge?

Although more than 90% of states and territories are currently committed to the implementation of the Standards, it is important to note that the CCSS movement did not emerge overnight. Its roots can be traced to a national standards movement that began in the 1990s, when the U.S.

government began to collect evidence that students were not performing as well as expected when compared with their international counterparts. Then, federal discussion around national standards diminished for several reasons. One explanation was that in the United States, education is a right of the state. Few states were inclined to allow the federal government to decide what their students should know and be able to do. A second difficulty arose in determining which standards the students should be required to meet. Disagreements over topics and instructional methods to be included in a set of national standards became the fodder for heated discussions in Washington, DC, as well as among educational organizations. As a result, national discussions quickly dwindled, and each state created its own set of standards. This was an ambitious move that led to varied, state-by-state expectations for students. Some students thrived. Others did not.

As time passed, the world continued to change, and students became more mobile. In 2006, ACT (formerly American College Testing) published *Reading Between the Lines: What the ACT Reveals About College Readiness in Reading*, a document that focused on steps for improving the reading skills of students attending our nation's high schools. New job skills began to emerge, and the United States experienced increased global competition. In 2008, a policy publication from ACT released data that showed that fewer than 2 in 10 eighth graders were on target to be ready for college-level work by the time they graduated from high school. The National Governors Association Center for Best Practices (NGA Center) and the Council of Chief State School Officers (CCSSO) collaborated to develop a state-led initiative that established a set of common standards in English language arts and mathematics to enable students to become college and career ready. The NGA Center and the CCSSO developed the Standards at the request of their members and with substantial encouragement and support from philanthropies, such as the Bill & Melinda Gates Foundation. The group began with a set of college and career readiness standards, which were drafted by a committee representing various education entities. The College and Career Readiness (CCR) Standards were released in draft form in September 2009. After feedback from states, organizations, and the public, the K–12 English Language Arts and Mathematics Common Core State Standards, based on the CCR Standards, were published in June 2010. It was also in 2010 that the federal Race to the Top grant program required state applicants to adopt a common set of standards. This gave many states considerable incentive to adopt the CCSS immediately.

What Is the Goal of the Common Core State Standards Initiative?

The Common Core State Standards Initiative adopted the ACT (2008) definition of college and career readiness, which is the "acquisition of the knowledge and skills a student needs to enroll and succeed in credit-bearing, first-year courses at a postsecondary institution, such as a two- or four-year college, trade school, or technical school...not needing to take remedial courses in college" (p. 1). The goal of the K–12 Common Core State Standards Initiative is for every student in the United States to be college and career ready by the end of high school. The Standards for English Language Arts and Literacy in History/Social Studies, Science, and Technical Subjects, as well as Mathematics, were created to ensure that students are prepared to meet the challenges of college and their future careers. *A First Look at the Common Core and College and Career Readiness*, an ACT (2010) publication using longitudinal college and career readiness data to estimate student performance on the Common Core Standards, reported that we are far from this goal.

What Are the ELA College and Career Readiness Anchor Standards?

As noted in the Common Core State Standards for English Language Arts (NGA Center & CCSSO, 2010), "The CCR standards anchor the document and define general, cross-disciplinary literacy expectations that must be met for students to be prepared to enter college and workforce training programs ready to succeed" (p. 4). The College and Career Readiness Anchor Standards are the foundation of the Common Core State Standards Initiative. In fact, the CCSS are organized according to the CCR Standards.

In the CCSS document, students who are college and career ready are characterized as being able to do the following:

- They demonstrate independence.
- They build strong content knowledge.
- They respond to the varying demands of audience, task, purpose, and discipline.
- They comprehend as well as critique.
- They value evidence.
- They use technology and digital media strategically and capably.
- They come to understand other perspectives and cultures. (NGA Center & CCSSO, 2010, p. 7)

What Are the Common Core State Standards?

The CCSS are comprised of multiple characteristics. According to the Common Core State Standards Initiative (2010), the Standards

- Are aligned with college and work expectations;
- Are clear, understandable and consistent;
- Include rigorous content and application of knowledge through high-order skills;
- Build upon strengths and lessons of current state standards;
- Are informed by other top performing countries, so that all students are prepared to succeed in our global economy and society; and
- Are evidence-based. (para. 4)

How Can the Appendixes in the Common Core State Standards Document Serve as Resources?

There are three ELA appendixes included in the CCSS document. The information in the first, Appendix A, focuses on research supporting key elements of the Standards and provides a glossary of key terms. Text exemplars and sample performance tasks are offered in Appendix B, and examples of student writing are presented in Appendix C.

Each of the appendixes is designed to further inform educators using the CCSS. For example, a rationale for standards focusing on text complexity, as well as a three-part model for measuring text complexity, is provided in Appendix A. In Appendix B, example texts, designated by type and grade level, are followed by a short list of performance tasks. Following each student writing sample in Appendix C, a list of annotations, or comments, about the student's writing is provided. This provides a model for teachers seeking to respond to similar types of writing in their classrooms.

How Are the Common Core K–12 English Language Arts Standards Organized?

The K–12 Common Core Standards are based on the College and Career Readiness Anchor Standards, which describe what students should know and be able to do by the time they enter college or the workplace after high school graduation. Backward mapping is then used in the K–12 Standards to describe what all students should know and be able to do at each grade level. Each standard is an end-of-grade expectation, beginning at kindergarten and advancing in a staircase of complexity to the conclusion of the 12th grade.

The CCR Anchor Standards for English Language Arts and Literacy in History/Social Studies, Science, and Technical Subjects are organized into

- 10 Reading Standards
- 10 Writing Standards
- 6 Speaking and Listening Standards
- 6 Language Standards (This includes two standards on conventions of standard English, one on knowledge of language, and three on vocabulary acquisition and use.)

The K–12 ELA Standards are organized according to the College and Career Readiness clusters: key ideas and details, craft and structure, integration of knowledge and ideas, and range of reading and level of text complexity. In this volume, we focus on the Reading Standards for grades K–5. The Reading Standards encompass the substrands Literature (K–12), Informational Text (K–12), and Foundational Skills (K–5 only). In the Overview of Common Core State Standards for K–5 English Language Arts chart, we delineate how the CCR Anchor Standards relate to the CCSS.

To date, almost all of the U.S. states and territories have adopted the Common Core Standards. Participating states are allowed to add up to 15% of their own content to the CCSS. For example, they might choose to expand the Standards to include a pre-K level or add information about reading comprehension strategies. Unfortunately, at this point, most states have added little content and made few, if any, changes.

The Common Core State Standards Initiative is a big plan indeed.

In Chapter 1, we continue our discussion of the CCSS by focusing on the effective use of both the CCR Anchor Standards and the CCSS. In the remainder of Part I, we explore formative and summative assessment in Chapter 2; implementing the Common Core in Chapter 3; how to address the needs of beginning readers in Chapter 4; concerns about English learners, students with disabilities, and gifted and talented learners in Chapter 5; and curricular issues in Chapter 6.

Overview of Common Core State Standards for K–5 English Language Arts

Standards Strand	Substrand	CCR Anchor Standards Cluster	Focus of Each Standard
Reading	Literature	• Key Ideas and Details	1. Supporting understanding of text; details; inference
			2. Retelling and summarizing, theme
			3. Characters, setting, events
		• Craft and Structure	4. Meanings of words and phrases
			5. Narrative text structure
			6. Point of view
		• Integration of Knowledge and Ideas	7. Visual and multimedia elements
			8. Not applicable to literature
			9. Comparing and contrasting elements and texts
		• Range of Reading and Level of Text Complexity	10. Reading grade-level literature
	Informational Text	• Key Ideas and Details	1. Supporting understanding of text; details; inference
			2. Main idea, summarizing
			3. Connections between events, ideas, and concepts
		• Craft and Structure	4. Meanings of words
			5. Informational text features and structures
			6. Point of view
		• Integration of Knowledge and Ideas	7. Visual and multimedia elements
			8. Author's reasons and evidence
			9. Comparing and contrasting texts
		• Range of Reading and Level of Text Complexity	10. Reading grade-level informational text
	Foundational Skills	• Print Concepts (K and 1)	1. Organization and features of print
		• Phonological Awareness (K and 1)	2. Spoken words, syllables, and sounds
		• Phonics and Word Recognition	3. Grade-level phonics and word analysis skills
		• Fluency	4. Fluent reading of grade-level text
Writing		• Text Types and Purposes	1. Opinion pieces
			2. Informative/explanatory texts
			3. Narrative texts
		• Production and Distribution of Writing	4. Development and organization (grades 3–5)
			5. Revising and editing
			6. Use of technology
		• Research to Build and Present Knowledge	7. Short research projects
			8. Varied sources
			9. Evidence to support analysis, reflection, and research (grades 4 and 5)
		• Range of Writing	10. Extended time frames, varied purposes (grades 3–5)
Speaking and Listening		• Comprehension and Collaboration	1. Collaborative conversations
			2. Main ideas of speaker and multimedia information
			3. Questioning speaker's reasons and evidence
		• Presentation of Knowledge and Ideas	4. Describe, tell, and report orally
			5. Visual and oral presentations
			6. Complete sentences, use of formal English
Language		• Conventions of Standard English	1. Grammar, usage
			2. Capitalization, punctuation, spelling
		• Knowledge of Language	3. Knowledge of language and conventions (grades 3–5)
		• Vocabulary Acquisition and Use	4. Unknown words and phrases
			5. Word relationships and nuances, figurative language
			6. Academic and domain-specific words and phrases

Note. CCR = College and Career Readiness. Reprinted from "The Common Core: Insights Into the K–5 Standards," by M. McLaughlin and B.J. Overturf, 2012, *The Reading Teacher, 66*(2), pp. 156–157.

References

ACT. (2006). *Reading between the lines: What the ACT reveals about college readiness in reading.* Iowa City, IA: Author.

ACT. (2008). *The forgotten middle: Ensuring that all students are on target for college and career readiness before high school.* Iowa City, IA: Author. Retrieved May 31, 2012, from www.act.org/research/policymakers/pdf/ForgottenMiddle.pdf

ACT. (2010). *A first look at the Common Core and college and career readiness.* Iowa City, IA: Author. Retrieved May 31, 2012, from www.act.org/commoncore/pdf/FirstLook.pdf

Common Core State Standards Initiative. (2010). *About the Standards.* Washington, DC: National Governors Association Center for Best Practices & Council of Chief State School Officers.

McLaughlin, M., & Overturf, B.J. (2012). The Common Core: Insights into the K–5 Standards. *The Reading Teacher, 66*(2), 153–164. doi:10.1002/TRTR.01115

National Governors Association Center for Best Practices & Council of Chief State School Officers. (2010). *Common Core State Standards for English language arts and literacy in history/social studies, science, and technical subjects.* Washington, DC: Authors. Retrieved August 3, 2012, from www.corestandards.org/assets/CCSSI_ELA%20Standards.pdf

Children's Literature Cited

Shea, B. (2008). *Big plans.* New York: Hyperion.

CHAPTER 1

How Can Teachers Effectively Use the Standards?

The Common Core State Standards (CCSS) are the focus of educators in more than 90% of the states, as well as in the U.S. territories, such as the U.S. Virgin Islands. This unexpected connection between educators and the Standards has resulted in a communal effort to use the Standards effectively. The movement has an energy about it that appears to be fueled by the need to know everything possible about the Common Core.

As participants in this undertaking, teachers are wondering about numerous aspects of the multifaceted Standards. How the College and Career Readiness (CCR) Anchor Standards support the English Language Arts Standards is a prime example of this. Others include the need to know how to align the Standards with teaching strategies and how to assess students as they engage with the Common Core.

In this chapter, we address teachers' needs. We explore how we, as educators, can effectively use the CCSS with our students. We share our thinking by responding to the following questions:

- How can we use the College and Career Readiness Anchor Standards to gain an overview of the expectations of the CCSS?
- How should we read the Common Core State Standards?
- How can we align the content of the Standards with viable teaching strategies?
- How should we assess students when using the CCSS?
- How should we plan to teach the English Language Arts CCSS?
- What can we do differently to help our students achieve?

How Can We Use the College and Career Readiness Anchor Standards to Gain an Overview of the Expectations of the CCSS?

Because the Common Core State Standards are multifaceted, using them is a complex task. To begin, the College and Career Readiness Anchor Standards provide a foundation for the CCSS. These Anchor Standards are what students should know and be able to do by the end of 12th grade to succeed in college and the workplace. The CCSS are organized according to the CCR Anchor Standards. The CCR Standards are the broader, more general anchors; the CCSS are the more specific benchmarks that underpin each anchor. The grade-specific Common Core State Standards connect to the CCR Standards as benchmarks of what students in each grade level, K–12, should know and be able to do to meet the CCR Standards by the time they graduate from high school. As represented in Table 1.1, the K–12 Common Core State Standards are divided into two general categories: English language arts and mathematics. (The CCSS in their entirety are available online at www.corestandards.org.)

The College Career and Readiness (CCR) Anchor Standards delineate what students must know and be able to do when they graduate from high school. In the English Language Arts Standards, there are four strands of CCR Anchor Standards: Reading, Writing, Speaking and Listening, and Language. Understanding the substance of each CCR Anchor Standard helps us clarify the content of the Common Core State Standards as a whole. For example, the CCR Anchor Standards for Reading are organized into four clusters: Key Ideas and Details, Craft and Structure, Integration of Knowledge and Ideas, and Range of Reading and Level of Text Complexity. Table 1.2 features an overview of the CCR Anchor Standards for Reading.

How Should We Read the Common Core State Standards?

The CCSS are organized by grade level to correspond with the categories of the CCR Anchor Standards. This structure allows teachers to read the Standards both vertically and horizontally.

The designations for the strands of the English Language Arts standards are

RL—Reading Literature

RI—Reading Informational Text

RF—Reading Foundational Skills

W—Writing

SL—Speaking and Listening

L—Language

Further, each standard has an assigned code that describes the strand, grade level, and standard number. For example, the designation RI.4.3 means **R**eading **I**nformational Text, Grade **4**, Standard **3**.

Table 1.1 Overview of the Common Core State Standards

English Language Arts and Literacy in History/Social Studies, Science, and Technical Subjects	Mathematics
Reading • Literature: K–12 • Informational Text: K–12 • Foundational Skills: K–5	Mathematical Practice: K–12 (same for every grade level) Mathematical Content: K–8 and High School
Writing: K–12	
Speaking and Listening: K–12	
Language: K–12 • Conventions • Vocabulary	
Literacy in History/Social Studies: 6–12	
Literacy in Science and Technical Subjects: 6–12	

Table 1.2 Overview of the College and Career Readiness Anchor Standards for Reading

Cluster	Standards
Key Ideas and Details	1. Read closely to determine what the text says explicitly and to make logical inferences from it; cite specific textual evidence when writing or speaking to support conclusions drawn from the text. 2. Determine central ideas or themes of a text and analyze their development; summarize the key supporting details and ideas. 3. Analyze how and why individuals, events, and ideas develop and interact over the course of a text.
Craft and Structure	4. Interpret words and phrases as they are used in a text, including determining technical, connotative, and figurative meanings, and analyze how specific word choices shape meaning or tone. 5. Analyze the structure of texts, including how specific sentences, paragraphs, and larger portions of the text (e.g., a section, chapter, scene, or stanza) relate to each other and the whole. 6. Assess how point of view or purpose shapes the content and style of a text.
Integration of Knowledge and Ideas	7. Integrate and evaluate content presented in diverse media and formats, including visually and quantitatively, as well as in words. 8. Delineate and evaluate the argument and specific claims in a text, including the validity of the reasoning as well as the relevance and sufficiency of the evidence. 9. Analyze how two or more texts address similar themes or topics in order to build knowledge or to compare the approaches the authors take.
Range of Reading and Level of Text Complexity	10. Read and comprehend complex literary and informational texts independently and proficiently.

Note. From *Common Core State Standards for English Language Arts and Literacy in History/Social Studies, Science, and Technical Subjects* (p. 10), by the National Governors Association Center for Best Practices and the Council of Chief State School Officers, 2010, Washington, DC: Authors.

Why Should We Read the Standards Vertically Within Each Grade Level?

Within the CCSS, we need to read vertically to gain a general understanding of how the Standards are structured and what the more specific expectations are for each grade level. For example, if we were teaching third grade, we would read the third-grade Reading Standards 1–10 as detailed in Table 1.3.

When we read all of the English Language Arts Standards for third grade vertically, it becomes clear that as reading teachers, we are responsible not only for the Reading Standards but also for the Writing, Speaking and Listening, and Language Standards. This is a critical point because essential topics, such as vocabulary, which we would traditionally expect to encounter in the Reading Standards, are included in the Language Standards.

Another reason to read the Standards vertically is to get a big picture of what students need to know and be able to do in English language arts by the end of each grade level. Understanding what students are expected to know before and after they are taught at a particular grade level provides the teacher with knowledge of what students should know coming into class and what they will need to know when they leave that class. This is necessary information for understanding students as well as for planning instruction.

Why Should We Read the Standards Horizontally Across Grade Levels?

Within each standard, we read horizontally to fully understand what each grade-level standard actually encompasses. The Common Core State Standards are not structured in a way that allows a

Table 1.3 Overview of the Common Core State Standards for Reading Literature for Grade 3

Cluster	Standards
Key Ideas and Details	1. Ask and answer questions to demonstrate understanding of a text, referring explicitly to the text as the basis for the answers. 2. Recount stories, including fables, folktales, and myths from diverse cultures; determine the central message, lesson, or moral and explain how it is conveyed through key details in the text. 3. Describe characters in a story (e.g., their traits, motivations, or feelings) and explain how their actions contribute to the sequence of events.
Craft and Structure	4. Determine the meaning of words and phrases as they are used in a text, distinguishing literal from nonliteral language. 5. Refer to parts of stories, dramas, and poems when writing or speaking about a text, using terms such as chapter, scene, and stanza; describe how each successive part builds on earlier sections. 6. Distinguish their own point of view from that of the narrator or those of the characters.
Integration of Knowledge and Ideas	7. Explain how specific aspects of a text's illustrations contribute to what is conveyed by the words in a story (e.g., create mood, emphasize aspects of a character or setting). 8. (Not applicable to literature) 9. Compare and contrast the themes, settings, and plots of stories written by the same author about the same or similar characters (e.g., in books from a series).
Range of Reading and Level of Text Complexity	10. By the end of the year, read and comprehend literature, including stories, dramas, and poetry, at the high end of the grades 2–3 text complexity band independently and proficiently.

Note. From *Common Core State Standards for English Language Arts and Literacy in History/Social Studies, Science, and Technical Subjects* (p. 12), by the National Governors Association Center for Best Practices and the Council of Chief State School Officers, 2010, Washington, DC: Authors.

fifth-grade teacher to teach only the fifth-grade standards. To fully understand what each standard requires of students, we need to ensure that all of the preceding standards within a given anchor are being met (see Table 1.4).

For example, the Reading Informational Text Standard 1 for fifth grade is "Quote accurately from a text when explaining what the text says explicitly and when drawing inferences from the text" (NGA Center & CCSSO, 2010, p. 14). However, the standards for grades K–4 for the same benchmark address the following (NGA Center & CCSSO, 2010, pp. 13–14):

Kindergarten: "With prompting and support, ask and answer questions about key details in a text."

Grade 1: "Ask and answer questions about key details in a text."

Grade 2: "Ask and answer such questions as *who, what, where, when, why,* and *how* to demonstrate understanding of key details in a text."

Grade 3: "Ask and answer questions to demonstrate understanding of a text, referring explicitly to the text as the basis for the answers."

Grade 4: "Refer to details and examples in a text when explaining what the text says explicitly and when drawing inferences from the text."

As a result, a more accurate phrasing that details what teachers and students need to know for grade 5's Standard 1 is: Ask and answer questions about key details in a text. Demonstrate

Table 1.4 Common Core State Standards 1–3 (Key Ideas and Details) for Reading Literature for Grades K–5

Grade	Standards
K	1. With prompting and support, ask and answer questions about key details in a text. 2. With prompting and support, retell familiar stories, including key details. 3. With prompting and support, identify characters, settings, and major events in a story.
1	1. Ask and answer questions about key details in a text. 2. Retell stories, including key details, and demonstrate understanding of their central message or lesson. 3. Describe characters, settings, and major events in a story, using key details.
2	1. Ask and answer such questions as *who, what, where, when, why,* and *how* to demonstrate understanding of key details in a text. 2. Recount stories, including fables and folktales from diverse cultures, and determine their central message, lesson, or moral. 3. Describe how characters in a story respond to major events and challenges.
3	1. Ask and answer questions to demonstrate understanding of a text, referring explicitly to the text as the basis for the answers. 2. Recount stories, including fables, folktales, and myths from diverse cultures; determine the central message, lesson, or moral and explain how it is conveyed through key details in the text. 3. Describe characters in a story (e.g., their traits, motivations, or feelings) and explain how their actions contribute to the sequence of events.
4	1. Refer to details and examples in a text when explaining what the text says explicitly and when drawing inferences from the text. 2. Determine a theme of a story, drama, or poem from details in the text; summarize the text. 3. Describe in depth a character, setting, or event in a story or drama, drawing on specific details in the text (e.g., a character's thoughts, words, or actions).
5	1. Quote accurately from a text when explaining what the text says explicitly and when drawing inferences from the text. 2. Determine a theme of a story, drama, or poem from details in the text, including how characters in a story or drama respond to challenges or how the speaker in a poem reflects upon a topic; summarize the text. 3. Compare and contrast two or more characters, settings, or events in a story or drama, drawing on specific details in the text (e.g., how characters interact).

Note. From *Common Core State Standards for English Language Arts and Literacy in History/Social Studies, Science, and Technical Subjects* (pp. 11 and 12), by the National Governors Association Center for Best Practices and the Council of Chief State School Officers, 2010, Washington, DC: Authors.

understanding of key details by asking and answering *who, what, where, when, why,* and *how* questions. Ask and answer questions to demonstrate understanding of a text, referring explicitly to the text. Refer to examples in the text when explaining the text and drawing inferences from it. Quote accurately from a text when explaining what the text says explicitly and when drawing inferences from the text.

Understanding the English language arts expectations for a particular grade level is important (reading vertically), but we must also be aware of the expectations that build to that grade level (reading horizontally).

How Can We Align the Content of the Standards With Viable Teaching Strategies?

Knowing the content of the Standards is essential for teaching students how to meet them. This requires studying each of the Standards in depth and aligning the content with viable teaching strategies. For example, Language Standard 4 for grade 2 (L.2.4) is "Determine or clarify the meaning of unknown and multiple-meaning words and phrases based on *grade 2 reading and content*, choosing flexibly from an array of strategies" (NGA Center & CCSSO, 2010, p. 27).

We could begin by examining a small part of the Standard: "Determine or clarify the meaning of unknown...words." Next, we could brainstorm strategies that we might use to help students meet this section of the Standard. Ideas such as the Semantic Map (Johnson & Pearson, 1984; see Chapter 11) and Semantic Feature Analysis (Johnson & Pearson, 1984; see Chapter 10) might be among those that come to mind.

How Should We Assess Students When Using the CCSS?

We need to assess students in relation to their ability to meet the Standards before we plan effective instruction. Formative assessments provide viable options to determine student knowledge. According to the International Reading Association (2012), formative assessments are ongoing measures that teachers use to obtain information about various aspects of students' literacy. Examples of formative assessments include teacher observations (of discussions, patterned partner reading, and whisper reading); strategy applications, such as the Semantic Question Map (McLaughlin, 2010), the Bookmark Technique (McLaughlin & Allen, 2009), retellings, and summaries; and brief written responses, such as Tickets Out (McLaughlin, 2012).

We can begin by using formative assessments to determine the degree of students' background knowledge. The results of such assessments provide a beginning point for effective instruction and illuminate any gaps in knowledge that may exist. Within each standard and across all of the standards, we can also use formative assessments to measure student progress.

Formative assessments occur every day during teaching and learning and provide information that informs multiple processes. Using formative assessments is not only an effective way to monitor student progress but also a viable way to glean information for planning future instruction. (Chapter 2 goes into further detail about formative assessment.)

How Should We Plan to Teach the English Language Arts CCSS?

According to the Common Core State Standards document, the ELA Standards are based on an integrated model of literacy, with expectations for research and media skills embedded throughout. Intentionally, there are no specific teaching strategies recommended. Instead, the document advocates flexibility in teaching methods. This means that teachers will need to find resources and plan curricula so their students can meet the English Language Arts Standards. First, however, teachers will need to study the Standards and decide what they mean.

What Can We Do Differently to Help Our Students Achieve?

The Common Core Standards are different from many state standards in terms of structure and content. For example, when considering structure, the CCSS are directly linked to the College and Career Readiness Standards, whereas state standards have traditionally stood on their own. When thinking about content, the English Language Arts Standards focus on skills such as interpretation, argumentation, and literary analysis, whereas more traditional standards focus on reader response and comprehension.

Elementary teachers who have been implementing the ELA Standards find that their thought processes about curricula, instruction, and assessment are being continually challenged. Even though standards for each grade level are provided, they are broad, and there is little direction about how to teach students to meet them. In fact, that is left for the teachers to determine. As stated in the introduction to the Common Core Standards (NGA Center & CCSSO, 2010), "By emphasizing required achievements, the Standards leave room for teachers, curriculum developers, and states to determine how those goals should be reached and what additional topics should be addressed" (p. 4). Yet, the expectations have clearly been set for students to be able to read texts on grade level with appropriate text complexity and write, speak, listen, and use language effectively. This has left educators wondering how to teach the aspects of literacy emphasized in the Standards.

Many teachers have been finding that they need to adapt their instruction to help students meet the expectations of the Standards. An example of how instruction may need to be different can be found in the challenges of Reading Standard 8 for Informational Text. It focuses on how an author uses reasoning and evidence to support points in informational text. It is associated with College and Career Readiness Reading Anchor Standard 8, which states that by the end of high school, students will be able to "delineate and evaluate the argument and specific claims in a text, including the validity of the reasoning as well as the relevance and sufficiency of the evidence" (NGA Center & CCSSO, 2010, p. 10). In Reading Standard 8 for Informational Text for grades K–5, teachers are responsible for helping students learn a progression of skills that lay the foundation for middle school and high school instruction about using formal arguments to persuade a reader. The K–5 skill progressions for this standard are delineated in Table 1.5.

Of course, before students can analyze a text to determine the validity of the author's reasoning and the sufficiency of evidence, the students must first be able to comprehend the text. Thus, reading comprehension strategies still need to be taught. A number of volumes about explicitly teaching reading comprehension strategies have been published (e.g., Harvey & Goudvis, 2007; McLaughlin, 2010; McLaughlin & Allen, 2009). The research purports that comprehension is a multifaceted process that typically involves strategies such as activating relevant background knowledge, monitoring, visualizing, self-questioning, inferring, summarizing, and evaluating. Teaching these strategies helps enable students in each grade level to meet the expectations of all the CCR Anchor Standards, but especially Substrand 10: Range of Reading and Level of Text Complexity.

Mary, a fourth-grade teacher in Kentucky, is an example of an educator who has experienced the challenge of teaching her students what they need to know to read successfully, while simultaneously focusing

Table 1.5 Common Core State Standard 8 for Reading Informational Text for Grades K–5

Grade	Standard
K	With prompting and support, identify the reasons an author gives to support points in a text.
1	Identify the reasons an author gives to support points in a text.
2	Describe how reasons support specific points the author makes in a text.
3	Describe the logical connection between particular sentences and paragraphs in a text (e.g., comparison, cause/effect, first/second/third in a sequence).
4	Explain how an author uses reasons and evidence to support particular points in a text.
5	Explain how an author uses reasons and evidence to support particular points in a text, identifying which reasons and evidence support which point(s).

Note. From *Common Core State Standards for English Language Arts and Literacy in History/Social Studies, Science, and Technical Subjects* (pp. 13 and 14), by the National Governors Association Center for Best Practices and the Council of Chief State School Officers, 2010, Washington, DC: Authors.

on the instructional methods and materials necessary for students to meet the Common Core Standards. She has also observed that her teaching emphases have changed. Mary notes,

> Before the Common Core, much of my reading instruction focused on teaching reading comprehension strategies. Our state standards were pretty explicit about what to teach. I knew exactly what to teach and which strategies to use. With the Common Core, I find myself working with other teachers, studying each standard, trying to decide what the standard means and what students should be able to do when they achieve it. Once we determine that, we need to think about what the Standards should look like in practice and determine what kind of instruction it will take to meet them. We also need to make sure we are using appropriate text complexity in instruction and integrating good formative assessments.

Previously, with state standards, Mary planned reading instruction with a focus on comprehension. She spent time introducing the text, teaching essential vocabulary, and encouraging students to make predictions and ask questions about the text. She taught comprehension strategies such as making connections, monitoring, visualizing, and summarizing. She also invited students to respond to the text in a variety of ways. Mary taught those skills and strategies that were clearly delineated in the state standards. She documented what she had taught and noted students' progress in meeting the state standards through formative assessments and required district measures.

To meet the CCSS, Mary knows that her students still need to be able to comprehend text. Consequently, in her teaching, Mary knows that she needs to continue teaching her students not only to use a repertoire of reading comprehension strategies, which are not emphasized in the CCSS, but also to learn other ideas that are stressed in the Common Core. As Mary notes, "I still teach comprehension strategies because my students definitely need them, but now I need to teach more."

Since they began teaching the Common Core State Standards, Mary and her colleagues have realized that teaching the concepts embedded in the English Language Arts Standards cannot be accomplished in a series of isolated lessons. The teachers know that they must integrate what they know about best practices in the teaching of reading, writing, speaking and listening, and language and the CCSS every day. Comprehension instruction remains a critical curricular component, as the Standards are interwoven in lessons across the curriculum. In Standards-based lessons, teaching methods need to be carefully planned, and the content needs to be well coordinated. Teaching the Common Core State Standards is a complex task. They cannot simply be checked off a list.

These teachers integrate the Standards when they plan instruction. For example, when teaching CCR Anchor Standard 2 for Reading for fourth grade, Mary integrates a number of Standards: Reading Literature Standards 1 and 6, Reading Informational Text Standard 8, Speaking and Listening Standards 1 and 2, Language Standard 6, and several Writing Standards. For example, Reading Standard 2 for fourth grade for Literature is "determine a theme of a story, drama, or poem from details in the text; summarize the text" (NGA Center & CCSSO, 2010, p. 12), and for Informational Text is "determine the main idea of a text and explain how it is supported by key details; summarize the text" (NGA Center & CCSSO, 2010, p. 14). To teach CCR Standard 2 for Reading for fourth grade, Mary plans lessons about inferring, how to determine an author's message, how to summarize, and how to prepare an explanation of the text. She rarely teaches a reading lesson that does not involve identifying text-based evidence to support conclusions, so she has to teach her students how to pull words from the text that will support their explanations (CCR Anchor Standard 1).

With literature, Mary teaches her students to infer the author's takeaway message (theme) and why the author values it (Reading Literature Standard 1). Her students learn that *theme* is the vocabulary word for *takeaway message*, plus they learn academic language found in the text selection. With informational text, students learn the term *main ideas* plus domain-specific vocabulary found in the text (Language Standard 6). Mary teaches her class to determine the author's point of view (Reading Literature Standard 6) because she believes that the point of view often reveals a lot about why the author may have written the text. For texts in which the author states an opinion, she teaches her students to determine claims the author has made and analyze the author's reasons and evidence that support those claims (Reading Informational Text Standard 8).

Mary uses many instructional techniques in which students participate in collaborative conversations about the theme or the main ideas and key details of the text (Speaking and Listening Standard 1). She also teaches her fourth-grade students to write narratives with an obvious theme (Writing Standards 3 and 9), develop opinion pieces that include reasons supported by facts and details (Writing Standard 1), and create informational essays that include supporting facts and details (Writing Standard 2). Mary states,

> For my students, learning a concept such as author's purpose now takes a lot of whole-group and small-group discussion about text, writing, use of graphic organizers, and interactive experiences involving art, drama, and technology. I need to engage my students in different types of lessons for them to become critical readers of text.

In Chapter 2, we discuss formative assessment: We define it, focus on the role that it plays in the successful implementation of the Common Core State Standards, and detail practical classroom applications.

ESSENTIAL RESOURCES

- Harvey, S., & Goudvis, A. (2007). *Strategies that work: Teaching comprehension for understanding and engagement* (2nd ed.). Portland, ME: Stenhouse.
- McLaughlin, M. (2010). *Guided Comprehension in the primary grades* (2nd ed.). Newark, DE: International Reading Association.
- McLaughlin, M., & Allen, M.B. (2009). *Guided Comprehension in grades 3–8* (Combined 2nd ed.). Newark, DE: International Reading Association.

References

Harvey, S., & Goudvis, A. (2007). *Strategies that work: Teaching comprehension for understanding and engagement* (2nd ed.). Portland, ME: Stenhouse.

International Reading Association. (2012). *Statement on formative assessment*. Newark, DE: Author.

Johnson, D.D., & Pearson, P.D. (1984). *Teaching reading vocabulary* (2nd ed.). New York: Holt, Rinehart and Winston.

McLaughlin, M. (2010). *Guided Comprehension in the primary grades* (2nd ed.). Newark, DE: International Reading Association.

McLaughlin, M. (2012). Tickets out. *The Reading Teacher, 65*(7), 477–479. doi:10.1002/TRTR.01071

McLaughlin, M., & Allen, M.B. (2009). *Guided Comprehension in grades 3–8* (Combined 2nd ed.). Newark, DE: International Reading Association.

National Governors Association Center for Best Practices & Council of Chief State School Officers. (2010). *Common Core State Standards for English language arts and literacy in history/social studies, science, and technical subjects.* Washington, DC: Authors. Retrieved August 3, 2012, from www.corestandards.org/assets/CCSSI_ELA%20 Standards.pdf

CHAPTER 2

Assessment and the Common Core

ssessment and the Common Core State Standards (CCSS) are inextricably linked. We use formative assessment while we teach, and we use summative assessments to determine what our students have learned. We also use Partnership for Assessment of Readiness for College and Careers (PARCC; 2010), Smarter Balanced (2010), and other assessment consortia–developed resources to assess how well students have met the Standards.

According to the International Reading Association (IRA; 2012), formative assessment is an ongoing, goal-based process that occurs during teaching and learning. The results of formative assessment are used to check student understanding and inform instruction, whereas summative assessment documents student learning and school accountability. Summative assessment occurs after learning. It includes high-stakes tests and typically receives more public attention. McTighe and O'Connor (2005) distinguish between formative and summative assessments by viewing formative assessment as a means of improving learning, and summative assessment as a way to provide reliable information about what has been achieved.

In this chapter, we focus on these two aspects of assessment as they relate to the CCSS: formative assessment, which we use every day in our classrooms to help us understand students' progress, and summative assessments, such as those that have been developed by the Common Core assessment consortia. The latter are administered annually to measure students' progress in meeting the Common Core Standards. We also explore how we can prepare students to be successful when engaging in both types of assessment.

Particular questions that we address in this chapter are the following:

- What is formative assessment?
- How does formative assessment relate to the CCSS?
- What are examples of formative assessment strategies that we can use in our teaching?
- What is summative assessment?
- What CCSS assessments are being developed by the federally funded consortia?

What Is Formative Assessment?

Formative assessment is a goal-based process that provides descriptive feedback to teachers and students for use in adjusting both teaching and learning. In formative assessment, teachers and students share responsibility for learning. Then, they use the results to improve student learning.

Peer and self-assessment can also be viewed as elements of formative assessment. As Heritage (2010) notes, both processes evince the depth of student thinking and how well they understand the learning goals.

It is important to note that formative assessment is not quizzes or tests. It is not graded. It is not associated with rubrics. It also has a research history that goes back more than 20 years and a teaching history that more than likely extends to the first teacher–student encounter.

Black and Wiliam (1998), often credited with writing about this topic first, note that formative assessment is everything in which teachers and students engage that provides information to be used as feedback to modify teaching and learning experiences. Shepard (2005) notes that formative assessment is a collaborative process in which how to improve learning is negotiated between the teacher and the student. Weber (1999, p. 26) proposes that formative assessment suggests future steps for teaching and learning. Such steps might result from observations that allow us to determine how well a student contributed to a class discussion, or informal writing that documents whether a student is able to apply a particular skill or strategy. Formative assessment not only helps reinforce how students learn and what students know but also helps identify what remains unclear.

Menken (2000) reminds us that effective assessments should be deeply entwined with teaching and learning driven by standards. Timely feedback on the part of both the teacher and the students is an essential ingredient of formative assessment. Figure 2.1 illustrates how teachers can base their instruction on the Common Core State Standards and use formative assessment to engage in continuous improvement.

Figure 2.1 Common Core State Standards Continuous Improvement Teaching Loop

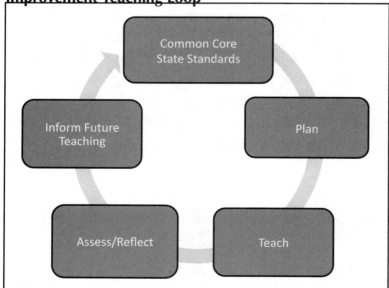

Formative assessment is a natural part of teaching and learning (McLaughlin, 2010a). Formative assessment strategies include informal writing, strategy applications, short written responses, and teacher observation, which occurs during everyday learning experiences.

Researchers agree that formative assessment is characterized by the following:

- *Specified learning goals*—Formative assessment has a purpose. It is goal based. Results of the assessment strategies provide information that can be actively used to show how well the students are meeting the goals and to improve teaching and learning.

- *Collaboration*—Both teachers and students have active roles in formative assessment. Teachers plan lessons that integrate formative assessment strategies. They also observe, review, and make changes in their teaching based on descriptive feedback provided through student responses. Students actively engage with multiple formative assessment strategies every day. They use descriptive feedback from teachers to improve their learning.

- *Dynamic nature*—Formative assessment is active. It occurs during teaching and learning, is interwoven into lessons, and changes based on the nature of the activity. Formative assessment is ongoing and provides multiple measures of student learning.

- *Descriptive feedback to teachers and students*—As students actively engage in learning, they create feedback about their performances that is provided to teachers. Teachers typically use observation to record descriptive feedback about students' engagement in formative assessment. Then, teachers provide specific suggestions to students about how to improve.

- *Continuous improvement*—Teachers and students use the descriptive feedback to make meaningful adjustments in teaching and learning. It is important to note that we, as teachers, should be as specific as possible in our feedback to students. Complimenting them on their work does not provide direction for their work. Specific comments, such as those that follow, provide focus and purpose for students' revisions:

  > "In your literature response journal, you said you liked *The Three Little Wolves and the Big Bad Pig* by Eugene Trivizas better than the *The True Story of the Three Little Pigs* by Jon Scieszka, but you didn't tell why. Will you please share at least two reasons why you like the *The Three Little Wolves and the Big Bad Pig* better? You might want to think about the characters, setting, problem, and how the problem was resolved."

  > "You need to develop your description of the main character in the story you wrote. Questions to consider could be, How old is she? What does she look like? What can you tell us about her background?"

Formative assessment helps teachers differentiate instruction and helps students increase their achievement. Both help close the gap between what students understand at a given point and their achievement of the desired learning goals. Teachers use the information they glean from formative assessment to continually inform their understanding of students' strengths and needs, and then they use what they have learned to provide the most appropriate instruction for each student (IRA, 2012). Formative assessment supports learning as it occurs. It is a multifaceted information source that helps us use assessment results to provide appropriate reading instruction for all students. It also provides students with multiple opportunities for success.

How Does Formative Assessment Relate to the CCSS?

Formative assessment is not new. As teachers, we have been using it for decades—if not for centuries. We teach, observe student responses, and plan our next steps based on the descriptive feedback provided by formative assessment. The good news about its relation to the Common Core State Standards is that its value has finally been acknowledged, and although summative measures such as PARCC (2010) and Smarter Balanced (2010) are also being employed, in everyday teaching and learning, formative assessment is the focus.

When considering formative assessment's relation to the CCSS, IRA (2012) notes that teachers can use formative assessment to gain insights into student progress in all areas, including interaction with increasingly complex text. Formative assessment measures student growth and informs teachers' ongoing efforts to help students reach the Common Core State Standards. Assessing students' needs and strengths is an integral facet of meeting the Standards. Formative assessment is unique in its ability to meet this need.

It is important to remember that formative assessment strategies often address more than one Standard. As the ELA Common Core Standards (NGA Center & CCSSO, 2010) document states, "While the Standards delineate specific expectations in reading, writing, speaking, listening, and language, each standard need not be a separate focus for instruction and assessment. Often, several standards can be addressed by a single rich task" (p. 5).

What Are Examples of Formative Assessment Strategies That We Can Use in Our Teaching?

We use numerous formative assessment strategies in our teaching every day. We use the results to gauge student understanding and to inform our practice. Examples that we focus on in this section are the Concept of Definition Map (Schwartz & Raphael, 1985), Bookmark Technique (McLaughlin & Allen, 2009), the Lyric Summary (McLaughlin, 2010b, 2012a), discussion, Tickets Out (McLaughlin, 2012b), and teacher observation. Other formative assessment strategies are featured in Chapters 7–16.

Concept of Definition Map

We use the Concept of Definition Map (Schwartz & Raphael, 1985) to teach students to make connections to a focus term by responding to questions such as "What is it?" "What is it like?" and "What are some examples?" Students build personal understandings by connecting the new information to prior knowledge. Then, they can create a Concept of Definition Map Summary based on their completed maps.

When we observe students completing these maps or review the completed graphic organizers, we can discern what students understand about the focus term and its various characteristics, as well as how well they can summarize.

This formative assessment strategy can be used to support CCSS, such as Language Standard 4, in which students are required to determine words' meanings.

Bookmark Technique

We encourage students to engage in the Bookmark Technique (McLaughlin & Allen, 2009) to monitor their comprehension while reading. Students make four decisions related to the text: (1) the most interesting part; (2) a vocabulary word that the whole class needs to discuss; (3) something that was confusing; and (4) a chart, map, graph, or illustration that helped them understand what they read.

As we observe students completing the bookmarks or review their final efforts, we can discover multiple types of information about student performance. These include students' understanding of the text, knowledge of vocabulary words, and ability to use supports such as maps, graphs, and illustrations. This formative assessment strategy can be used to support the multiple CCSS that require students to read narrative or informational text, such as Reading Standard 2 and Reading Standard 10 for both literature and informational text.

Lyric Summary

The Lyric Summary (McLaughlin, 2010b) offers an alternative format for students to create text summaries. This small-group approach to summarizing provides opportunities for students to use an alternative representation of thinking to share summaries. To begin, students gather in small groups and brainstorm lists of facts that they know about a topic of informational text or about the elements in narrative text. Next, they choose a song that they all know. Then, using their brainstormed lists, they write new lyrics to the song. Finally, each small group sings its Lyric Summary for the class.

When we observe students creating and performing their Lyric Summaries, we gain insights into their ability to work collaboratively, brainstorm ideas, summarize what they know, and transform the information into song lyrics.

This formative assessment strategy can be used to support CCSS, such as Reading Literature Standard 2, Reading Informational Text Standard 2, Writing Standard 8, and Speaking and Listening Standard 2, in which students are required to summarize narrative or informational text.

Discussion

Discussions are "forums for collaboratively constructing meaning and for sharing responses" (Almasi, 1996, p. 2). Gambrell (1996) notes that these collaborations integrate listening, speaking, and thinking skills. Because of the dynamic nature of these discussions, the meanings that readers construct are continually transformed by their experiences, interactions with others, and information from the text (Almasi, 1996). This social interaction is another aspect of literacy that is underpinned by Vygotsky's (1978) research. Discussion is a process that has cognitive, social, and affective dimensions. It affords students opportunities to engage in higher order thinking, interact with others, and take ownership of their learning (Almasi, 1996). Assessment feedback can be recorded through teacher observation or peer review.

This formative assessment strategy can be used to support many Common Core State Standards, particularly Speaking and Listening Standard 1, in which students are asked to participate in collaborative conversations.

Tickets Out

When using Tickets Out (McLaughlin, 2012b), students reflect on what they have learned and share two types of information: (1) What is the most important thing that you learned during class today? and (2) What questions do you have about what you learned today? Each student's response to what he or she learned that day is recorded on the front of an index card or blackline, and one question that the students may have is written on the back of the card or on the blackline. Students need only about five minutes to complete their tickets.

This type of writing is called Tickets Out because we collect the tickets as we stand at the door at the end of class. When the students hand us their tickets, they are able to leave the classroom.

After the students leave, it takes just a few minutes to read their tickets. We collect the tickets with the front side facing up so we can quickly read all the responses about the most important thing the students learned. As we read, we should be careful to set aside any responses that may need clarification. Then, we turn over the class tickets and read the questions that students have about their learning. As we read these, we should set aside questions that we think we need to respond to in a whole-group setting. This is often only four or five questions because several of them may be similar. Reading the tickets only takes about five minutes. The next day, we can begin class by clarifying any necessary information and responding to the students' questions.

This formative assessment strategy can be used to support CCSS, such as Reading Informational Text Standards 2 and 10.

Using Observation to Glean Student Feedback From Formative Assessment

When we integrate formative assessment in our teaching, we need to have a way to record and maintain information about each student. Observation provides opportunities for us to gather such information about students' engagement in all aspects of literacy. For example, we can observe if we want to assess students' fluency, record ideas about their engagement, or comment on students' roles in collaborative activities. Observation allows us to capture the essence of a live performance by watching students as they engage in a task. Observations are purposeful and offer evidence of student motivation, communication, interaction, risk taking, collaboration, and critical and creative thinking.

Before we begin observing, we need to establish a purpose and determine how we will use the information we glean. For example, if we are observing a student who is doing an oral retelling, we can use a checklist that includes information such as the characters, setting, problem, attempts to resolve, resolution, and a section for recording additional comments. In contrast, if we are observing a student's contribution to a cooperative activity, our checklist might include items such as the student's preparation for the group's work, engagement with peers, and contributions.

One way to organize and manage observations is to use a clipboard (McLaughlin, 2010a). We attach a sheet of mailing labels to a clipboard, with a label for each student in the class; student names are preprinted on each label. After we observe a student, we record our notes on a mailing label and date it. Then, we remove the label from the clipboard and place it on a piece of paper either in the student's portfolio or in his or her observation folder. The names of students who have not yet been observed remain on the clipboard. When all students have been observed, the mailing labels are replenished. As students are observed multiple times, the completed labels are placed chronologically on the designated sheet in either the portfolio or observation folder. This ongoing record of observations offers a running history of the student's engagement with formative assessments throughout a marking period and, eventually, throughout the year.

Observation annotations can help us remember specific attributes of student performance, while simultaneously providing informal assessment information for each student. Keeping a dated record of student observations accommodates Tomlinson and McTighe's (2006) suggestion that we gather a "photo album" rather than a "snapshot" of evidence of student performance (p. 60). Using the results of multiple measures helps us differentiate instruction based on more accurate assessments of our students' learning needs.

It is important to note that there is no magic number of observations that should be completed each day. Starting slowly is a good way to begin. After all the students have been observed a few times, we typically find a comfort level with the timing of this process.

What Is Summative Assessment?

As teachers, we use both formative and summative assessment. Each of these types of assessment has particular characteristics, ranging from how often students engage in them to their informal and formal natures. For example, formative assessment is ongoing, classroom based, and informal. Summative assessment usually occurs at definitive times, such as the end of a chapter, a theme, or grading period and is a more formal type of assessment. Accountability is measured on a single day with a single summative test, but accountability is established across the school year when formative assessment is used on a regular basis in the classroom.

Summative assessments are usually more complex than formative assessments and take a longer period of time to complete. Examples of summative assessments include exhibitions, inquiry-based projects, and teacher-designed or textbook-related tests. These assessments are typically evaluated through the use of rubrics, or scoring guides, which we share with students before the assessment begins.

What CCSS Assessments Are Being Developed by the Federally Funded Consortia?

Five federally funded state assessment consortia have been approved: two comprehensive consortia, two alternate assessment consortia, and an English-language proficiency assessment consortium. The work of each is detailed in the Center for K–12 Assessment & Performance Management at ETS (K–12 Center at ETS; 2012) guide *Coming Together to Raise Achievement: New Assessments for the Common Core State Standards*. The publication provides a general overview of both standards and assessments, describes what it means for states involved in the consortia, and updates the progress of the five state assessment consortia. It also includes the future opportunities for each. The five assessment consortia are PARCC (2010), the Smarter Balanced Assessment Consortium (2010), the Dynamic Learning Maps (DLM) Consortium, the National Center and State Collaborative (NCSC) Consortium, and the Assessment Services Supporting ELs through Technology Systems (ASSETS) of the Wisconsin Department of Public Instruction and the World-Class Instructional Design and Assessment (WIDA) Consortium.

As we discuss the new assessments, we should consider the following seven elements viewed as common to successful assessment systems:

1. The student assessment process is guided by common standards and grounded in a thoughtful, standards-based curriculum. It is managed as part of a tightly integrated system of standards, curriculum, assessment, instruction, and teacher development.
2. A balance of assessment measures that includes evidence of actual student performance on challenging tasks that evaluate applications of knowledge and skills.
3. Teachers are integrally involved in the development of curriculum and the development and scoring of assessment measures for both the on-demand portion of state or national examinations and local tasks that feed into examination scores and course grades.

4. Assessment measures are structured to continuously improve teaching and learning.

5. Assessment and accountability systems are designed to improve the quality of learning and schooling.

6. Assessment and accountability systems use multiple measures to evaluate students and schools.

7. New technologies enable greater assessment quality and information systems that support accountability. (Darling-Hammond, 2010, pp. 3–5)

PARCC and Smarter Balanced

The publication *Coming Together to Raise Achievement: New Assessments for the Common Core State Standards* (K–12 Center at ETS, 2012) recounts the developments in PARCC (2010) and Smarter Balanced (2010), both of which received competitive grants from the U.S. Department of Education to develop new assessment systems by consortia of 15 or more states.

Both PARCC and Smarter Balanced committed to building assessment systems for grades 3–8 and high school that meet the following criteria:

- Builds upon **shared standards** in mathematics and English language arts (ELA) for college- and career-readiness;
- Measures **individual growth** as well as proficiency;
- Measures the extent to which each student is on track, at each grade level tested, toward **college or career readiness** by the time of high school completion; and
- Provides **information that is useful** in informing:
  - Teaching, learning, and program improvement;
  - Determinations of school effectiveness;
  - Determinations of principal and teacher effectiveness for use in evaluations and the provision of support to teachers and principals; and
  - Determinations of individual student college- and career-readiness, such as determinations made for high school exit decisions, college course placement to credit-bearing classes, or college entrance. (K–12 Center at ETS, 2012, p. 15)

Both consortia expect to be prepared with field-tested, technology-based assessments by the 2014–2015 school year.

PARCC has designed model content frameworks to help educators understand how to align curricula with the CCSS for the new assessments.

> The purpose of the PARCC system is to increase the rates at which students graduate from high school prepared for success in college and the workplace. To reach this goal, PARCC intends the assessments to help educators increase student learning by providing data throughout the school year to inform instruction, interventions, and professional development as well as to improve teacher, school, and system effectiveness. The assessments will be designed to provide valid, reliable, and timely data; provide feedback on student performance; help determine whether students are college- and career-ready or on track; support the needs of educators in the classroom; and provide data for accountability, including measures of growth. (K–12 Center at ETS, 2012, p. 16)

(To keep pace with PARCC's continuing developments, visit parcconline.org.)

The design of the Smarter Balanced Assessment Consortium (Smarter Balanced) is intended to strategically "balance" summative, interim, and formative assessment through an integrated system of standards, curriculum, assessment, instruction, and teacher development, while providing accurate year-to-year indicators of students' progress toward college- and career-readiness. (K–12 Center at ETS, 2012, p. 24)

Smarter Balanced contracted with a national panel of experts in **fall 2012** to develop exemplar modules of formative assessment tasks and tools in ELA and mathematics for Grades 3–8 and 11. Six exemplar instructional modules will be developed for each grade level, three in mathematics and three in ELA. Each module will address one or two learning progressions and will include formative tasks, scoring rubrics and samples of student work at multiple performance levels. (K–12 Center at ETS, 2012, p. 31)

(To stay informed about updates concerning Smarter Balanced, visit www.smarterbalanced.org.)

Dynamic Learning Maps and the National Center and State Collaborative

Two alternate assessment consortia were also federally funded: the DLM and the NCSC (K–12 Center at ETS, 2012). These consortia were charged to create assessments "for those students with the most significant cognitive disabilities, who are unable to participate in general state assessments even with appropriate accommodations" (K–12 Center at ETS, 2012, p. 33). These measures were also planned to be ready for use by the 2014–2015 school year. The Wisconsin Department of Public Instruction, in collaboration with the Consortium, created ASSETS, the English-language proficiency assessment project. This was planned to be implemented for the 2015–2016 school year.

These new alternate assessments will be aligned to the Common Core State Standards (CCSS) and are expected to fit cohesively within the comprehensive assessment systems under development by the federal grant recipients: the Partnership for Assessment Readiness for College and Careers (PARCC) and the Smarter Balanced Assessment Consortium (Smarter Balanced). Both DLM and NCSC are to be ready for use by the 2014–15 school year, the same year in which the comprehensive assessment systems will be operational. (K–12 Center at ETS, 2012, p. 33)

The purpose of the DLM assessment system is to significantly improve the academic outcomes of students with the most significant cognitive disabilities, thereby improving their preparedness for postsecondary options and the world of work. The assessment system will be designed to provide useful, timely diagnostic information and strong instructional support to teachers through a highly customizable system of instructionally embedded and end-of-year assessments.
In addition, professional development resources will be developed by DLM to provide Individualized Education Program (IEP)[1] teams with clear, consistent guidelines for the identification of students for the alternate assessment and to train teachers in the use of the assessment system. (K–12 Center at ETS, 2012, p. 34)

(To stay informed about updates concerning DLM, visit dynamiclearningmaps.org.)

The NCSC is developing a comprehensive system that addresses the curriculum, instruction, and assessment needs of students with the most significant cognitive disabilities by:

1) producing technically defensible summative assessments;

2) incorporating evidence-based instruction and curriculum models; and

3) developing comprehensive approaches to professional development delivered through state-level Communities of Practice.

These resources will support educators and Individualized Education Program (IEP) teams as they design and implement appropriate instruction that addresses content and skill expectations aligned to the Common Core State Standards (CCSS), as well as help prepare students with the most significant cognitive disabilities for postsecondary life. When complete, the assessment system and accompanying resources will be made available to all states, regardless of their participation in the original grant. (K–12 Center at ETS, 2012, p. 38)

To help teachers translate the CCSS into effective instruction, NCSC is developing curriculum resource guides for the concepts in math and ELA that are considered to be "big ideas" within the academic content. These guides will provide information on instruction within the general education setting (e.g., how the area can be taught to typically developing students); teaching and applying skills in meaningful contexts; linking skills to other content areas; differentiation of instruction through Universal Design for Learning; considerations for providing instruction of more basic skills to some students as embedded within instruction of grade level content; and tools for tiered interventions. (K–12 Center at ETS, 2012, p. 40)

(To remain informed of developments with the NCSC's comprehensive system, visit www .ncscpartners.org.)

Figure 2.2 details the similarities and differences among the assessments being developed by the two comprehensive consortia and the two alternate assessment consortia. The assessments featured are PARCC, Smarter Balanced, DLM, and NCSC.

ASSETS

English learners are the focus of ASSETS, a Common Core assessment that was developed by WIDA. WIDA's (2012) mission is to advance "academic language development and academic achievement for linguistically diverse students through high quality standards, assessments, research, and professional development for educators" (n.p.). Detailed information about ASSETS, as excerpted from *Coming Together to Raise Student Achievement: New Assessments for the Common Core State Standards*, follows. (More detailed information about English learners and the Common Core appears in Chapter 5.)

To support the development of next generation assessments of English proficiency, the U.S. Department of Education's 2011 competitive Enhanced Assessment Grant provided funding for the development of new assessments by consortia of 15 or more states. In addition to producing results that are valid, reliable and fair for the intended purpose, the new assessment system had to meet additional criteria, including:

- Be based on a common definition of English learner adopted by all Consortium states;

- Include diagnostic (e.g. screener or placement) and summative assessments;

- Assess English language proficiency across the four language domains of reading, writing, speaking and listening for each grade level from kindergarten through Grade 12;

- Produce results that indicate whether individual students have attained a level and complexity of English proficiency that is necessary to participate fully in academic instruction in English;

- Be accessible to all English learners with the one exception of those who are eligible for alternate assessments based on alternate academic standards; and

Figure 2.2 Side-by-Side Comparison of Four Common Core State Standards Assessment Systems

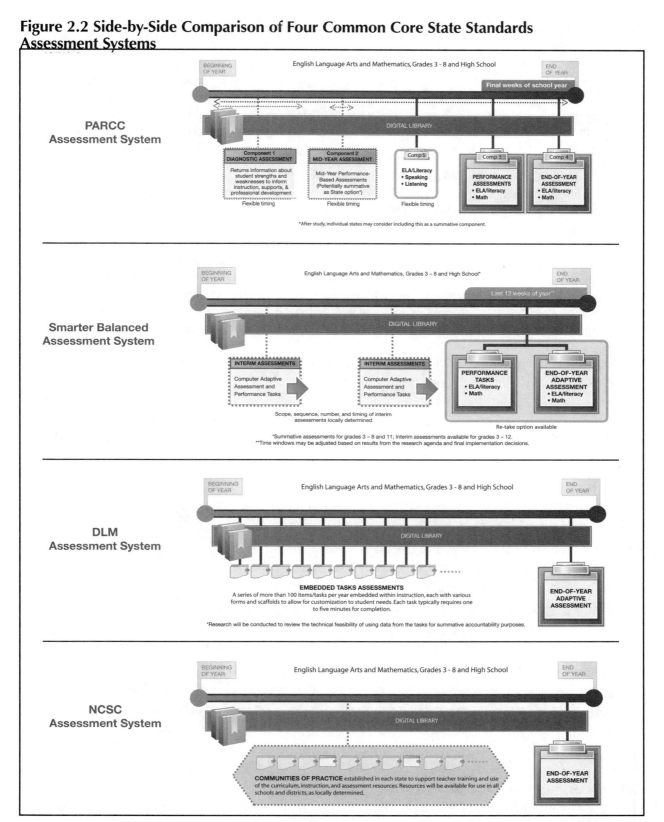

Note. DLM = Dynamic Learning Maps. NCSC = National Center and State Collaborative. PARCC = Partnership for Assessment of Readiness for College and Careers. Reprinted from *Coming Together to Raise Achievement: New Assessments for the Common Core State Standards* (p. 42), by Center for K–12 Assessment & Performance Management at ETS. (2012, April), Austin, TX: Author.

- Use technology to the maximum extent appropriate to develop, administer, and score assessments.

The sole award was given to the Wisconsin Department of Public Instruction, in collaboration with the World-Class Instructional Design and Assessment (WIDA) Consortium. The assessment system under development, called **Assessment Services Supporting ELs through Technology Systems** (ASSETS) is to be ready for use by the 2015–16 school year. A summary and illustration of the design of ASSETS can be found...at www.k12center.org/publications.html. (K–12 Center at ETS, 2012, p. 43)

The ASSETS Consortium will develop a next generation, technology-based language assessment system for students in grades K–12 who are learning English. The system will include a summative language assessment, an on-demand diagnostic screener, classroom interim assessments, and formative assessment tools for use in instruction, as well as accompanying professional development materials. All of these components will be grounded in English development standards linked to the Common Core State Standards (CCSS) in English language arts and mathematics. This Consortium will leverage the work of a Consortium formed in 2002 under another Enhanced Assessment Grant that included many of the same member states. ASSETS member states will govern the development of ASSETS. The assessments and tools developed by this Consortium will be available to all states. (K–12 Center at ETS, 2012, p. 44)

(To keep informed about new developments concerning ASSETS, visit www.k12center.org/publications/english_language_proficiency.html.)

Whether formative or summative, assessment permeates teaching and learning. Assessment is a shared responsibility. Motivating our students to join us in taking an active role in such measures is essential.

ESSENTIAL RESOURCES

- Center for K–12 Assessment & Performance Management at ETS. (2012, April). *Coming together to raise achievement: New assessments for the Common Core State Standards.* Austin, TX: Author. Available at www.k12center.org/publications/raise_achievement.html
- Darling-Hammond, L. (2010). *Performance counts: Assessment systems that support high-quality learning.* Washington, DC: Council of Chief State School Officers. Available at www.ccsso.org/Documents/2010/Performance_Counts_Assessment_Systems_2010.pdf
- Heritage, M. (2010, September). *Formative assessment and next-generation assessment systems: Are we losing an opportunity?* Washington, DC: Council of Chief State School Officers. Available at www.ccsso.org/Documents/2010/Formative_Assessment_Next_Generation_2010.pdf

References

Almasi, J.F. (1996). A new view of discussion. In L.B. Gambrell & J.F. Almasi (Eds.), *Lively discussions! Fostering engaged reading* (pp. 2–24). Newark, DE: International Reading Association.

Black, P., & Wiliam, D. (1998). Assessment and classroom learning. *Assessment in Education: Principles, Policy & Practice, 5*(1), 7–74.

Center for K–12 Assessment & Performance Management at ETS. (2012, April). *Coming together to raise achievement: New assessments for the Common Core State Standards*. Austin, TX: Author. Retrieved August 3, 2012, from www.k12center.org/rsc/pdf/Coming_Together_April_2012_Final.PDF

Darling-Hammond, L. (2010). *Performance counts: Assessment systems that support high-quality learning*. Washington, DC: Council of Chief State School Officers. Retrieved August 3, 2012, from www.ccsso.org/Documents/2010/Performance_Counts_Assessment_Systems_2010.pdf

Gambrell, L.B. (1996). What research reveals about discussion. In L.B. Gambrell & J.F. Almasi (Eds.), *Lively discussions! Fostering engaged reading* (pp. 25–38). Newark, DE: International Reading Association.

Heritage, M. (2010, September). *Formative assessment and next-generation assessment systems: Are we losing an opportunity?* Washington, DC: Council of Chief State School Officers. Retrieved August 3, 2012, from www.ccsso.org/Documents/2010/Formative_Assessment_Next_Generation_2010.pdf

International Reading Association. (2012). *Formative assessment* (Position statement). Newark, DE: Author.

McLaughlin, M. (2010a). *Content area reading: Teaching and learning in an age of multiple literacies*. Boston: Allyn & Bacon.

McLaughlin, M. (2010b). *Guided Comprehension in the primary grades* (2nd ed.). Newark, DE: International Reading Association.

McLaughlin, M. (2012a). *Guided Comprehension for English learners*. Newark, DE: International Reading Association.

McLaughlin, M. (2012b). Tickets out. *The Reading Teacher, 65*(7), 477–479. doi:10.1002/TRTR.01071

McLaughlin, M., & Allen, M.B. (2009). *Guided Comprehension in grades 3–8* (Combined 2nd ed.). Newark, DE: International Reading Association.

McTighe, J., & O'Connor, J. (2005). Seven practices for effective learning. *Educational Leadership, 63*(3), 10–17.

Menken, K. (2000, September). *What are the critical issues in wide-scale assessment of English language learners?* (Issue Brief No. 6). Washington, DC: Center for the Study of Language & Education, National Clearinghouse for Bilingual Education. Retrieved August 3, 2012, from www.ncela.gwu.edu/files/rcd/BE020919/What_Are_The_Critical_Issues.pdf

National Governors Association Center for Best Practices & Council of Chief State School Officers. (2010). *Common Core State Standards for English language arts and literacy in history/social studies, science, and technical subjects*. Washington, DC: Authors. Retrieved August 3, 2012, from www.corestandards.org/assets/CCSSI_ELA%20Standards.pdf

Partnership for Assessment of Readiness for College and Careers. (2010). *The Partnership for Assessment of Readiness for College and Careers (PARCC) application for the Race to the Top comprehensive assessment systems competition*. Retrieved October 2, 2010, from www.fldoe.org/parcc/pdf/apprtcasc.pdf

Schwartz, R.M., & Raphael, T.E. (1985). Concept of definition: A key to improving students' vocabulary. *The Reading Teacher, 39*(2), 198–205.

Shepard, L.A. (2005). Linking formative assessment to scaffolding. *Educational Leadership, 63*(3), 66–70.

Smarter Balanced Assessment Consortium. (2010). *Race to the Top assessment program application for new grants: Comprehensive assessment systems*. Retrieved August 3, 2012, from www2.ed.gov/programs/racetothetop-assessment/applicant.html

Tomlinson, C.A., & McTighe, J. (2006). *Integrating differentiated instruction and understanding by design: Connecting content and kids*. Alexandria, VA: Association for Supervision and Curriculum Development.

Vygotsky, L.S. (1978). *Mind in society: The development of higher psychological processes* (M. Cole, V. John-Steiner, S. Scribner, & E. Souberman, Eds. & Trans.). Cambridge, MA: Harvard University Press.

Weber, E. (1999). *Student assessment that works: A practical approach*. Boston: Allyn & Bacon.

World-Class Instructional Design and Assessment. (2012). Who we are & the WIDA story. Retrieved from www.wida.us/aboutus/mission.aspx

CHAPTER 3

Implementation of the Common Core Standards

The Common Core State Standards Initiative is progressing at lightning speed. Every day, new policy statements, documents to support implementation, and resources related to the Common Core State Standards (CCSS) are emerging. States are either actively engaged in implementation or in the planning stages. Future implementations will build on current efforts.

As we contemplate teaching the Standards, we can think about implementation efforts as the responsibility of every educator. Even though the Common Core State Standards Initiative began as a policy decision, professionals organizations, publishers, states, universities, districts, and schools are pulling together to create tools, resources, and materials to help with implementation.

In this chapter, we respond to the following questions:

- What is the role of professional development in the implementation of the Common Core State Standards?

- How can national organizations, professional associations, and publishers support implementation of the Standards?

- How can multistate regions support implementation of the CCSS?

- How can states support professional development and Standards implementation?

- How can institutions of higher education support teacher preparation and professional development in CCSS implementation?

- How can school districts support schools and administrators in professional development and CCSS implementation?

- How can schools support teachers in professional development and Standards implementation?

In this chapter, we respond to these questions with a variety of suggestions for implementing the Common Core State Standards. Examples of implementation plans at various levels are also presented.

What Is the Role of Professional Development in the Implementation of the Common Core State Standards?

At first glance, it may seem to some educators that the Common Core Standards represent little change from the standards that they have been using. However, educators who have been involved in the in-depth implementation of the CCSS are finding the Standards quite different from any previous state standards. There is an intentional focus on informational text, and classrooms are abuzz with terms that may be unfamiliar, such as *close reading, text complexity, argumentation*, and *text-based evidence*. Researchers at the Center on Policy Education (Kober & Rentner, 2012) noted that most educators in the survey believed that the Common Core Standards are more rigorous than previous state standards. In the same survey, Kober and Rentner found that providing professional development in sufficient quality and quantity to ensure that teachers and administrators are prepared for the new demands will be quite a challenge.

Yet, it stands to reason that intensive, ongoing professional development will be the key to quality Standards implementation. Teachers and administrators working together to interpret the CCSS, ensure a common understanding, align curricula at the state and local levels, and plan for lessons, units, and related assessments is paramount. To meet this challenge, teachers need time for extensive group planning, as well as access to a variety of instructional resources and necessary funding. To successfully implement the Standards, educators at every level need to begin with a Common Core Implementation Model (see Figure 3.1).

When using the Model, states, districts, and schools should clearly delineate participants and their responsibilities, as well as create a timeline of professional development and strategic tasks. The resulting Common Core Implementation Plan should be thoughtful, extensive, and connected to all relevant Common Core initiatives. For example, if a state has a grant to implement components of the CCSS that extends to districts, this effort should be reflected in both the state and district Common Core Implementation Plans. If districts have Common Core–based expectations for teachers, the ideas should be supported by professional development opportunities. This should appear in the Common Core Implementation Plans for both the district and the school. It should be clear how the Standards initiative is connected and will be implemented.

Figure 3.1 The Common Core Implementation Model

Resources to assist in implementation of such plans are beginning to emerge in a variety of Web-based and traditional publications. The Essential Resources section at the end of this chapter includes specific links to many of these resources.

How Can National Organizations, Professional Associations, and Publishers Support Implementation of the Standards?

National organizations, professional associations, and educational publishers are rallying around the Common Core State Standards. Each is making efforts to provide information and resources that are being connected across the United States in a rapid and unprecedented manner. National organizations, such as the Council of Chief State School Officers (CCSSO) and the National Governors Association Center for Best Practices (NGA Center), have been leading the Common Core implementation at the national level by providing tools and resources for state and district leadership. Many other national organizations are also involved in developing resources to support professional development and implementation at the state, district, and classroom level. Examples of these include the following:

- The CCSSO (www.ccsso.org) is a co-leader of the Common Core State Standards Initiative and has developed a list of resources that is continually being updated for parents, teachers, principals, and higher education to help with implementation.

- The NGA Center (www.nga.org) is the other co-leader of the charge and has created a Common Core implementation guide aimed at assisting state governors with transition to the Standards.

- Achieve (www.achieve.org), an organization focused on college and career readiness, has developed a wealth of materials to assist in Common Core planning and implementation for policymakers and state and district leaders.

- The Hunt Institute (www.hunt-institute.org) has sponsored a series of videos on YouTube about the Standards and what they mean.

- Student Achievement Partners (www.achievethecore.org) has been instrumental in the Common Core initiative and is building a bank of resources and lesson plans with video examples of classroom practice and examples of student work that demonstrate the instructional shifts required by the Common Core Standards.

- The National PTA (www.pta.org) has developed the *Parents' Guide to Student Success* (www .pta.org/4446.htm), a set of grade-level guides explaining to parents what students should know and be able to do to meet the expectations of the CCSS.

- Learning Forward (www.learningforward.org) has published a collection of studies and materials to support professional development and implementation of the Standards.

- PARCC and Smarter Balanced, the national assessment consortia discussed in Chapter 2, are developing resources aligned with the Standards and the related assessments.

These are a few examples of the type of support being developed to assist educators and policymakers as they grapple with the implications of implementation across the United States.

Professional associations have also responded to lend support to educators in their implementation of the Common Core. For example, the International Reading Association Common Core State Standards (CCSS) Committee (2012) has developed the white paper *Literacy Implementation Guidance for the ELA Common Core State Standards* to guide teachers, administrators, curriculum developers, and publishers to make sound instructional decisions as they align literacy and content area curriculum, plan lessons and assessment, and create resources to meet individual student needs. These principles address the following topics:

1. Use of challenging texts
2. Foundational skills

3. Comprehension

4. Vocabulary

5. Writing

6. Disciplinary literacy

7. Diverse learners

IRA has also created webinars, resources, and professional development institutes. Further, it sponsors a Q and A about the Common Core on the Association's website. The IRA Annual Convention also has featured sessions, institutes, and strands based on Common Core Standards issues, literacy components, and approaches to implementation.

Other professional organizations have supported professional development and implementation of the Common Core. Examples of these include, but are not limited to, the National Council of Teachers of English (www.ncte.org), ASCD (www.ascd.org), and the National Association of Elementary School Principals (www.naesp.org). Professional associations are continually updating information for their members and the general public on their websites.

Publishers are aligning their materials to the Common Core State Standards and developing new curricular materials and supplemental resources to support teachers in the implementation of the CCSS. Publishers are also supporting professional development for teachers transitioning to the Common Core. A quick look at most educational publisher websites will yield a variety of resources or opportunities for professional development. For example, Pearson Education (www .pearsoned.com) has developed a series of webinars explaining different aspects of the Common Core Standards. McGraw-Hill Education has published materials to be used in lesson planning and professional development, which can be found on their Common Core Solutions website (www .commoncoresolutions.com). Creative Commons (www.creativecommons.org) and the Association of Educational Publishers (www.aepweb.org) have begun a collaborative project involving the major Internet search engines (Google, Yahoo, and Bing). Together, they are partnering in a project called the Learning Resource Metadata Initiative (www.lrmi.net) that will develop a tagging system to help educators find specific Internet resources about the Common Core. Further, a number of publishers and nonprofit organizations are assisting with the Learning Resource Metadata Initiative tagging system so the Common Core tags are accurate and useful for teachers.

Links to these organizations and other helpful resources from national organizations, professional associations, and publishers can be found in the Essential Resources section at the end of this chapter. The resulting responsibilities for professional development and implementation of the Standards rest with educators in states, institutions of higher education, school districts, and schools.

How Can Multistate Regions Support Implementation of the CCSS?

In some instances, groups of states are uniting to pool expertise and resources to create implementation tools. For example, leaders from Massachusetts, New York, and Rhode Island, facilitated by Achieve, collaborated to develop the Tri-State Quality Review Rubric for Lessons and Units: ELA/Literacy (Grades 3–5) and ELA (Grades 6–12). The rubric is intended to be used when evaluating Common Core–aligned curricular resources in developing lessons and units that represent the rigor of the Common Core's English language arts expectations. This is an excellent resource for any classroom teacher or school administrator. (To see the latest version of the Tri-State Rubric, visit www.achieve.org.)

How Can States Support Professional Development and Standards Implementation?

The Common Core State Standards are a state-led initiative. Consequently, states have the responsibility to ensure that districts and schools have the support they need to implement the CCSS in ways that connect seamlessly with other state initiatives and requirements. States have the following responsibilities:

- Add content to the CCSS, including information concerning pre-K students, struggling readers, English learners, and special-needs students.
- Provide funding to facilitate the changes necessitated by the CCSS.
- Require quality, meaningful assessment of the CCSS.
- Provide opportunities and resources for quality professional development that focuses on the content of the Standards, curricular alignment, and the development of related assessments for educators at multiple levels, including state departments of education, school administrators, curriculum planners, supervisors, specialists, classroom teachers, and teacher educators.

When contemplating implementation, states may choose to use a regional approach to ensure that knowledge and implementation of the Standards is comprehensive. Kentucky, which was the first state to adopt the Standards, is a model of a state that has ensured a statewide, systemic approach to professional development on the Standards (Overturf, 2011). In 2009, the legislature of the state of Kentucky voted to overhaul the state's education system. Senate Bill 1 required the Kentucky Department of Education to create a new system of standards and assessments by the spring of 2012. Because the Common Core Standards were being developed at the same time, Kentucky decided to join the effort. Educators in Kentucky provided feedback on the CCR Anchor Standards as well as the K–12 Common Core Standards. Kentucky used an interim assessment to measure students' achievement of the CCSS in spring 2012.

To prepare educators for this massive undertaking, the Kentucky Department of Education led regional, monthly CCSS implementation sessions as part of the Kentucky Content Leadership Network. The sessions were comprised of teams of teachers and school administrators from every school district in the state, as well as university professors from all institutions of higher learning within the state, who were required to participate in ongoing professional development to ensure the successful implementation of the Common Core. The purpose of the regional sessions was to analyze the Standards, develop assessments, plan for instruction, and learn from one another. Educators then returned to their classrooms to implement their new learning and share with others in their schools. It was—and continues to be—a truly collaborative effort.

The Kentucky Department of Education website (www.education.ky.gov) features a variety of instructional resources for school districts and teachers that were developed by regional representatives. These resources, many of which emerged from the monthly regional meetings, include the state's Model Curriculum Framework, English Language Arts Deconstructed Standards with learning targets, and webcasts about the Standards. Kentucky also distributes an electronic newsletter every month that includes updates and resources for teaching the Standards, and hosts periodic Twitter days when educators share resources that they are using to teach the Standards. Kentucky is developing the state-of-the-art Continuous Instructional Improvement Technology System, which will connect the Standards, electronically stored instructional resources, curriculum, formative assessment strategies, and lessons. Many of these resources were developed by Kentucky educators working together across the state in the Content Leadership Network and other state-led professional development, but the plan is to also include outside resources. Kentucky is also involved in a partnership with Learning Forward to develop a statewide, comprehensive professional learning system to support educators in Kentucky's implementation of the Common Core.

There are many other examples of leadership from state departments of education. For example, the New Mexico Department of Education has developed a clear, coherent website that provides information and resources. The Kansas Department of Education has created a website with numerous resources for implementation of the Common Core, including excellent materials for understanding text complexity. The New York Department of Education has created a website called EngageNY, with resources and videos focused on implementation. Additionally, the Ohio Department of Education has created a model curriculum that includes teaching ideas and strategies. The links to these and other selected state resources can be found in Table 3.1.

Table 3.1 Selected State Resources

- *Kansas Department of Education: Common Core Resources*—Includes a collection of tools for use in understanding and measuring text complexity: www.ksde.org/Default.aspx?tabid=4778
- *Kentucky Department of Education: Content Leadership Networks deliverables*—Contains resources to use in implementation of the ELA Standards, including standards "placemats" and gap alignment tools: www.education.ky.gov/kde/administrative+resources/school+improvement/instructional+support +network/leadership+networks+-+deliverables.htm
- *Kentucky Department of Education: English Language Arts Deconstructed Standards*—Created through a collaboration of Kentucky educators, including teachers, district administrators, higher education faculty, regional consultants, and department of education consultants: www.education.ky.gov/KDE/ Instructional+Resources/Curriculum+Documents+and+Resources/English+Language+Arts +Deconstructed+Standards.htm
- *New Mexico Public Education Department: Common Core State Standards*—Contains a wealth of information for students, parents, teachers, and administrators: newmexicocommoncore.org
- *New York State Education Department: EngageNY: Common Core*—Includes videos explaining the instructional shifts in the Common Core Standards: engageny.org/common-core
- *Ohio Department of Education: English Language Arts Model Curriculum*—Includes strategies for students with disabilities, gifted students, and English learners: www.education.ohio.gov/GD/ Templates/Pages/ODE/ODEDetail.aspx?page=3&TopicRelationID=1696&ContentID=83819
- *Utah Education Network: Utah Core Standards for Mathematics & English Language Arts*—Includes resources and videos to support the ELA Common Core Standards: www.uen.org/commoncore/ #eresources

How Can Institutions of Higher Education Support Teacher Preparation and Professional Development in CCSS Implementation?

Institutions of higher education have the responsibility to prepare preservice and inservice teachers for the increased demands of teaching in a Common Core world. Participants in this effort should include faculty and administrators in teacher preparation programs, graduate literacy programs, and the arts and sciences.

College and university faculties who are involved in preservice teacher preparation should study the Standards and engage in collaborative discussions and projects to help develop their knowledge of the Standards and the challenges of implementation. Faculty members should take every opportunity to engage with schools that are transitioning to the Common Core State Standards and participate fully in professional learning communities at the university level. Preservice coursework, assignments, assessments, and field-based experiences should be aligned with the CCSS to ensure that preservice candidates are prepared for the Common Core expectations in public schools.

At the inservice level, teachers and administrators need research-based support from institutions of higher education to make appropriate instructional decisions and design suitable assessments. Higher education faculty members should be in a position to help provide that support, which means that universities need to be fully engaged in and knowledgeable about the Standards and the expectations for public school educators. Graduate faculty need to address the Standards and provide research-based theoretical underpinnings as well as practical, classroom-based assignments and strategies for their students.

National projects are underway to involve institutions of higher education fully in the Common Core Standards initiative. The American Association of State Colleges and Universities, the Council of Chief State School Officers, and the State Higher Education Executive Officers are collaborating to lead an initiative called the College Readiness Partnership. This partnership currently involves teams from seven states who are working to create resources outlining how institutions of higher education and states can work together to ensure Standards implementation and college and career readiness.

How Can School Districts Support Schools and Administrators in Professional Development and CCSS Implementation?

School district offices have a responsibility to ensure that educators in their districts are equipped to implement the Common Core. That includes a plan to do so. Local school districts and schools have the following responsibilities:

- Address the needs of struggling readers, English learners, students with disabilities, and pre-K students in relation to the Standards.
- Provide opportunities and resources for quality professional development that focuses on the content of the Standards, curricular alignment, instructional methods, and the development of related assessments for teachers and building-level administrators.

- Provide resources, including time and materials, for teachers attempting to learn best teaching practices for the CCSS.
- Design and implement instruction and formative assessments that will help all students achieve.

To lead CCSS initiatives at the school district levels, administrative personnel need to be proactive in supporting building-level administrators and teachers, providing material and financial resources, ensuring curricular alignment support, and leading professional development opportunities. For example, in the first year of implementation of the Common Core, Kentucky's Jefferson County Public Schools developed a summer institute to introduce the CCSS to elementary teachers. Representatives from each elementary school participated in the professional development institute and prepared to lead CCSS professional development in their schools. The district then placed all professional development materials online. These include links to the Standards, materials from the training sessions, directions for developing a Standards-based writing workshop, and a document containing Standards-related terminology. Ongoing district support included posting tools for implementing the ELA Standards that featured grade K–5 curriculum standards maps, K–5 curriculum unit maps, K–12 Standards progression documents, and sets of reading tools such as posters, rubrics (scoring guides), and resource lists. Jefferson County also created Standards-based guided practice documents that feature student passages, related questions, and additional queries that require students to compare and contrast passages. Teacher support materials, including detailed lesson plans on how to teach to help students reach the Standards, were incorporated in these documents. The district also sent sets of texts representing required text complexity at each grade level to be made available for teachers in schools' library/media centers.

The New York City Department of Education is another example of a school district that has supported teachers with excellent CCSS resources. The NYC Department of Education website features a Common Core Library section with resources for teacher teams, including professional development materials and lesson plans with rubrics and examples of annotated student work. Many other school districts will engage in these types of efforts as the Standards implementation progresses.

How Can Schools Support Teachers in Professional Development and Standards Implementation?

Schools have the ultimate responsibility for ensuring that faculty members are knowledgeable, skillful, and thoughtful about implementation of the Common Core. At the school level, administrators in Kentucky have found that their efforts to help teachers understand and teach the CCSS is a massive task that requires time, funding, and instructional resources. For example, Stacey is a principal in a Kentucky elementary school that is implementing the Standards. She has found that most of her school's professional development resources for the first year of implementation needed to be focused on supporting teachers in learning the Standards. To facilitate group learning and planning, a strategic professional plan, consisting of multiple levels of professional development, was put into place to support implementation of the CCSS. This included a five-day, school-based summer institute for the entire faculty and establishing professional learning communities (PLCs) focused on the Common Core. As a principal, Stacey also engaged teachers in meetings with grade-level teams, extended faculty meetings, and after-school professional development opportunities. She notes, "We were compelled to do a tremendous amount of professional development in our school because the Standards were so very different from what we had used in the past."

During the five-day summer institute, teachers met in grade-level teams to deconstruct the CCSS and plan for the first six weeks of the school year. Participants took active roles in a variety of activities designed to help them explore the Standards and determine vertical and horizontal alignment for the grade levels they were teaching. This was an eye-opening experience for many teachers. As Stacey notes,

> When my teachers saw the vertical alignment for the first time, they were amazed at the jumps in conceptual development from some grade levels to the next. We realized then that instruction can no longer be viewed as a primary set of goals and an intermediate set of goals. It is about consistency in K–5, on into middle school, and then into high school.

Because of gaps in student knowledge about the concepts represented in the Standards, the teachers in Stacey's school realized that they would need to become intentional about meeting individual students' needs. To begin to accommodate their students, teams of teachers developed formative assessments, including questions to informally gauge students' knowledge and ability to contend with each standard. For example, in an informal survey of students' knowledge of appropriate grade-level content vocabulary (Reading Informational Text Standard 4), teachers asked, "Have you seen the word? Do you know what the word means? Can you use the word?" These teams also worked on curriculum maps and developed plans for assessing student progress in meeting the Standards.

To further support the implementation of the Standards, the school's master schedule was redesigned to ensure that grade-level teams had common planning time and that teachers could continue to work together during the school year. Each team also worked together in a PLC once a month. PLCs are characterized by shared leadership, collective creativity, shared values and vision, supportive conditions, and shared personal practice. The schedule provided time for each PLC to work together for four hours during the school day, two hours for English Language Arts Common Core Standards implementation planning, and two hours for Mathematics Standards implementation planning. The PLCs afforded teachers much needed time to discuss horizontal alignment and share ideas from classrooms at the same grade level, as well as analyze assessments and set learning goals. Teachers created formative assessments and analyzed data from district assessments to identify instructional gaps.

In addition, the PLCs worked collaboratively to develop prompts and applications, as well as the vocabulary needed to understand each standard at each grade level. For example, Reading Informational Text Standard 5 for grade 5 is, "Compare and contrast the overall structure (e.g., chronology, comparison, cause/effect, problem/solution) of events, ideas, concepts, or information in two or more texts" (NGA Center & CCSSO, 2010, p. 14). The PLC decided that using a prompt, a paragraph frame, and teaching informational text structures could be employed to help the students meet the standard. The compare/contrast paragraph frame that students completed is featured in Figure 3.2. Vocabulary, which was also a factor in teaching informational text structures, included *text structure*, *chronology*, *comparison*, *cause/effect*, *problem/solution*, *events*, *ideas*, and *concepts*.

In extended faculty meetings, teachers met with groups across grade levels to ensure continuity from kindergarten through grade 5. After-school professional development opportunities, entitled Marvelous Mondays and Fabulous Fridays, gave teachers the chance to continue to study the Standards through teacher demonstration lessons and plan for implementation in six-week intervals. Teachers conducted backward planning: reviewing important vocabulary that students should know, writing assessments, and developing lesson plans together. Teachers also began study groups, participated in webinars, and read professional books and articles to continue to learn about the Standards. Stacey believes that the students in her school have directly benefited from the time the school personnel spent engaging in professional development. She notes, "We have learned a great deal by analyzing and working with the Standards as a learning community."

Implementing the ELA Standards is a complex task, but teachers across the country are working diligently to meet the challenge. As Stacey notes,

> Without our CCSS Implementation Plan—the work we did last summer, our professional development days throughout the school year, the time we spent analyzing data, quartile planning, teacher-created instructional materials and assessments, and the teamwork—we would not be where we are now. We have much more to do, but as a team, we believe we are on the path to success.

Implementation of the Common Core Standards is a colossal endeavor, one that requires a great deal of time, effort, and collaboration among all who have responsibility for student achievement. Implementing the CCSS must, most assuredly, be a united effort.

In Chapter 4, we focus on the Common Core and how it affects beginning readers, specifically considering the foundational skills of literacy. We present research-based ideas for teaching phonemic awareness, phonics, fluency, vocabulary, and comprehension.

Figure 3.2 Compare/Contrast Paragraph Frame

I can compare and contrast _____ and _____ based on the _____ (events, ideas, concepts). _____ and _____ are alike because in the text, it says _____ and _____. _____ and _____ are different because in the text, it says _____ and _____.

ESSENTIAL RESOURCES

- ASCD has created a number of Common Core resources: www.ascd.org/common-core-state-standards/common-core.aspx.
- The Council of Chief State School Officers has created a list of resources for implementing the Standards: www.ccsso.org/Resources/Programs/The_Common_Core_State_Standards_Initiative.html.
- The Hunt Institute has published a series of YouTube videos with information and explanations of the Standards: www.youtube.com/user/TheHuntInstitute.

- The International Reading Association has a webpage dedicated to the ELA Standards, as well as publications and other resources for professional development: www.reading.org/Resources/ResourcesByTopic/CommonCore-resourcetype/CommonCore-rt-overview.aspx.
- The National Council of Teachers of English has a webpage focused on the Common Core Standards and resources for professional development: www.ncte.org/standards/commoncore.
- The National PTA has created a parents' guide to explain the Common Core at each grade level entitled the *Parents' Guide to Student Success*: www.pta.org/4446.htm.
- Open Educational Resources has developed a collection of online, copyright-free teaching and learning materials available in the public domain with a section specifically focused on resources for the Common Core: www.oercommons.org.
- Pearson Education provides resources for teachers, as well as a series of webinars about the Standards: commoncore.pearsoned.com/index.cfm?locator=PS11T9.
- *Publishers' criteria*—David Coleman and Susan Pimentel, two of the major writers of the Common Core State Standards, have published two publishers' criteria guides for publishers and curriculum developers. The guidelines are helpful for districts, schools, and teachers as they work to plan lessons and units focused on the ELA/Literacy Standards.

    - Revised Publishers' Criteria for the Common Core State Standards in English Language Arts and Literacy, Grades K–2: www.corestandards.org/assets/Publishers_Criteria_for_K-2.pdf
    - Revised Publishers' Criteria for the Common Core State Standards in English Language Arts and Literacy, Grades 3–12: www.corestandards.org/assets/Publishers_Criteria_for_3-12.pdf
- Student Achievement Partners has created examples of lesson plans for demonstrating the instructional shifts in the ELA Standards, which includes video and examples of student work: www.achievethecore.org.
- The Teaching Channel's website includes a section with videos of teaching practices related to the Common Core: www.teachingchannel.org/videos?categories=topics_common-core.
- Tri-State Quality Review Rubric for Lessons and Units: ELA/Literacy (Grades 3–5) and ELA (Grades 6–12) was developed by Massachusetts, New York, and Rhode Island: www.achieve.org.

References

International Reading Association Common Core State Standards (CCSS) Committee. (2012). *Literacy implementation guidance for the ELA Common Core State Standards* [White paper]. Newark, DE: Author. Available at www.reading.org/ccssguidelines

Kober, N., & Rentner, D.S. (2012, January). *Year two of implementing the Common Core State Standards: States' progress and challenges*. Washington, DC: Center on Education Policy. Retrieved August 3, 2012, from www.cep-dc.org/displayDocument.cfm?DocumentID=391

National Governors Association Center for Best Practices & Council of Chief State School Officers. (2010). *Common Core State Standards for English language arts and literacy in history/social studies, science, and technical subjects*. Washington, DC: Authors. Retrieved August 3, 2012, from www.corestandards.org/assets/CCSSI_ELA%20Standards.pdf

Overturf, B.J. (2011). Kentucky leads the US in implementing Common Core Standards. *Reading Today*, 29(2), 24–25.

CHAPTER 4

Beginning Readers, the Teaching of Reading, and the Common Core

Beginning readers are deserving of special consideration when striving to achieve the Common Core. Some accommodations have already been made. For example, the writers of the Reading Standards have included a special section focused on foundational skills to support learners in grades K–5. Topics addressed in the Foundational Skills section of the Standards include concepts of print, phonological awareness, phonics and word recognition, and fluency.

The preface to the Common Core Reading Standards Foundational Skills (National Governors Association Center for Best Practices & Council of Chief State School Officers, 2010) notes,

> These foundational skills are not an end in and of themselves; rather, they are necessary and important components of an effective, comprehensive reading program designed to develop proficient readers with the capacity to comprehend texts across a range of types and disciplines. (p. 15)

We agree that the skills addressed in this section are part of a comprehensive reading program. What makes this an intricate issue is trying to understand why some of the essential pillars of literacy addressed by the National Reading Panel (National Institute of Child Health and Human Development [NICHD], 2000) are included but not all. For example, the Standards do not address vocabulary in great depth; nor do they require the teaching of metacognitive reading comprehension strategies.

In this chapter, we consider a fuller understanding of beginning reading by exploring the pillars of literacy addressed by the National Reading Panel (NICHD, 2000). We present research-based ideas for teaching phonemic awareness, phonics, fluency, vocabulary, and comprehension (c.f. McLaughlin, 2010b, pp. 196–209). The definition of each term is followed by a summary of its research base, practical ideas for teaching it, and suggestions for further reading. Questions that guided our inquiry included the following:

This chapter is adapted from Appendix B, "Research-Based Resources for Teaching Phonemic Awareness, Phonics, Fluency, Vocabulary, and Comprehension," in *Guided Comprehension in the Primary Grades* (2nd ed., pp. 196–209), by M. McLaughlin, 2010, Newark, DE: International Reading Association. Copyright 2010 by the International Reading Association.

- What do we know about this topic?

- What are some practical ideas for teaching these topics to ensure that our students can meet the CCSS?

- What are some essential resources for these topics that we can read and share with our colleagues?

Phonemic Awareness

What Do We Know About Phonemic Awareness?

Phonological awareness—the broader term—is part of the Foundational Skills Substrand of the Common Core State Standards. Phonemic awareness falls under the umbrella of phonological awareness and is considered to be an essential area of beginning reading (Adams, 1990). According to Yopp and Yopp (2000),

> Phonemic awareness is the awareness that the speech stream consists of a sequence of sounds—specifically phonemes, the smallest unit of sound that makes a difference in communication. It is a phoneme that determines the difference between the words *dog* and *hog*, for instance, and between *look* and *lick*. These differences influence meaning. (p. 130)

Harris and Hodges (1995) concur, stating, "Phonemic awareness is the awareness of the sounds (phonemes) that make up spoken words" (p. 185). Note the distinction between phonemic awareness and phonics: Phonics correlates phonemes (the smallest units of sound) with graphemes (written letters). Ehri and Nunes (2002) elaborate on this distinction by observing, "Whereas PA is a specific skill that involves manipulating sounds in speech, *phonics* is a method of teaching reading" (p. 113).

Researchers agree that phonemic awareness is a powerful predictor of reading and spelling acquisition (Ball & Blachman, 1991; Ehri & Nunes, 2002). We also know that phonemic awareness can be taught, but Yopp and Yopp (2000) caution that its instruction needs to be situated in a broader reading program to be effective. The National Reading Panel (NICHD, 2000) presents similar conclusions, noting that teaching children to manipulate phonemes in words has been highly effective under a variety of teaching conditions with a variety of learners.

What Are Some Practical Ideas for Teaching Phonemic Awareness to Ensure That Our Students Can Meet the CCSS?

There are numerous practical, motivational, and fun ways to teach different aspects of phonemic awareness. Frequently hearing, saying, and creating rhymes; manipulating sounds; and singing songs adapted to promote phonemic awareness are among the many ways found to be effective. According to Ehri and Nunes (2002), phonemic awareness tasks include the following:

1. Phoneme isolation, which requires recognizing individual sounds in words, for example, "Tell me the first sound in *paste*." (/p/)

2. Phoneme identity, which requires recognizing the common sound in different words, for example, "Tell me the sound that is the same in *bike*, *boy*, and *bell*." (/b/)

3. Phoneme categorization, which requires recognizing the word with the odd sound in a sequence of three or four words, for example, "Which word does not belong? *Bus, bun,* or *rug*." (*rug*)

4. Phonemic blending, which requires listening to a sequence of separately spoken sounds and combining them to form a recognizable word, for example, "What word is /s/ /k/ /u/ /l/?" (*school*)

5. Phoneme segmentation, which requires breaking a word into its sounds by tapping out or counting the sounds, or by pronouncing and positioning a marker for each sound, for example, "How many phonemes in *ship*?" (three: /š/ /l/ /p/)

6. Phoneme deletion, which requires stating the word that remains when a specified phoneme is removed, for example, "What is *smile* without the /s/?" (*mile*) (pp. 111–112)

Yopp and Yopp (2000) note, "Phonemic awareness supports reading development only if it is part of a broader program that includes—among other things—development of students' vocabulary, syntax, comprehension, strategic reading abilities, decoding strategies, and writing across all content areas" (p. 142). A discussion of a number of ideas for teaching phonemic awareness follows.

Rhyme

Read books with rhyming texts to the students. After they become familiar with the rhyme scheme, pause and encourage them to predict the next rhyming word. Nancy Shaw's sheep books, such as *Sheep in a Jeep* (1986), *Sheep in a Shop* (1991), *Sheep out to Eat* (1995), and *Sheep Trick or Treat* (1997), are examples of texts that work well.

Syllable Manipulation

The song "Clap, Clap, Clap Your Hands" can be adapted for language manipulation. The following version of the song encourages blending syllables; the first two verses are part of the original song, and the last two verses are an adaptation (Yopp & Yopp, 2000):

Clap, clap, clap your hands,
Clap your hands together.
Clap, clap, clap your hands,
Clap your hands together.

Snap, snap, snap your fingers.
Snap your fingers together.
Snap, snap, snap your fingers.
Snap your fingers together.

Say, say, say these parts.
Say these parts together.
Say, say, say these parts,
Say these parts together:
Teacher: moun (pause) tain (children respond, "mountain!")
Teacher: love (pause) ly (children respond, "lovely!")
Teacher: un (pause) der (children respond, "under!")
Teacher: tea (pause) cher (children respond, "teacher!") (p. 138)

Phoneme Manipulation

Singing traditional songs with lyrics revised to promote phonemic awareness can be used to promote a variety of aspects of phonemic awareness, including sound isolation, sound addition or deletion, and full segmentation.

Sound Isolation Activities. Yopp (1992) suggests that children may be given a word and asked to tell what sound occurs at the beginning, middle, or end of the word. In this activity, students sing new lyrics to the well-known children's song "Old MacDonald Had a Farm." The following lyrics focus on isolating beginning sounds:

> What's the sound that starts these words:
> *Turtle*, *time*, and *teeth*?
> /t/ is the sound that starts these words:
> *Turtle*, *time*, and *teeth*.
> With a /t/, /t/ here, and a /t/, /t/ there,
> Here a /t/, there a /t/, everywhere a /t/, /t/.
> /t/ is the sound that starts these words:
> *Turtle*, *time*, and *teeth*.

Chicken, *chin*, and *cheek* would be another option for the song.

Bear, Invernizzi, Templeton, and Johnston (2012) have created Beginning-Middle-End, an activity that involves three steps. First, the teacher places the letters of a three- or four-letter word face down in a pocket chart so the students cannot see them. Then, the teacher says the word for the students (e.g., *hat*). Next, the teacher and students sing the following brief song to the tune of "Are You Sleeping, Brother John?":

> Beginning, middle, end; beginning, middle, end
> Where is the sound? Where is the sound?
> Where's the /t/ in hat? Where's the /t/ in hat?
> Let's find out. Let's find out.

After the song, one student comes forward, picks the sound position (beginning, middle, or end), and turns around the letter card.

Sound Addition or Deletion Activity. Students may add or substitute sounds in words in familiar songs. In this activity, students sing the traditional verses of the well-known children's song "Row, Row, Row Your Boat," but they sing different beginning sounds in the repeated words in the chorus (Yopp, 1992). For example, the traditional chorus is "merrily, merrily, merrily, merrily, life is but a dream." In alternate versions of the song designed to promote phonemic awareness, the beginning sound of *merrily* may be replaced by any consonant. It doesn't matter if the word created is a nonsense word. The lyrics to "Row, Row, Row Your Boat" that follow focus on substituting beginning sounds:

Row, row, row your boat
Gently down the stream
Merrily, merrily, merrily, merrily
Life is but a dream
(Berrily, berrily, berrily, berrily)
(Terrily, terrily, terrily, terrily)

Full Segmentation.   In full segmentation, the word is segmented or separated into individual sounds. In this activity, students sing new lyrics to the classic children's song "Twinkle, Twinkle, Little Star" (Yopp, 1992). The lyrics that follow focus on presenting a word—in this case *face*—and then segmenting or separating the individual sounds that make up the word:

Listen, listen to my word,
Then tell me the sounds you heard: *face*
/f/ is one sound
/a/ is two,
/s/ is the last sound it's true.
Thanks for listening to my words,
And telling me the sounds you heard.

Phonics

What Do We Know About Phonics?

Phonics is "a way of teaching reading and spelling that stresses symbol sound relationships, used especially in beginning instruction" (Harris & Hodges, 1995, p. 186). According to Norman and Calfee (2004),

> The goal of early reading instruction is to help students move as quickly as possible toward independent comprehension of a broad range of texts. Phonics instruction is one gateway toward this goal by providing students with the skills to decode unfamiliar words encountered in new and challenging passages. (p. 42)

Stahl, Duffy-Hester, and Stahl (1998, pp. 339–343) report that good phonics instruction

- Develops the alphabetic principle
- Develops phonological awareness
- Provides a thorough grounding in the letters
- Does not teach rules, need not use worksheets, should not dominate instruction, and does not need to be boring
- Provides sufficient practice in reading words
- Leads to automatic word recognition
- Is one part of reading instruction

Researchers also note that students differ in their needs for phonics instruction and concur with Stahl and colleagues' (1998) belief that phonics is just one component of a balanced reading program (Cunningham & Cunningham, 2002; NICHD, 2000). The National Reading Panel (NICHD, 2000) reports that systematic phonics instruction produces significant benefits for students in kindergarten through grade 6 and for children having difficulty with learning to read.

What Are Some Practical Ideas for Teaching Phonics to Ensure That Our Students Can Meet the CCSS?

Cunningham and Cunningham (2002) suggest that children should spend a majority of their time reading and writing and that phonics instruction should be taught through a variety of multilevel activities that emphasize transfer. Numerous teaching ideas support this thinking. What follows is a sampling of activities that have proven to be effective.

Alphabet Scrapbook

For Alphabet Scrapbook (Bear et al., 2012), prepare a blank dictionary for each child by stapling together sheets of paper. (Seven sheets of paper folded and stapled in the middle is enough for one letter per page.) Children can use this book in a variety of ways.

- Practice writing uppercase and lowercase forms of the letter on each page.
- Cut out letters in different fonts or styles from magazines and newspapers and paste them into their scrapbooks.
- Draw and label pictures and other things that begin with that letter sound.
- Cut and paste magazine pictures onto the corresponding letter page. These pictures can be labeled, too.
- Add sight words as they become known to create a personal dictionary.

Making Words

In Making Words (adapted from Cunningham, 2009), students manipulate a group of letters to create words of varying lengths. They may create the words based on clues or just list as many words as possible. Then, they guess the mystery word—the source of the random letters. When creating the words, students may manipulate plastic letters or arrange magnetic letters on a cookie sheet.

Making and Writing Words. In Making and Writing Words (Rasinski, 1999a), students follow the same procedure as in Making Words, but instead of manipulating the letters, they write them.

Making and Writing Words Using Letter Patterns. In Making and Writing Words Using Letter Patterns (Rasinski, 1999b), students use rimes (word families) and other patterns, as well as individual letters, to write words. Then, the students transfer their knowledge to create new words. Finally, they cut up the organizer to create word cards, which they can use to practice the words in games and sorts.

Onset and Rime Word Wall and Portable Word Wall

Choose onsets and use these 37 common rimes (Stahl, 1992) to create a classroom word wall:

-ack	-an	-aw	-ick	-ing	-op	-unk
-ain	-ank	-ay	-ide	-ink	-or	
-ake	-ap	-eat	-ight	-ip	-ore	
-ale	-ash	-ell	-ill	-ir	-uck	
-all	-at	-est	-in	-ock	-ug	
-ame	-ate	-ice	-ine	-oke	-ump	

Use the word wall as a resource for students' reading and writing. Extend this idea, or any word wall, by encouraging students to create Portable Word Walls that they can use in other instructional settings or at home. This is easily accomplished by using manila folders to house the word wall and having students use markers to copy the words onto the inside of their individual folders.

Fluency

What Do We Know About Fluency?

According to Rasinski (2010), fluency is the ability to read quickly, effortlessly, and efficiently with good, meaningful expression and comprehension. Harris and Hodges (1995) note that fluency is "1. the clear, easy, written or spoken expression of ideas. 2. freedom from word-identification problems that might hinder comprehension in silent reading or the expression of ideas in oral reading; automaticity" (p. 85). The National Reading Panel (NICHD, 2000) reports that fluent readers read orally with speed, accuracy, and expression.

Rasinski (2010) stresses fluency's connection to reading comprehension, noting that the more fluent readers are, the more they can focus on comprehending what they are reading. Other researchers agree that oral reading fluency contributes to comprehension (Nathan & Stanovich, 1991; NICHD, 2000). The National Reading Panel (NICHD, 2000) also reports that repeated oral reading procedures that include guidance from teachers, peers, or parents have significant and positive impacts on the word recognition, fluency, and comprehension of both good and poor readers.

What Are Some Practical Ideas for Teaching Fluency to Ensure That Our Students Can Meet the CCSS?

To become fluent readers, students need to have good models, access to text, and time to read. To practice fluency, students engage in techniques such as choral reading and repeated readings. To do this independently, students need to have access to text that they can read without teacher assistance. The following activities provide a good starting point for building fluency in beginning readers.

Modeling Fluent Reading

Providing fluent reading models for students helps them become fluent readers. Teachers, parents, cross-age volunteers, and audiobooks can provide good fluency models for students.

Choral Reading

In choral reading, the teacher and the students read together. When engaging in choral reading, the pressure is off the individual reader, so there is more of a tendency to focus on the fluent manner in which the poem or text segment is being read. Choral reading also provides everyone engaged with good fluency models.

Echo Reading

To engage in echo reading, the teacher reads a short selection (e.g., a poem) segment by segment (e.g., line by line). As the teacher reads, the students echo, or repeat, what the teacher read. In this activity, the teacher's reading provides a fluent model for the students.

Repeated Reading

Repeated reading of text helps students read more fluently (Samuels, 2006). In this process, students work with partners; pairing a strong reader with a less able reader is preferable. In each pair, students take turns assuming the role of teacher and student. The teacher looks at the words in the text while listening to the student read orally. The passage is read four times, with the partners swapping roles after each reading. This improves comprehension, because as the reading becomes more fluent, less emphasis is placed on decoding and more on constructing meaning.

Readers Theatre

Readers Theatre does not involve producing a class play; it is like a read-through of a script. A narrator often introduces the work, sets the scene, and provides transitional information during the performance. The readers use their voices to create the scene and bring the characters to life. Books that have a lot of dialogue can be used for Readers Theatre. A number of websites also provide scripts for this technique. Examples include Timeless Teacher Stuff (www.timelessteacherstuff.com) and Teaching Heart's Reader's Theater Scripts and Plays (www.teachingheart.net/readerstheater.htm).

Vocabulary

What Do We Know About Vocabulary?

Vocabulary development is "1. the growth of a person's stock of known words and meanings. 2. the teaching-learning principles and practices that lead to such growth, as comparing and classifying word meanings, using context, analyzing root words and affixes, etc." (Harris & Hodges, 1995, p. 275). Pearson, Hiebert, and Kamil (2007) note that vocabulary may seem simple, but it is complex. Words relate to our experiences and knowledge, and their meanings change depending on the context in which they are used.

Researchers agree that if our students do not know the words in a given context, they will have difficulty comprehending what they are reading (Blachowicz, Fisher, Ogle, & Watts-Taffe, 2006; Duke, 2007; McLaughlin & Allen, 2009; NICHD, 2000). Vocabulary instruction leads to gains in comprehension, but the methods must be appropriate to the age and ability of the reader (NICHD, 2000). Baumann and Kame'enui (1991) report that direct instruction of vocabulary and learning from context should be balanced. Blachowicz and Fisher (2000) note that the following four guidelines emerge from existing research about vocabulary instruction:

1. That students should be active in developing their understanding of words and ways to learn them.
2. That students should personalize word learning.
3. That students should be immersed in words.
4. That students should build on multiple sources of information to learn words through repeated exposures. (p. 504)

According to Kucan (2012),

> Students need vocabulary instruction that allows them to build rich representations of words. Such instruction cannot only be incidental. Teachers need to plan and implement vocabulary lessons that can support students in developing the kind of high-quality lexical representations that will endure and be available for reading and writing. (p. 366)

Kucan further suggests that vocabulary lessons should involve the following: (1) explaining words meanings in ways that make sense to students, (2) engaging students in meaningful activities and using the words in a variety of contexts, and (3) using assessments that determine students' depth of knowledge about the words.

What Are Some Practical Ideas for Teaching Vocabulary to Ensure That Our Students Can Meet the CCSS?

Descriptions of a variety of ideas for teaching vocabulary are included in this book. These include Semantic Maps (see Chapter 11, page 135) and Semantic Feature Analysis (Chapter 10, page 122).

Numerous other ideas for teaching vocabulary can be found in current academic journals and professional books. "Fun With Vocabulary" (Towell, 1997), which is summarized below, is an example of the former; *Word Nerds: Teaching All Students to Learn and Love Vocabulary* (Overturf, Montgomery, & Smith, in press) is an example of the latter.

V   *Visual-Auditory-Kinesthetic-Tactile*—This is a multisensory technique in which students trace the target word with a finger while pronouncing each syllable until it can be written from memory.

O   *Onsets and rimes*—The onset is the part of the word before the vowel; the rime is the vowel and the rest of the letters in the word.

C   *Clusters*—For vocabulary instruction to be meaningful, words should be presented in semantic frameworks through categories or clusters. A cluster is a set of words that relate to a single concept.

A *ABC books and anagrams*—Students create their own alphabet books and discover words through illustrations on the basis of their prior knowledge or schemata. Anagrams are another fun and interesting way to learn vocabulary or spelling words.

B *Book boxes*—Create boxes of related reading materials for the students.

    Boxes for visual configuration—This visual discrimination technique involves drawing around words to emphasize their length and shape.

    Word banks—Students should have personal word banks for storing and remembering their self-selected and teacher-selected words, such as spelling words.

U *Unknown words*—A strategy for primary grades is beep it, frame it, begin it, split it, and find it in the dictionary.

L *Language Experience Approach*—A student tells a story, the teacher creates a book using the student's words, and the student reads the book.

A *Active involvement*—Students must be actively involved in learning and using vocabulary.

R *Repetition, rhymes, riddles, and roots*—Encountering the words they have learned in multiple settings, engaging in word play (e.g., books by Fred Gwynne and Marvin Terban), and engaging in structural analysis support students' vocabulary development.

Y *Yarns*—Using their vocabulary to spin yarns or tall tales is a fun way for students to use words that they have learned. The stories can be shared through storytelling or writing.

Reading Comprehension

What Do We Know About Reading Comprehension?

Reading comprehension researchers, including Duke and Pearson (2002), Hilden and Pressley (2002), and Pressley (2001), note that reading comprehension strategies can be taught in the primary grades. Pressley suggests that students begin learning comprehension skills and a few strategies as early as kindergarten. Pearson (2001) reports that the three most important things that we have learned about comprehension in the past 30 years are that (1) students benefit from using comprehension strategies and routines; (2) having opportunities to read, write, and talk matters; and (3) knowledge helps comprehension by providing a starting point—where readers are and what they know.

Duke and Pearson (2002) note, "Comprehension is a consuming, continuous, and complex activity, but one that, for good readers, is both *satisfying and productive*" (p. 206). According to Harris and Hodges (1995), comprehension is

> the construction of the meaning of a written or spoken communication through a reciprocal, holistic interchange of ideas between the interpreter and the message in a particular communicative context. *Note:* The presumption here is that meaning resides in the intentional problem-solving, thinking processes of the interpreter during such an interchange, that the content of meaning is influenced by that person's prior knowledge and experience, and that the message so constructed by the receiver may or may not be congruent with the message sent. (p. 39)

Much of what we know about comprehension is based on studies of good readers—readers who are actively engaged in the reading process, who have set clear goals, and who constantly monitor the relation between their goals and the text that they are reading (Duke & Pearson, 2002; Pressley, 2000). Good readers use a repertoire of comprehension strategies to facilitate the construction of meaning (Duke & Pearson, 2002; McLaughlin, 2010a, 2010b, 2012; McLaughlin & Allen, 2009; NICHD, 2000; Palincsar & Brown, 1984, 1986; Roehler & Duffy, 1984).

What Are Some Practical Ideas for Teaching Reading Comprehension to Ensure That Our Students Can Meet the CCSS?

Although the Common Core State Standards do not explicitly address the teaching of reading comprehension strategies, we suggest many comprehension skill and strategy applications as teaching ideas throughout this volume. These include skills such as using text structures and strategies, such as summarizing (see Chapter 11, this volume).

We can also consider using other strategy applications. The following list offers an example for each reading comprehension strategy.

- *Previewing*—Storybook Introductions (Clay, 1991)
- *Self-questioning*—Draw and Write "I Wonder" Statements (McLaughlin, 2010b)
- *Making connections*—Draw and Write Connections (McLaughlin, 2010b)
- *Visualizing*—Draw and Write Visualizations (McLaughlin, 2010b)
- *Monitoring*—Say Something (Short & Harste, 1996)
- *Knowing how words work*—Semantic Question Map (McLaughlin, 2010b)
- *Summarizing*—Paired Summarizing (Vaughn & Estes, 1986)
- *Evaluating*—Discussion Webs (Alvermann, 1991)

ESSENTIAL RESOURCES

Phonemic Awareness

- Ehri, L.C., & Nunes, S.R. (2002). The role of phonemic awareness in learning to read. In A.E. Farstrup & S.J. Samuels (Eds.), *What research has to say about reading instruction* (3rd ed., pp. 110–139). Newark, DE: International Reading Association.
- Yopp, H.K., & Yopp, R.H. (2000). Supporting phonemic awareness development in the classroom. *The Reading Teacher, 54*(2), 130–143.

Phonics

- Bear, D.R., Invernizzi, M., Templeton, S., & Johnston, F. (2012). *Words their way: Word study for phonics, vocabulary, and spelling instruction* (5th ed.). Boston: Pearson.
- Cunningham, P.M. (2009). *Phonics they use: Words for reading and writing* (5th ed.). Boston: Pearson.
- Stahl, S.A., Duffy-Hester, A.M., & Stahl, K.A.D. (1998). Everything you wanted to know about phonics (but were afraid to ask). *Reading Research Quarterly, 33*(3), 338–355.

Fluency

- Rasinski, T.V. (2010). *The fluent reader: Oral and silent reading strategies for building fluency, word recognition, and comprehension* (2nd ed.). New York: Scholastic.
- Rasinski, T.V. (2012). Why fluency should be hot! *The Reading Teacher, 65*(8), 516–522.
- Samuels, S.J. (2006). Toward a model of reading fluency. In S.J. Samuels & A.E. Farstrup (Eds.), *What research has to say about fluency instruction* (pp. 24–46). Newark, DE: International Reading Association.

Vocabulary

- Blachowicz, C.L.Z., Fisher, P.J.L., Ogle, D., & Watts-Taffe, S. (2006). Vocabulary: Questions from the classroom. *Reading Research Quarterly, 41*(4), 524–539.
- Kucan, L. (2012). What is most important to know about vocabulary? *The Reading Teacher, 65*(6), 360–366.
- Overturf, B.J., Montgomery, L.H., & Smith, M.H. (in press). *Word nerds: Teaching all students to learn and love vocabulary*. Portland, ME: Stenhouse.

Reading Comprehension

- McLaughlin, M. (2010). *Guided Comprehension in the primary grades* (2nd ed.). Newark, DE: International Reading Association.
- McLaughlin, M. (2012). *Guided Comprehension for English learners*. Newark, DE: International Reading Association.
- McLaughlin, M., & Allen, M.B. (2009). *Guided Comprehension in grades 3–8* (Combined 2nd ed.). Newark, DE: International Reading Association.

Children's Literature

- Shaw, N. (1986). *Sheep in a jeep*. Boston: Houghton Mifflin.
- Shaw, N. (1991). *Sheep in a shop*. Boston: Houghton Mifflin.
- Shaw, N. (1992). *Sheep out to eat*. Boston: Houghton Mifflin.
- Shaw, N. (1997). *Sheep trick or treat*. Boston: Houghton Mifflin.

References

Adams, M.J. (1990). *Beginning to read: Thinking and learning about print*. Cambridge, MA: MIT Press.

Alvermann, D.E. (1991). The discussion web: A graphic aid for learning across the curriculum. *The Reading Teacher, 45*(2), 92–99.

Ball, E.W., & Blachman, B.A. (1991). Does phoneme awareness training in kindergarten make a difference in early word recognition and developmental spelling? *Reading Research Quarterly, 26*(1), 49–66. doi:10.1598/RRQ.26.1.3

Baumann, J.F., & Kame'enui, E.J. (1991). Research on vocabulary instruction: Ode to Voltaire. In J. Flood, J.M. Jensen, D. Lapp, & J.R. Squire (Eds.), *Handbook of research on teaching the English language arts* (pp. 604–632). New York: Macmillan.

Bear, D.R., Invernizzi, M., Templeton, S., & Johnston, F. (2012). *Words their way: Word study for phonics, vocabulary, and spelling instruction* (5th ed.). Boston: Pearson.

Blachowicz, C.L.Z., & Fisher, P. (2000). Vocabulary instruction. In M.L. Kamil, P.B. Mosenthal, P.D. Pearson, & R. Barr (Eds.), *Handbook of reading research* (Vol. 3, pp. 503–523). Mahwah, NJ: Erlbaum.

Blachowicz, C.L.Z., Fisher, P.J.L., Ogle, D., & Watts-Taffe, S. (2006). Vocabulary: Questions from the classroom. *Reading Research Quarterly, 41*(4), 524–539. doi:10.1598/RRQ.41.4.5

Clay, M.M. (1991). Introducing a new storybook to young readers. *The Reading Teacher, 45,* 264–273.

Cunningham, P.M. (2009). *Phonics they use: Words for reading and writing* (5th ed.). Boston: Pearson.

Cunningham, P.M., & Cunningham, J.W. (2002). What we know about how to teach phonics. In A.E. Farstrup & S.J. Samuels (Eds.), *What research has to say about reading instruction* (3rd ed., pp. 87–109). Newark, DE: International Reading Association.

Duke, N. (2007, October). *Comprehension throughout the day.* Paper presented at the annual meeting of the Alaska State Literacy Association, Anchorage, AK.

Duke, N.K., & Pearson, P.D. (2002). Effective practices for developing reading comprehension. In A.E. Farstrup & S.J. Samuels (Eds.), *What research has to say about reading instruction* (3rd ed., pp. 205–242). Newark, DE: International Reading Association.

Ehri, L.C., & Nunes, S.R. (2002). The role of phonemic awareness in learning to read. In A.E. Farstrup & S.J. Samuels (Eds.), *What research has to say about reading instruction* (3rd ed., pp. 110–139). Newark, DE: International Reading Association. doi:10.1598/0872071774.6

Harris, T.L., & Hodges, R.E. (Eds.). (1995). *The literacy dictionary: The vocabulary of reading and writing.* Newark, DE: International Reading Association.

Hilden, K., & Pressley, M. (2002, December). *Can teachers become comprehension strategies teachers given a small amount of training?* Paper presented at the 52nd annual meeting of the National Reading Conference, Miami, FL.

Kucan, L. (2012). What is most important to know about vocabulary? *The Reading Teacher, 65*(6), 360–366. doi:10.1002/TRTR.01054

McLaughlin, M. (2010a). *Content area reading: Teaching and learning in an age of multiple literacies.* Boston: Allyn & Bacon.

McLaughlin, M. (2010b). *Guided Comprehension in the primary grades* (2nd ed.). Newark, DE: International Reading Association.

McLaughlin, M. (2012). *Guided Comprehension for English learners.* Newark, DE: International Reading Association.

McLaughlin, M., & Allen, M.B. (2009). *Guided Comprehension in grades 3–8* (Combined 2nd ed.). Newark, DE: International Reading Association.

Nathan, R.G., & Stanovich, K.E. (1991). The causes and consequences of differences in reading fluency. *Theory Into Practice, 30*(3), 176–184. doi:10.1080/00405849109543498

National Governors Association Center for Best Practices & Council of Chief State School Officers. (2010). *Common Core State Standards for English language arts and literacy in history/social studies, science, and technical subjects.* Washington, DC: Authors. Retrieved August 3, 2012, from www.corestandards.org/assets/CCSSI_ELA%20Standards.pdf

National Institute of Child Health and Human Development. (2000). *Report of the National Reading Panel. Teaching children to read: An evidence-based assessment of the scientific research literature on reading and its implications for reading instruction* (NIH Publication No. 00-4769). Washington, DC: U.S. Government Printing Office.

Norman, K.A., & Calfee, R.C. (2004). Tile test: A hands-on approach for assessing phonics in the early grades. *The Reading Teacher, 58*(1), 42–52. doi:10.1598/RT.58.1.4

Overturf, B.J., Montgomery, L.H., & Smith, M.H. (in press). *Word nerds: Teaching all students to learn and love vocabulary.* Portland, ME: Stenhouse.

Palincsar, A.S., & Brown, A.L. (1984). Reciprocal teaching of comprehension-fostering and monitoring activities. *Cognition and Instruction, 1,* 117–175.

Palincsar, A.S., & Brown, A.L. (1986). Interactive teaching to promote independent learning from text. *The Reading Teacher, 39*(8), 771–777.

Pearson, P.D. (2001). *Comprehension strategy instruction: An idea whose time has come again.* Paper presented at the annual meeting of the Colorado Council of the International Reading Association, Denver, CO.

Pearson, P.D., Hiebert, E.H., & Kamil, M.L. (2007). Vocabulary assessment: What we know and what we need to learn. *Reading Research Quarterly, 42,* 282–296.

Pressley, M. (2000). What should comprehension instruction be the instruction of? In M.L. Kamil, P.B. Mosenthal, P.D. Pearson, & R. Barr (Eds.), *Handbook of reading research* (Vol. 3, pp. 545–561). Mahwah, NJ: Erlbaum.

Pressley, M. (2001, December). *Comprehension strategies instruction: A turn of the century status report.* Paper presented at the 51st annual meeting of the National Reading Conference, San Antonio, TX.

Rasinski, T. (1999a, February). Making and writing words. *Reading Online.* Retrieved August 4, 2012, from www.readingonline.org/articles/words/rasinski.html

Rasinski, T. (1999b, September). Making and writing words using letter patterns. *Reading Online.* Retrieved August 4, 2012, from www.readingonline.org/articles/art_index.asp?HREF=/articles/rasinski/index.html

Rasinski, T.V. (2010). *The fluent reader: Oral and silent reading strategies for building fluency, word recognition, and comprehension* (2nd ed.). New York: Scholastic.

Roehler, L.R., & Duffy, G.G. (1984). Direct explanation of comprehension processes. In G.G. Duffy, L.R. Roehler, & J. Mason (Eds.), *Comprehension instruction: Perspectives and suggestions* (pp. 265–280). New York: Longman.

Samuels, S.J. (2006). Toward a model of reading fluency. In S.J. Samuels & A.E. Farstrup (Eds.), *What research has to say about fluency instruction* (pp. 24–46). Newark, DE: International Reading Association.

Short, K.G., & Harste, J.C. (with Burke, C.). (1996). *Creating classrooms for authors and inquirers* (2nd ed.). Portsmouth, NH: Heinemann.

Stahl, S.A. (1992). Saying the "p" word: Nine guidelines for exemplary phonics instruction. *The Reading Teacher, 45*(8), 618–625.

Stahl, S.A., Duffy-Hester, A.M., & Stahl, K.A.D. (1998). Everything you wanted to know about phonics (but were afraid to ask). *Reading Research Quarterly, 33*(3), 338–355. doi:10.1598/RRQ.33.3.5

Towell, J. (1997). Fun with vocabulary. *The Reading Teacher, 51*(4), 356–358.

Vaughn, J.L., & Estes, T.H. (1986). *Reading and reasoning beyond the primary grades.* Boston: Allyn & Bacon.

Yopp, H.K. (1992). Developing phonemic awareness in young children. *The Reading Teacher, 45*(9), 696–703.

Yopp, H.K., & Yopp, R.H. (2000). Supporting phonemic awareness development in the classroom. *The Reading Teacher, 54*(2), 130–143. doi:10.1598/RT.54.2.2

English Learners, Students With Disabilities, Gifted and Talented Learners, and the Common Core

As we plan to implement the Common Core State standards, it is important to remember that all students are responsible for achieving the Standards. This means that populations such as English learners, students with disabilities, and gifted and talented learners are also accountable for them. Unfortunately, the Common Core initiative has barely addressed these students' needs.

The Common Core State Standards for English Language Arts were written for regular education students, and at this point, there are no plans to modify them in any way. Consequently, English learners, students with disabilities, and gifted and talented learners have neither Standards nor related materials that accommodate their needs.

In this chapter, we focus on these learners. We respond to a variety of queries about each, including what research has to say and how we can differentiate instruction. The questions that guide our exploration of these topics include

- What do we know about these learners?
- What connections can we make to the CCSS?
- What types of instructional considerations need to occur?

English Learners

What Do We Know About English Learners?

According to Young and Hadaway (2006), English learners (ELs) are the fastest growing educational population. Goldenberg (2010) further notes, "ELL students in the United States come from over 400 different language backgrounds; however, by far the largest proportion—80%—is Spanish speakers" (p. 17).

When teaching ELs, we need to view their previous experiences as strengths and maintain high expectations for their performance. As Helman (2009) has observed, "When students' knowledge and background experiences, as well as their abilities, languages, and family heritage, are seen as strengths, students are empowered to be successful at school" (p. 9).

August and Shanahan (2008) have found that ELs learning to read in English benefit from the explicit teaching of the components of literacy (e.g., phonemic awareness, phonics, vocabulary, comprehension, writing), just as English speakers learning to read in English do. Goldenberg (2010) notes, "ELLs appear to be capable of learning at levels comparable to those of English speakers, if they are provided with good, structured, explicit teaching" (p. 27).

A wide range of accessible text at a variety of levels should be available to English learners. Further, an array of supports, including pictures, wait time, and collaboration, should be included in our teaching.

When assessing ELs, we need to be particularly aware of their language development. Our goal is to ensure that language issues do not interfere with the content of the assessments. We can monitor English learners' progress through formative assessment. Observing their progress through formative assessments provides us with ongoing insights into their thinking and abilities. This information helps us understand whether the supports we provided were effective or need to be changed.

What Connections Can We Make to the CCSS?

The National Governors Association Center for Best Practices and the Council of Chief State School Officers (2010a) have created a document entitled "Application of Common Core State Standards for English Language Learners." The authors suggest that English learners should be held to the high expectations of the Common Core State Standards. They further note that "these students may require additional time, appropriate instructional support, and aligned assessments as they acquire both English language proficiency and content area knowledge" (p. 1).

The document also notes that to meet the Standards, it is essential that ELs have access to the following:

- Teachers and personnel at the school and district levels who are well prepared and qualified to support ELLs while taking advantage of the many strengths and skills they bring to the classroom;
- Literacy-rich school environments where students are immersed in a variety of language experiences;
- Instruction that develops foundational skills in English and enables ELLs to participate fully in grade-level coursework;
- Coursework that prepares ELLs for postsecondary education or the workplace, yet is made comprehensible for students learning content in a second language (through specific pedagogical techniques and additional resources);
- Opportunities for classroom discourse and interaction that are well-designed to enable ELLs to develop communicative strengths in language arts;
- Ongoing assessment and feedback to guide learning; and
- Speakers of English who know the language well enough to provide ELLs with models and support. (NGA Center & CCSSO, 2010a, pp. 1–2)

What Types of Instructional Considerations Need to Occur?

Jamal is a fourth-grade student who immigrated to the United States from Senegal with his family last year. He is an English learner who uses multiple supports while reading. To begin, Jamal reads better when he finds the text engaging, so having access to motivational text is essential for him. He also appreciates texts that are culturally relevant. His favorite reading topics are Senegal and aspects of African culture. His teacher, Mrs. Downing, integrates Jamal's culture into her teaching. She views his rich history as a class resource.

When engaging Jamal in learning, Mrs. Downing is careful to use a variety of instructional settings, including small group and paired. Jamal seems more comfortable responding in smaller settings. His teacher is also aware that supports, such as pictures, wait time, and short written responses, work well for him.

Mrs. Downing focuses on encouraging Jamal to take an active role in reading. She uses techniques such as Language Experience Approach (Allen & Allen, 1970), Discussion Circles (McLaughlin, 2010), and integrating technology to motivate him. She makes sure to use culturally relevant text when explicitly teaching the reading comprehension strategies to Jamal. She also encourages him to engage in discussion and various types of journal writing, including response and dialogue.

Our goal is to teach the English learners in our classes to become active, engaged readers. To help our students do this, we need to understand all that we can about how to teach them (Young & Hadaway, 2006). According to McLaughlin (2012), there are numerous ways in which we can modify our teaching to accommodate these students, including the following:

- Emphasize student motivation and engagement
- Employ a structured literacy lesson format with appropriate supports
- Teach students to generate and respond to questions
- Teach patterns for narrative and informational texts
- Read aloud texts that present content, useful language patterns, or vocabulary in context to help foster oral language development
- Interact with text to make content more comprehensible
- Encourage students to engage in written responses to provide time for thought and reflection
- Provide numerous daily opportunities for students to engage in discussion
- Integrate visual aids to support and extend understanding, including picture books as supports for English learners of all ages
- Teach integrated, engaging, and enriching lessons that deepen understandings (p. 6)

An additional strategy is to encourage students to represent their thinking in multiple ways (e.g., dramatization, music, photography).

Helman (2009) notes, "Educational factors that influence the literacy learning of ELLs involve in-class instruction, the types and quality of lessons, involvement of the students and their communities, teacher knowledge, and students' opportunities to use language in cognitively challenging activities" (p. 13). As English learners strive to meet the Common Core Standards, high-quality instruction will support their efforts.

Students With Disabilities

What Do We Know About Students With Disabilities?

Since 1975, federal laws have been in place to provide accommodations for learning and other types of disabilities. Currently, four federal regulations govern special education in the United States: the Individuals with Disabilities Education Act, Section 504 of the Rehabilitation Act, the Americans with Disabilities Act, and the No Child Left Behind Act. One of the qualifications for special-education services is that a student must be in need of specially designed instruction to receive a free, appropriate public education in the least restrictive environment that conforms to an individualized education plan (IEP). Once the student is eligible to receive special-education services, there are a multitude of policies that govern those services, the process for receiving them, and the student's privacy (Osborne & Russo, 2007).

Response to Intervention (RTI) is often associated with special education but is actually a general education system. The National Center on Response to Intervention (2010) defines RTI as such:

> Response to Intervention integrates assessment and intervention within a multi-level prevention system to maximize student achievement and to reduce behavioral problems. With RTI, schools use data to identify students at risk for poor learning outcomes, monitor student progress, provide evidence-based interventions and adjust the intensity and nature of those interventions depending on a student's responsiveness, and identify students with learning disabilities or other disabilities. (p. 2)

Each state has its own particular guidelines for RTI; however, the bottom line is that districts are required to have an RTI process in place before referring a student for special education. The RTI system is designed to provide information about students' achievement, provide learning supports to students who need them, and put in place a monitoring system that allows students to acquire the supports as needed. Students can be referred for special education services after receiving interventions in the regular classroom. Only after a student has demonstrated that he or she still needs specialized instruction after interventions in the regular education setting can the student be referred for special education services. For many students, RTI interventions are focused on reading achievement.

According to researchers in the field of reading disabilities, students with learning disabilities may display poor phonological awareness, which affects their reading ability in other areas (Shankweiler et al., 1995). Students may have problems with auditory, visual, phonological, or language processing or may have difficulties with memory or attention. Some students have physical disabilities such as visual or hearing impairment that affect reading achievement. Each student who qualifies for special education has an IEP that is specifically designed to meet his or her particular needs. A student's IEP in reading, based on assessment, is likely to be focused on gaps in basic skills knowledge in phonemic awareness or phonics, fluency issues, lack of vocabulary development, comprehension strategies, written language processing, or a combination of these areas. The IEP includes specially designed instruction (SDI) to specify evidence-based practice, and may note modification and/or accommodations for the student on reading assessments should the reading disability negatively impact expected reading behaviors. Reading instruction for students with disabilities is always required; accommodations are not a replacement for effective instruction and student practice.

What Connections Can We Make to the CCSS?

The Common Core Standards document includes a caveat for students with disabilities. A brief document attached to the Standards is entitled "Application to Students With Disabilities" (NGA Center & CCSSO, 2010b). The writers of this document state that students who are eligible under the Individuals with Disabilities Education Act "must be challenged to excel within the general curriculum" (p. 1). In other words, students with disabilities are expected to participate fully in instruction based on the CCSS. The Standards should not be made easier; instead, students should be provided supports and accommodations to achieve within the expectations of the Common Core (Council for Exceptional Children, 2011).

To promote a culture of high expectations, the CCSS document goes on to recommend three types of supports and services for students with disabilities:

- Instructional supports for learning—based on the principles of Universal Design for Learning (UDL)...

- Instructional accommodations (Thompson, Morse, Sharpe & Hall, 2005)—changes in materials or procedures—which do not change the standards...

- Assistive technology devices and services to ensure access to the general education curriculum and the Common Core State Standards. (NGA Center & CCSSO, 2010b, pp. 1–2)

What Types of Instructional Considerations Need to Occur?

Thomas, a fourth grader, is eligible for special education services in reading. When other students read and discuss main ideas and key details in science articles or read literature closely, Thomas struggles with basic comprehension. He has an IEP with accommodations for reading. In the Common Core classroom, students with disabilities that affect their reading progress still need specialized instructional attention provided by a literacy expert. These students should receive small-group comprehension instruction geared to meet their particular literacy needs. However, Thomas also needs to be part of the whole-class instruction in lessons relating to the ELA Standards. Thomas's teacher, Ms. Lee, needs to plan instruction for her class with supports for learning based on the principles of the Universal Design for Learning (UDL; CAST, 2011).

The UDL Model is a framework to address curricular planning that meets the needs of all learners. This framework was created to anticipate the needs of diverse learners when designing a curriculum, but its principles can be used when planning classroom units and lessons as well. The three principles are as follows (CAST, 2011, p. 5):

- Provide multiple means of representation.
- Provide multiple means of action and expression.
- Provide multiple means of engagement.

These can essentially be summarized as using multiple modes of teaching, learning, and engagement.

Multiple Means of Representation

Multiple means of representation relates to the "what" of learning—the ways that learners perceive and comprehend information. To provide multiple means of representation means students have a variety of ways to acquire information. We must understand student needs based on assessment and plan to use different modes (e.g., visual, auditory, language) when planning instructional activities and assessing reading performance. This can be accomplished through the use of technology as well as research-based teaching methods and strategies that take into account the different ways that children learn. For special-education students, indeed for all students, assessment is used to help them build on knowledge that they already possess to build new knowledge.

For students with reading disabilities, instruction in the Common Core Standards needs to be explicit. For struggling readers like Thomas to be able to participate in the instruction and meet the expectations, Ms. Lee engages in explicit instruction: modeling for her students, scaffolding their learning, giving multiple opportunities for her students to practice, and planning frequent check-ins using formative assessment. She intentionally models the thinking processes that she wants Thomas and his classmates to be able to use when approaching a literacy task focused on the CCSS. She is transparent in her teaching, talking in detail about what she is doing and why. She knows what to emphasize and ensures that she is clear when talking to her students about what they need to learn. Ms. Lee provides learning supports for Thomas's reading of more complex text. These include using highlighting tape to focus on vocabulary words, providing pictures or examples if there are none in the text, and preparing a digital recording of the text if he needs to listen to the passage. Ms. Lee provides numerous learning supports so Thomas can attempt to achieve the Standards.

Multiple Means of Action and Expression

Multiple means of action and expression in UDL addresses the "how" of learning—the ways in which students demonstrate their learning. To provide multiple means of expression means to ensure that students have varied options to demonstrate what they have learned. For Thomas, this means Ms. Lee provides increased opportunities to respond in lessons focused on the Common Core Standards, and she accepts different ways for him to communicate. Thomas and his classmates can dramatize passages or create illustrations to demonstrate interpretations of the text, as well participate in explicit writing instruction of the types of texts required to meet the Standards. He can also participate in academic discussions of the ideas found in the text.

Multiple Means of Engagement

Multiple means of engagement in UDL has to do with the "why" of learning—the reasons students learn. Multiple means of engagement means teachers know their students well enough to know their interests and abilities, and the teachers know what it takes to motivate the students to learn at high levels. For Thomas, Ms. Lee offers options for individual choice and autonomy, provides instruction that is culturally responsive and relevant to his interests, and helps him develop skills and procedures for tasks so he can gain a sense of academic confidence. Thomas and several other students in the class may need more or extended time, so Ms. Lee plans for that. She helps her students learn to set goals for success that will be valuable in helping them meet the appropriate Common Core Standards.

When we design classroom instruction following the principles of UDL, we increase the likelihood that the needs of students with disabilities will be met. A student who meets the eligibility criteria under the Individuals with Disabilities Education Act will have an IEP. It may designate that teachers will provide instructional modifications within mainstream classroom instruction. Any instructional modifications should support instruction in the Common Core Standards. The expectation is that if students with disabilities can meet the CCSS, they must be engaged in appropriate instruction to do so. More information about the UDL principles can be found at www.udlcenter.org/aboutudl/udlguidelines.

Gifted and Talented Students

What Do We Know About Gifted and Talented Students?

Although there are no federal mandates to serve gifted and talented students at this time, the federal definition of gifted and talented, included in the Elementary and Secondary Education Act (2004), states that gifted and talented learners are

> students, children, or youth who give evidence of high achievement capability in areas such as intellectual, creative, artistic, or leadership capacity, or in specific academic fields, and who need services and activities not ordinarily provided by the school in order to fully develop those capabilities. (National Association for Gifted Children, 2008, para. 1)

Catron and Wingenbach (1986) define gifted readers as "students who have been identified both as gifted and as reading on a level two or more years beyond their chronological grade placement" (p. 134). They make a distinction between a gifted reader and a good reader, saying that

> the gifted reader is quick to integrate prior knowledge and experience with text information, is comfortable and productive in the application of higher level thinking skills (analysis, synthesis, evaluation) to the written text, and is capable of communicating the outcome of this individualized processing of print. (p. 134)

Gifted readers appear to effortlessly employ comprehension skills such as anticipation of meaning based on visual cues, organization of text, and syntax; reader and text interaction through use of prior knowledge and experience; and metacognitive awareness. Gifted readers, according to these researchers, process "text for immediate comprehension, going directly from visual features to meaning" (p. 135). Catron and Wingenbach add that gifted readers generally add so much of their own knowledge and experience as they comprehend text that sometimes it interferes with literal levels of comprehension.

There have been few studies examining effective instructional programs for gifted and talented readers, but experts and advocates of gifted education consistently agree about the nature of instruction for these readers. Wood (2008) discusses what gifted and talented readers need from an instructional reading program, including

- Opportunities to read challenging materials
- Deeper reading comprehension instruction

- Critical reading of text, including interpretation and analysis
- Development of an appreciation of diverse, multicultural literature
- Opportunities for group discussion of selected texts
- Development of creative reading behaviors, including writing and dramatic interpretation
- Choice and self-selection of texts to promote motivation and reading enjoyment

Experts in gifted and talented education have recommended that an instructional program for these readers should include flexible grouping based on reading level and interest, acceleration, enrichment, discussion opportunities, challenging literature, and reading that is critical, creative, and inquiry-based (Wood, 2008).

What Connections Can We Make to the CCSS?

The introduction to the English Language Arts Standards includes a statement that the CCSS "do not define the nature of advanced work for students who meet the Standards prior to the end of high school" (NGA Center & CCSSO, 2010c, p. 6). In Appendix A of the Standards, the issue of text complexity for advanced readers is addressed with this statement:

> *Students reading well above and well below grade-band level need additional support.* Students for whom texts within their text complexity grade band (or even from the next higher band) present insufficient challenge must be given the attention and resources necessary to develop their reading ability at an appropriately advanced pace. (NGA Center & CCSSO, 2010d, p. 9)

Beyond these statements there is little direction for teachers regarding gifted and talented readers in the Common Core Standards. However, as teachers, we know that there will be students who are advanced beyond the CCSS at that particular grade level. Although details are lacking, the expectation of the writers of the Standards is that gifted and talented readers will have the opportunity to learn at levels of which they are capable. These students must have special consideration in the planning of curriculum, instruction, and assessment in order for their needs to be met. Gifted readers have the right to carefully planned instruction that allows them to achieve at their greatest potential in the comprehension of more challenging materials and to more sophisticated methods of response within the Common Core classroom.

What Types of Instructional Considerations Need to Occur?

Maria began reading before she started school and quickly progressed to chapter books by the end of first grade. By the beginning of third grade, she was reading and enjoying books such as *The Secret Garden* by Frances Hodgson Burnett and the Harry Potter series by J.K. Rowling. At home, Maria spent time creating elaborate projects with text, including a newspaper based on book characters. She read magazines about science and social studies topics that she found interesting and discussed her reading with an e-mail friend. Maria had an extensive vocabulary, understood the concepts of morphology, and could identify the meanings of many unfamiliar, multisyllabic words in her reading. However, at school she participated in a reading curriculum based on a series of phonics workbooks and basal readers of prescribed stories. Maria could not understand phonics because she had already internalized the concepts and was applying them automatically in her reading.

Consequently, she consistently failed basic phonics tests. In her reading group, she read all the basal stories the first day that she received the book and then paid little attention during instruction, appearing disinterested and inattentive. Maria appeared to be a student who was not progressing in reading. The truth was, Maria was a highly gifted reader trapped in the wrong type of instruction. Assessment geared toward discovering Maria's strengths could have unveiled her talents with text. A teacher who understood her needs could have provided alternative instruction geared to Maria's abilities to help her thrive to even higher levels.

Although this was the type of story we heard repeatedly during the Reading First years with the focus on struggling readers, the potential is the same when implementing the Common Core State Standards with gifted and talented readers. The National Association for Gifted Children (2008) notes that for advanced students, "fidelity to grade-level standards will limit learning" (para. 23). These readers need instructional considerations that stretch beyond the grade-level boundaries of the CCSS. Students who demonstrate the characteristics of gifted and talented readers in their early primary years need opportunities to analyze and discuss text to the extent of their abilities, rather than focusing on the beginning expectations of the Standards.

In the Common Core classroom, we need to ensure that gifted and talented readers have opportunities to engage in Standards instruction that allows them to use their abilities for text comprehension and analysis with materials that are appropriately challenging for their needs. The possibilities for text analysis, writing, research, speech and debate, and multimedia presentations are endless for gifted and talented readers in grades K–5 if teachers look ahead to the ELA Standards expectations in the grade levels to come.

English learners, students with disabilities, and gifted and talented learners are three types of students whose needs must be considered as we implement the Common Core State Standards. Because there are relatively few CCSS resources available for these students, we need to be especially diligent in ensuring that they can reach their maximum potential in our classrooms.

ESSENTIAL RESOURCES

- Chi, Y., Garcia, R.B., Surber, C., & Trautman, L. (2012). *Alignment study between the Common Core State Standards in English language arts and mathematics and the WIDA English language proficiency standards, 2007 Edition, prekindergarten through grade 12.* Retrieved July 29, 2012, from www.wida.us/Research/agenda/Alignment

- McLaughlin, M. (2012). *Guided Comprehension for English learners.* Newark, DE: International Reading Association.

- National Governors Association Center for Best Practices & Council of Chief State School Officers. (2010). *Application of Common Core State Standards for English language learners.* Retrieved July 29, 2012, from www.corestandards.org/assets/application-for-english-learners.pdf

- National Governors Association Center for Best Practices & Council of Chief State School Officers. (2010). *Application to students with disabilities.* Retrieved July 29, 2012, from www.corestandards.org/assets/application-to-students-with-disabilities.pdf

References

Allen, R.V., & Allen, C. (1970). *Language experiences in reading* (Vols. 1 & 2). Chicago: Encyclopedia Britannica.

August, D., & Shanahan, T. (Eds.). (2008). *Developing reading and writing in second-language learners: Lessons from the report of the National Literacy Panel on language-minority children and youth.* New York: Routledge; Washington, DC: Center for Applied Linguistics; Newark, DE: International Reading Association.

CAST. (2011). *Universal Design for Learning (UDL) guidelines version 2.0.* Wakefield, MA: Author. Retrieved August 4, 2012, from www.udlcenter.org/aboutudl/udlguidelines

Catron, R.M., & Wingenbach, N. (1986). Developing the potential of the gifted reader. *Theory Into Practice, 25*(2), 134–140. doi:10.1080/00405848609543213

Council for Exceptional Children. (2011). Common Core Standards: What special educators need to know. *CEC Today.* Retrieved July 10, 2012, from www.cec.sped.org/AM/Template.cfm?Section=CEC_Today1&TEMPLATE=/CM/ContentDisplay.cfm&CONTENTID=15269

Goldenberg, C. (2010). Improving achievement for English learners: Conclusions from recent reviews and emerging research. In G. Li & P.A. Edwards (Eds.), *Best practices in ELL instruction* (pp. 15–43). New York: Guilford.

Helman, L. (2009). Factors influencing second-language literacy development: A road map for teachers. In L. Helman (Ed.), *Literacy development with English learners: Research-based instruction in grades K–6* (pp. 1–17). New York: Guilford.

McLaughlin, M. (2010). *Content area reading: Teaching and learning in an age of multiple literacies.* Boston: Allyn & Bacon.

McLaughlin, M. (2012). *Guided Comprehension for English learners.* Newark, DE: International Reading Association.

National Association for Gifted Children. (2008). *Frequently asked questions.* Retrieved July 11, 2012, from www.nagc.org/index2.aspx?id=548

National Center on Response to Intervention. (2010, April). *Essential components of RTI—a closer look at Response to Intervention.* Washington, DC: U.S. Department of Education, Office of Special Education Programs, National Center on Response to Intervention. Retrieved August 22, 2012, from www.rti4success.org/pdf/rtiessentialcomponents_042710.pdf

National Governors Association Center for Best Practices & Council of Chief State School Officers. (2010a). *Application of Common Core State Standards for English language learners.* Retrieved July 29, 2012, from www.corestandards.org/assets/application-for-english-learners.pdf

National Governors Association Center for Best Practices & Council of Chief State School Officers. (2010b). *Application to students with disabilities.* Retrieved August 7, 2012, from www.corestandards.org/assets/application-to-students-with-disabilities.pdf

National Governors Association Center for Best Practices & Council of Chief State School Officers. (2010c). *Common Core State Standards for English language arts and literacy in history/social studies, science, and technical subjects.* Washington, DC: Authors. Retrieved August 4, 2012, from www.corestandards.org/assets/CCSSI_ELA%20Standards.pdf

National Governors Association Center for Best Practices & Council of Chief State School Officers. (2010d). *Common Core State Standards for English language arts and literacy in history/social studies, science, and technical subjects: Appendix A: Research supporting key elements of the Standards and glossary of key terms.* Washington, DC: Authors. Retrieved August 7, 2012, from www.corestandards.org/assets/Appendix_A.pdf

Osborne, A.G., Jr., & Russo, C.J. (2007). *Special education and the law: A guide for practitioners* (2nd ed.). Thousand Oaks, CA: Corwin.

Shankweiler, D., Crain, S., Katz, L., Fowler, A., Liberman, A., Brady, S., et al. (1995). Cognitive profiles of reading-disabled children: Comparison of language skills in phonology, morphology, and syntax. *Psychological Science, 6*(3), 149–156. doi:10.1111/j.1467-9280.1995.tb00324.x

Wood, P.F. (2008). Reading instruction with gifted and talented readers: A series of unfortunate events or a sequence of auspicious results? *Gifted Child Today, 31*(3), 16–25.

Young, T.A., & Hadaway, N.L. (Eds.). (2006). *Supporting the literacy development of English learners: Increasing success in all classrooms.* Newark, DE: International Reading Association.

CHAPTER 6

Reshaping Curriculum to Accommodate the Common Core and the Teaching of Reading

When we review the Common Core State Standards, several dichotomies emerge between what the Standards are suggesting and what we, as reading teachers, know to be research-based best practices. Examples of such issues include the following:

1. Current best practices purport that reading is a social-constructivist process, but close reading advocates that our students read with little or no activation of background knowledge.

2. Metacognitive reading comprehension strategies are not included in the CCSS.

3. The Reading Standards note that students will read complex text at their grade levels, but the CCSS do not discuss how to analyze such text.

4. Although the Standards require that students ask and answer questions, there appears to be little emphasis on divergent and evaluative thinking.

Each of these points has an impact on curriculum, instruction, and assessment. Consequently, it is crucial that we, as literacy professionals, develop curricula that integrate what research and best practices support as essential for the high-quality teaching of reading—as well as what the Common Core requires. As we engage in this discussion, it is important to remember that each state has the opportunity to add 15% to the content of the Common Core State Standards. These topics are among those that states might consider including in their versions of the CCSS.

In this chapter, we address these issues by responding to the following questions:

• How can we reconcile reading as a social-constructivist process with the CCSS's reliance on close reading?

• What can we do to ensure that our students continue to learn reading comprehension strategies?

• How can we address the Standards' requirement for students to read complex text?

- How can we make certain that our students learn higher levels of thinking and questioning?
- How can we ensure that all students receive appropriate reading instruction?

How Can We Reconcile Reading as a Social-Constructivist Process With the CCSS's Reliance on Close Reading?

To understand reading comprehension as a social-constructivist process, we must first understand constructivism as a theory about knowledge and learning. From a constructivist perspective, learning "is understood as a self-regulated process of resolving inner cognitive conflicts that often become apparent through concrete experience, collaborative discourse, and reflection" (Brooks & Brooks, 1993, p. vii). Constructivists believe that students construct knowledge by linking what is new to what is already known. They construct meaning through these connections when educators pose relevant problems, structure learning around primary concepts, seek and value students' ideas, and assess student learning in context (Brooks & Brooks, 1993).

Cambourne (2002) suggests that instructional principles emerge from constructivist theory. These include:

- Creating a classroom culture that encourages deep engagement with effective reading.
- Using strategies that are a blend of explicitness, systematicity, mindfulness, and contextualization.
- Creating continuous opportunities to develop intellectual unrest.
- Encouraging students to develop their conscious awareness of how text functions and how we create meaning.
- Designing and using tasks that will support the authentic use of the processes and understandings that are implicit in reading behavior.

Constructivism is manifested in classrooms that are characterized by engagement, accessible text, student-generated ideas, discussion, interaction, higher levels of thinking, and personal construction of meaning (McLaughlin, 2010). In such contexts, authentic literacy tasks assimilate real-world experiences, provide a purpose for learning, and encourage students to take ownership of learning (Hiebert, 1994).

In reading, constructivism is reflected in schema-based learning development, which purports that learning takes place when new information is integrated with what is already known. Prior knowledge is the key factor in this process. The more students know about a particular topic, the easier it is for them to make connections between what they know and what they are learning (Anderson, 1994; Anderson & Pearson, 1984). Constructivists view comprehension as

> the construction of the meaning of a written or spoken communication through a reciprocal, holistic interchange of ideas between the interpreter and the message in a particular communicative context. *Note:* The presumption here is that meaning resides in the intentional problem-solving, thinking processes of the interpreter during such an interchange, that the content of meaning is influenced by that person's prior knowledge and experience, and that the message so constructed by the receiver may or may not be congruent with the message sent. (Harris & Hodges, 1995, p. 39)

Vygotsky's principles enhance the constructivist perspective by addressing the social context of learning (Dixon-Krauss, 1996). According to Vygotsky, a student should be taught within his or her zone of proximal development (Forman & Cazden, 1994; Vygotsky, 1978), which is the level at which the student can learn with the support of a more knowledgeable other. As the student's understanding increases, the support from the more knowledgeable other decreases, and the student takes on more responsibility. This gradual release of responsibility is also known as scaffolding instruction.

Instruction within the zone should incorporate both scaffolding and social mediation. When discussing this Vygotskian principle, Dixon-Krauss (1996) notes that language concepts are learned through discussion—social dialogue—with more capable others. Such social interaction encourages students to think and share their ideas. However, current beliefs about best practices in the teaching of reading and close reading appear to remain in opposition. In close reading, a great deal of attention is paid to how the author presents ideas, intentional word choice, and the message being conveyed based on minute clues in the text. In informational and argumentative text, readers also need to examine the author's claims and the evidence provided to support those claims. Close reading examples beginning as early as third grade are posted as models on websites such as that of Student Achievement Partners (2012; www.achievethecore.org). In such examples, students are expected to read complex text independently and then participate in a whole-group discussion based on text-dependent questions asked by the teacher.

College and Career Readiness (CCR) Reading Anchor Standard 1 states, "Read closely to determine what the text says explicitly and to make logical inferences from it; cite specific textual evidence when writing or speaking to support conclusions drawn from the text" (NGA Center & CCSSO, 2010, p. 10). Common Core Reading Standard 1 builds to CCR Reading Anchor Standard 1 by expecting early primary children to be able to ask and answer questions about key details in a text. By grade 5, and with increasing sophistication up through grade 12, students are expected to read closely and cite textual evidence to support logical conclusions per the ELA Reading Literature and Reading Informational Standards. The same is expected in grades 6–12 for literacy in history/social studies, science, and technical subjects.

Proponents of close reading advocate that teachers should not provide background information about the text, should not engage students in prereading activities, and should not teach lessons in reading strategies. Instead, students should approach a text to glean what they can about the author's message and ideas, and to engage in a "productive struggle," a term used in the *Publishers' Criteria for the Common Core State Standards in ELA and Literacy, Grades 3–12* (Coleman & Pimentel, 2012b). In a productive struggle, students first read the text with no help and then participate in discussion to figure out the meaning of words and the author's message. In a video explaining the concept of close reading, Coleman (2011), one of the chief contributing writers of the ELA Standards and an author of the publishers' criteria for the CCSS, puts forth statements about prereading, such as "predicting what's in a text before you read it is not an essential college- and career-ready skill" (2:14). Coleman also dismisses the idea of teaching a "generic reading strategy" (2:34) before a close reading of a complex text. These and similar statements have sparked a debate over the use of close reading (Gewetz, 2012). Such statements have the potential to negate decades of research on how students learn to read. As reading teachers, we know that students who cannot read well enough to comprehend today's classroom materials are not going to magically develop the skills and strategies they need to read and analyze complex text independently.

When commenting on close reading, literacy experts have shared thinking that provides insights into its nature. For example, Fisher and Frey (personal communication, July 7, 2012) see close reading as an important aspect of reader response. As they observe,

> Rosenblatt (1995) cautioned, "The reader must remain faithful to the author's text and must be alert to the potential clues concerning character and motive" (p. 11). This requires a careful reading and often re-reading of the same text, which has not been common practice.

Pearson (personal communication, July 7, 2012) notes,

> Empson (1930) in no way meant to divorce close reading from the deployment of existing knowledge and insight in the interpretive process. Knowledge has to be tamed, sometimes even held at bay, but it is intimately involved at every step.

Pearson also suggests a series of probes to support the use of close reading. They begin with "What do you think?" and "What makes you think so?" Next, he suggests that readers follow up with one of the following prompts, which he notes range from literal to interpretive to critical and even evaluative:

- What's the point of this piece?
- What's the flow of the author's fundamental argument? What's the nature of the author's evidence base?
- What other piece from this year's syllabus does it most remind you of?
- Does this author know anything about _____ (subject of the text)?
- How would this author have responded to _____ (another piece of fiction or nonfiction)?

Pearson further elaborates,

> Another way of thinking about close reading is that it puts the reader into a frame of conducting what some would call a textual reading (in contrast to a writerly reading—focusing on authorial moves and history, or a readerly reading—focusing on examining the text in light of reader's knowledge, response preferences, and dispositions). Still another way of thinking about close reading is that it gives due respect to the text—not, by the way, to the author, but to the text.

Finally, Pearson notes, "The real truth is that close reading is as grounded in knowledge and context as it is in text. It just ensures that text has a role—and a voice—at the table."

Calfee (personal communication, July 8, 2012) concludes that the Introduction to the Common Core State Standards

> lays out a full and rich portrayal of the concept of literacy—in all its forms—as a tool that serves individuals for thinking and communicating. "Close reading" and "reading closely" are mentioned, once in the Introduction, and as part of Anchor Standard 1. In reasonable proportion and with appropriate developmental attention, this idea certainly has a place in what we would expect of a high school graduate, but it does not warrant placement as the keystone in the arch of literacy that is portrayed by the Standards.

Our students are asked to read complex text to meet college and career goals, but they must be able to use comprehension strategies to read such texts. Therefore, the teaching of reading comprehension strategies needs to remain the focus of reading instruction at the K–5 level. Close reading experiences should be introduced through read-alouds in K–1 and occasionally in lessons in grades 2–5 as students learn to read more complex texts.

What Can We Do to Ensure That Our Students Continue to Learn Reading Comprehension Strategies?

The primary difficulty with the Common Core's failure to include reading comprehension strategies is that most school curricula will be built on the Standards—and will not include the additional content that teachers know students need. The fact is that a good number of states have adopted the CCSS without making any changes to content—much less the 15% that they have been invited to add. Individual states need to include the teaching of reading comprehension strategies in their versions of the Standards.

Studies have demonstrated that explicit instruction of comprehension strategies improves students' comprehension of new texts and topics (Dole, Duffy, Roehler, & Pearson, 1991; Duffy et al., 1987; Hiebert, Pearson, Taylor, Richardson, & Paris, 1998). Research supports the teaching of reading comprehension strategies beginning in the primary grades (Duffy, 2001; Duke & Pearson, 2002; Hilden & Pressley, 2002; McLaughlin, 2002). In fact, Duke and Pearson (2002) suggest incorporating "both explicit instruction in specific comprehension strategies and a great deal of time and opportunity for actual reading, writing, and discussion of text" (p. 207).

Fielding and Pearson (1994) recommend a framework for comprehension instruction that encourages the gradual release of responsibility from teacher to student. This four-step approach includes teacher modeling, guided practice, independent practice, and application of the strategy in authentic reading situations. This framework is underpinned by Vygotsky's (1978) work on instruction within the zone of proximal development and also supported by scaffolding, the gradual relinquishing of support as students become more competent in using the strategy.

Linking skills and strategies can facilitate comprehension. Comprehension strategies are generally more complex than comprehension skills and often require the orchestration of several skills. Effective instruction links comprehension skills and strategies to promote strategic reading. For example, the comprehension skills of sequencing, making judgments, noting details, making generalizations, and using text structure can be linked to summarizing, which is a comprehension strategy (Lipson, 2001). These and other skills, including generating questions, making inferences, distinguishing between important and less important details, and drawing conclusions, facilitate students' use of one or more comprehension strategies. Generating questions is an example of a skill that permeates all reading comprehension skills. Several such skills, including asking and answering questions, are addressed in the Reading Standards (see Reading Standard 1.1).

After explaining and modeling skills and strategies, we can scaffold instruction to provide the support necessary as students attempt new tasks. As we observe students gaining competence in using the strategies, we can gradually release responsibility for learning to the students, who apply the strategies independently after practicing them in a variety of settings.

In the Key Design Considerations section in the Introduction to the Common Core State Standards, reading comprehension strategies are addressed in a subsection labeled "A focus on results rather than means." It details the Standards' results-oriented approach:

> By emphasizing required achievements, the Standards leave room for teachers, curriculum developers, and states to determine how those goals should be reached and what additional topics should be addressed. Thus, the Standards do not mandate such things as a particular writing process or the full range of metacognitive strategies that students may need to monitor and direct their thinking and learning. Teachers are thus free to provide students with whatever tools and knowledge their professional judgment and experience identify as most helpful for meeting the goals set out in the Standards. (NGA Center & CCSSO, 2010, p. 4)

How Can We Address the Standards' Requirement for Students to Read Complex Text?

CCR Reading Anchor Standard 10 states that students will "Read and comprehend complex literary and informational texts independently and proficiently" (NGA Center & CCSSO, 2010, p. 10). As reading teachers, we can support the need for students to read increasingly complex texts, but we also know that not all students are capable of reading such texts, particularly at grade level. As the authors of the publishers' criteria for the CCSS note, "Many students will need careful instruction—including effective scaffolding—to enable them to read at the level required by the Common Core State Standards" (Coleman & Pimentel, 2012a, p. 8; Coleman & Pimental, 2012b). The complex nature of text is not new to those of us who teach reading. We fully understand its multifaceted features and its relation to readers. As Hiebert (2012) has observed,

- The complexity of a text is a function of the reader's proficiency. There are complex beginning reading texts, there are complex middle-grade texts, etc.
- Numerous features can make a text complex.
- Typically: Complex texts have complex ideas and, usually, complex ideas are conveyed with rare and infrequent vocabulary. (slide 8)

In 2006, ACT (formerly American College Testing) based its definition of text complexity on three levels of increasingly complex text: uncomplicated, more challenging, and complex. ACT (2006) further delineated the characteristics of text on its continuum as

- Relationships (interactions among ideas or characters)
- Richness (amount and sophistication of information conveyed through data or literary devices)
- Structure (how the text is organized and how it progresses)
- Style (author's tone and use of language)
- Vocabulary (author's word choice)
- Purpose (author's intent in writing the text) (p. 15)

Table 6.1 shows further details of ACT's definition.

Although several of the characteristics developed by ACT are rooted more in literary analysis than in reading, ACT's three categories of text complexity—uncomplicated, more challenging, and complex—strongly parallel the terms used by literacy professionals when discussing text levels:

Table 6.1 Characteristics of Uncomplicated, More Challenging, and Complex Texts on the ACT Reading Test

Aspect of Text	Degree of Text Complexity		
	Uncomplicated	**More Challenging**	**Complex**
Relationships	Basic, straightforward	Sometimes implicit	Subtle, involved, deeply embedded
Richness	Minimal/limited	Moderate/more detailed	Sizable/highly sophisticated
Structure	Simple, conventional	More involved	Elaborate, sometimes unconventional
Style	Plain, accessible	Richer, less plain	Often intricate
Vocabulary	Familiar	Some difficult, context-dependent words	Demanding, highly context dependent
Purpose	Clear	Conveyed with some subtlety	Implicit, sometimes ambiguous

Note. From *Reading Between the Lines: What the ACT Reveals About College Readiness in Reading* (p. 14), by ACT, 2006, Iowa City, IA: Author. Copyright 2006 by ACT. Reprinted with permission.

independent, instructional, and frustration. Students can read at the independent level with no assistance, and they can read at the instructional level with some assistance from the teacher. Frustration-level text is often shared in different ways, including teacher read-alouds and books on CD.

As reading teachers, we know that students have diverse reading abilities; not all students are capable of reading text at their grade level. There are general guidelines for determining students' reading levels related to word accuracy, comprehension, and fluency. For word accuracy, the text is considered easy if students can read it with 95–100% accuracy, provided their fluency and comprehension are appropriate. The instructional level is reached when students can read most of the text but have some challenges with words or content. This is usually between 90% and 94% accuracy. Students who read a text with accuracy below 90% often struggle with fluency and comprehension because they must use so much of their cognitive focus to figure out unknown words. This is considered the frustration level. At this level, keywords are often misunderstood, and comprehension is compromised.

In addition to word accuracy, comprehension must also be assessed. This often involves determining students' background knowledge as well as their ability to retell or summarize what was read, effectively discuss the text, or predict what will happen next. If a student is unable to successfully complete such tasks, the text may be too difficult.

Fluency, the third factor, is directly related to comprehension. In fact, Rasinski (2010) notes that fluency is the ability to read accurately and expressively at a natural rate with good phrasing and good comprehension. Fluency checks, which can easily be completed during Guided Reading, contribute to our understanding when creating appropriate student–text matches.

When we assess students' word accuracy, comprehension, and fluency, we gain insights into their reading abilities. Although the results of these informal measures are approximations, they provide a starting point for making appropriate student–text matches for guided and independent practice.

How Can We Make Certain That Our Students Learn Higher Levels of Thinking and Questioning?

The Common Core State Standards are built on the CCR Anchor Standards, which purport to ensure that our students are prepared for their future endeavors. However, when reviewing the CCSS, it becomes clear that there is little, if any, emphasis on students' ability to engage in higher level thinking, a necessity for their future success. The emphases within the K–5 Standards appear to be on finding answers to text-dependent questions. Consequently, we, as teachers, must continue to teach students how to think at higher levels.

Importantly, although the writers of the Common Core created the Standards, they also noted that teaching is in the hands of the educators. For example, Reading Literature Standard 1 for grades K–3 focuses on asking and answering questions. While this standard is limited in grades K and 1, because the questions are literal in nature, we can still teach students to generate questions at higher levels, including the convergent, divergent, and evaluative levels. In Reading Literature Standard 1 for second grade, a more detailed wording is presented. It notes that students should "ask and answer such questions as *who, what, where, when, why,* and *how* to demonstrate understanding of key details in a text" (NGA Center & CCSSO, 2010, p. 11).

Again, the focus is on understanding what appears in the text. Four of the question starters—who, what, where, and when—are literal in nature. The remaining question prompts, how and why, raise students' thinking to the convergent level. Similar standards about asking and answering questions in the primary grades appear in the Reading Informational Text Standards and the Speaking and Listening Standards.

Another area in which literal thinking is emphasized is Reading Informational Text Standard 2 for grades K–5. In this standard, students are asked to recall the main ideas and details within a text. Similar information also appears in the Common Core State Standards for Speaking and Listening.

To continue to engage our students in higher level thinking, we can follow Ciardiello's (1998, 2007) suggestions for teaching students how to generate and respond to questions at four levels: memory, convergent, divergent, and evaluative. Ciardiello also provides question prompts for each level. When teaching students in the elementary grades, we can describe the memory level as "in the text." In fact, we can teach our students that they can put their fingers on the answers in the text. We can describe the convergent level as the why and how level, the divergent level as the imagine level, and the evaluative level as What do you think? Ciardiello's questioning levels, including signal words and cognitive operations for each category, are featured in Table 6.2.

Table 6.2 Ciardiello's Levels of Questioning

Question Level	Signal Words and Phrases	Cognitive Operations
Memory	*Who?, What?, Where?, When?*	Naming, defining, identifying, designating
Convergent thinking	*Why?, How?, In what ways?*	Explaining, stating relationships, comparing/contrasting
Divergent thinking	*imagine, suppose, predict, if/then*	Predicting, hypothesizing, inferring, reconstructing
Evaluative thinking	*defend, judge, justify, What do you think?*	Valuing, judging, defending, justifying

How Can We Ensure That All Students Receive Appropriate Reading Instruction?

In 2000, the International Reading Association published a set of children's literacy rights in response to the growing concern about narrowed reading instruction. The document states, "We must ensure that all children receive the excellent instruction and support they need to learn to read and write" (p. 1). We think this statement is as true today as it was then. All students have the right to engage in the social-constructivist nature of reading, use reading comprehension strategies, read increasingly challenging text, and understand how to successfully engage in higher order thinking. As teachers, we can honor these rights by providing our students with a full range of research-based, best literacy practices when implementing the ELA Common Core Standards. Examples of using such practices to accommodate the CCSS can be found in Chapters 7–16.

References

ACT. (2006). *Reading between the lines: What the ACT reveals about college readiness in reading.* Iowa City, IA: Author. Retrieved August 22, 2012, from www.act.org/research/policymakers/pdf/reading_report.pdf

Anderson, R.C. (1994). Role of the reader's schema in comprehension, learning, and memory. In R.B. Ruddell, M.R. Ruddell, & H. Singer (Eds.), *Theoretical models and processes of reading* (4th ed., pp. 469–482). Newark, DE: International Reading Association.

Anderson, R.C., & Pearson, P.D. (1984). A schema-theoretic view of basic processes in reading comprehension. In P.D. Pearson, R. Barr, M.L. Kamil, & P. Mosenthal (Eds.), *Handbook of reading research* (pp. 255–291). New York: Longman.

Brooks, J.G., & Brooks, M.G. (1993). *In search of understanding: The case for constructivist classrooms.* Alexandria, VA: Association for Supervision and Curriculum Development.

Cambourne, B. (2002). Holistic, integrated approaches to reading and language arts instruction: The constructivist framework of an instructional theory. In A.E. Farstrup & S.J. Samuels (Eds.), *What research has to say about reading instruction* (3rd ed., pp. 25–47). Newark, DE: International Reading Association. doi:10.1598/0872071774.2

Ciardiello, A.V. (1998). Did you ask a good question today? Alternative cognitive and metacognitive strategies. *Journal of Adolescent & Adult Literacy, 42*(3), 210–219.

Ciardiello, A.V. (2007). *Puzzle them first! Motivating adolescent readers with question-finding.* Newark, DE: International Reading Association.

Coleman, D. (2011, July 31). *Close reading of text: Letter from Birmingham jail, Martin Luther King, Jr.* [Video]. Albany, NY: EngageNY. Retrieved June 24, 2012, from engageny.org/resource/close-reading-of-text-mlk -letter-from-birmingham-jail/

Coleman, D., & Pimentel, S. (2012a, May). *Revised publishers' criteria for the Common Core State Standards in English language arts and literacy, grades K–2.* Washington, DC: National Governors Association, Council of Chief State School Officers, Achieve, Council of the Great City Schools, & National Association of State Boards of Education. Retrieved July 12, 2012, from corestandards.org/assets/Publishers_Criteria_for_K-2.pdf

Coleman, D., & Pimentel, S. (2012b, April). *Revised publishers' criteria for the Common Core State Standards in English language arts and literacy, grades 3–12.* Washington, DC: National Governors Association, Council of Chief State School Officers, Achieve, Council of the Great City Schools, & National Association of State Boards of Education. Retrieved August 4, 2012, from corestandards.org/assets/Publishers_Criteria_for_3-12.pdf

Dixon-Krauss, L. (1996). *Vygotsky in the classroom: Mediated literacy instruction and assessment.* White Plains, NY: Longman.

Dole, J.A., Duffy, G.G., Roehler, L.R., & Pearson, P.D. (1991). Moving from the old to the new: Research on reading comprehension instruction. *Review of Educational Research, 61*(2), 239–264.

Duffy, G.G. (2001, December). *The case for direct explanation of strategies.* Paper presented at the 51st annual meeting of the National Reading Conference, San Antonio, TX.

Duffy, G.G., Roehler, L.R., Sivan, E., Rackliffe, G., Book, C., Meloth, M.S., et al. (1987). Effects of explaining the reasoning associated with using reading strategies. *Reading Research Quarterly*, 22(3), 347–368. doi:10.2307/747973

Duke, N.K., & Pearson, P.D. (2002). Effective practices for developing reading comprehension. In A.E. Farstrup & S.J. Samuels (Eds.), *What research has to say about reading instruction* (3rd ed., pp. 205–242). Newark, DE: International Reading Association.

Empson, W. (1930). *Seven types of ambiguity*. London: Chatto & Windus.

Fielding, L.G., & Pearson, P.D. (1994). Reading comprehension: What works. *Educational Leadership*, 51(5), 62–68.

Forman, E.A., & Cazden, C.B. (1994). Exploring Vygotskian perspectives in education: The cognitive value of peer interaction. In R.B. Ruddell, M.R. Ruddell, & H. Singer (Eds.), *Theoretical models and processes of reading* (4th ed., pp. 155–178). Newark, DE: International Reading Association.

Gewetz, C. (2012). Common standards ignite debate over prereading. *Education Week*, 31(29), 1, 22–23.

Harris, T.L., & Hodges, R.E. (Eds.). (1995). *The literacy dictionary: The vocabulary of reading and writing*. Newark, DE: International Reading Association.

Hiebert, E.H. (1994). Becoming literate through authentic tasks: Evidence and adaptations. In R.B. Ruddell, M.R. Ruddell, & H. Singer (Eds.), *Theoretical models and processes of reading* (4th ed., pp. 391–413). Newark, DE: International Reading Association.

Hiebert, E.H. (2012, February). *Seven actions that teachers can take right now: Text complexity*. Retrieved June 22, 2012 from textproject.org/assets/Uploads/Hiebert_2012-03-10_CRLP-slides.pdf

Hiebert, E.H., Pearson, P.D., Taylor, B.M., Richardson, V., & Paris, S.G. (1998). *Every child a reader*. Ann Arbor, MI: Center for the Improvement of Early Reading Achievement.

Hilden, K., & Pressley, M. (2002, December). *Can teachers become comprehension strategies teachers given a small amount of training?* Paper presented at the 52nd annual meeting of the National Reading Conference, Miami, FL.

International Reading Association. (2000). *Making a difference means making it different: Honoring children's rights to excellent reading instruction*. Newark, DE: International Reading Association.

Lipson, M.Y. (2001). *A fresh look at comprehension*. Paper presented at the Reading/Language Arts Symposium, Chicago, IL.

McLaughlin, M. (2002). *Guided Comprehension in the primary grades: Curricularizing strategy instruction*. Paper presented at the 52nd annual meeting of the National Reading Conference, Miami, FL.

McLaughlin, M. (2010). *Content area reading: Teaching and learning in an age of multiple literacies*. Boston: Allyn & Bacon.

National Governors Association Center for Best Practices & Council of Chief State School Officers. (2010). *Common Core State Standards for English language arts and literacy in history/social studies, science, and technical subjects*. Washington, DC: Authors.

Rasinski, T.V. (2010). *The fluent reader: Oral and silent reading strategies for building fluency, word recognition, and comprehension* (2nd ed.). New York: Scholastic.

Rosenblatt, L.M. (1995). *Literature as exploration* (5th ed.). New York: Modern Language Association of America.

Student Achievement Partners. (2012). *Close reading exemplars*. Retrieved June 27, 2012, from www.achievethecore.org/steal-these-tools/close-reading-exemplars

Vygotsky, L.S. (1978). *Mind in society: The development of higher psychological processes* (M. Cole, V. John-Steiner, S. Scribner, & E. Souberman, Eds. & Trans.). Cambridge, MA: Harvard University Press.

PART II

Teaching the Common Core State Standards for Reading

The Common Core State Standards (CCSS) are based on the set of 10 College and Career Readiness (CCR) Anchor Standards. The CCR Anchor Standards describe what college students should know and be able to do in the areas of reading (for both literature and informational text), writing, speaking and listening, and language (which includes conventions of standard English, knowledge of language, and vocabulary acquisition and use). It is safe to say that the Anchor Standards for Reading are the basis for the English Language Arts (ELA) Common Core State Standards. Students are expected to read and comprehend, and perform more sophisticated tasks with text than ever before to prepare for college and careers in the future. Each expectation in the CCSS begins with a text of some sort—a book, story, magazine article, poem, play, brochure, webpage, digital resource, piece of student writing, and so forth. Meeting the CCR Anchor Standards for Reading is key to achieving the Standards across the curriculum.

In Part II, we describe each CCR Anchor Standard for Reading and its corresponding Common Core State Standards for kindergarten through grade 5. As we contemplated the Standards, we assigned each an icon as a helpful way to remember the focus of each standard. The College and Career Readiness Anchor Standards for Reading chart provides a quick reference to the concepts and expectations that each icon and related Standards represent.

Each of the CCR Anchor Standards for Reading is discussed in a chapter that follows. Our exploration of the Standards is guided by these five queries:

1. What does this CCR Anchor Standard mean for college success?

2. How do the K–5 CCSS build to this CCR Anchor Standard?

3. What literacy skills and strategies support this reading standard at each grade level?

4. How can we teach this reading standard so our students achieve?

5. What other ELA Standards can be integrated with this reading standard?

Details concerning each question follow.

College and Career Readiness Anchor Standards for Reading

CCR Reading Anchor Standard 1		
Reading closely		Thinking like a detective

CCR Reading Anchor Standard 2		
Central idea/theme		Getting to the point

CCR Reading Anchor Standard 3		
Development of characters, events, and ideas		Following the thread

CCR Reading Anchor Standard 4		
Word meanings		Knowing the word

CCR Reading Anchor Standard 5		
Text structures		Examining how the text is built

CCR Reading Anchor Standard 6		
Point of view		Seeing in different ways

CCR Reading Anchor Standard 7		
Content in diverse media		Putting it together

CCR Reading Anchor Standard 8		
Reasons and evidence		Hearing the argument

CCR Reading Anchor Standard 9		
Comparing and contrasting		Weighing the works

CCR Reading Anchor Standard 10		
Text complexity		Stepping higher

What Does This CCR Anchor Standard Mean for College Success?

The Common Core State Standards were created by taking each College and Career Readiness Anchor Standard and backward mapping to what the earliest primary-grade students would need to know and be able to do to build a foundation for the expectations of the CCR Anchor Standard. The first section of each chapter focuses on an examination of the rationale for the CCR Standard.

How Do the K–5 CCSS Build to This CCR Anchor Standard?

In the second section of each chapter, we include the vertical alignment from kindergarten to grade 5 for each standard. We describe special considerations that we may need to think through when planning to teach the standard at each grade level.

What Literacy Skills and Strategies Support This Reading Standard at Each Grade Level?

In the next section of each chapter, we list and discuss the skills and concepts that students will need to achieve the Common Core Standard at each grade level. We keep in mind that some students may not have mastered the skills and concepts from the previous grades, so it is important to plan instruction that meets the additional needs of students in the class.

How Can We Teach This Reading Standard So Our Students Achieve?

In the fourth section of each chapter, we include a collection of teaching ideas that we can use in our classrooms to teach the literacy skills and strategies that support each standard. At the close of this section, a rich task, which integrates several standards, is discussed.

What Other ELA Standards Can Be Integrated With This Reading Standard?

The CCSS were not designed to be used as a checklist and should not be taught in isolation. They must be part of a carefully designed curriculum and include comprehensive instruction that integrates related standards. We believe that the effective teaching of the Reading Standards means integrating the ELA Standards into a series of rich, connected, instructional tasks. Attention to Writing, Speaking and Listening, and Language Standards are naturally integrated into any authentic reading task.

In the last section of each chapter, we include other ELA Standards that can be integrated with the focus reading standard for the chapter. This provides an opportunity to study the Common Core Standards carefully and decide how particular ELA standards can be combined and taught within the content expectations of their district or school. In particular, we should consider the following when planning to integrate ELA standards.

Reading

For each reading standard, there are a number of other reading standards that can be taught together. The Reading Standards were designed so reading can be used as a tool for learning. Most of the Reading Standards support the ability to read complex text closely and deliberately. Few of them can be deeply taught in isolation.

Writing

Reading and writing are inextricably linked, so writing is a natural part of reading instruction. Writing from sources, writing text-based answers, and engaging in brief research tasks can lead to writing to explore ideas and demonstrate learning in social studies, science, and other content areas. Writing longer pieces and deriving ideas from a variety of texts, including digital sources, are also student focuses. Writing Standards 1–3 describe expectations for three types of writing: (1) writing opinion pieces (called argumentation in grades 6–12), (2) writing informative/explanatory texts, and (3) writing narratives. Writing Standards 4–6 support the standards for the writing process, which should be addressed in every formal writing experience. Writing Standards 7–9 are the standards for conducting research, including the use of technology. Writing Standard 10 establishes the expectation for students to write for varied time frames.

Speaking and Listening

The Speaking and Listening Standards establish an expectation that students collaborate with one another, discuss ideas and content, listen carefully to others, and present their learning in different ways, including multimedia presentations. The Common Core Standards cannot be taught in a classroom in which students consistently sit quietly with no interaction. Teaching the CCSS for Reading requires active learning that addresses multiple modalities, including lots of opportunities for academic conversation.

Language

There are two main parts to the Language Standards. Language Standards 1–3 support writing conventions and language usage and should be considered in every lesson that includes writing. Language Standards 4–6 target vocabulary acquisition and use. Direct instruction and learning from context should be balanced in the elementary grades. The vocabulary standards should always be addressed when teaching the Reading Standards.

Part II is an important resource when planning for the ELA Standards at the state, district, school, team, and classroom levels. Each of the chapters that follow is focused on one of the CCR Anchor Standards. Chapters 7–16 are especially valuable resources as we develop a curriculum, units, and lessons to help our students achieve the Standards.

CHAPTER 7

CCR Reading Anchor Standard 1: Reading Closely and Citing Textual Evidence

Thinking Like a Detective

College and Career Readiness Reading Anchor Standard 1
Read closely to determine what the text says explicitly and to make logical inferences from it; cite specific textual evidence when writing or speaking to support conclusions drawn from the text. (NGA Center & CCSSO, 2010a, p. 10)

What Does CCR Reading Anchor Standard 1 Mean?

The aim of College and Career Readiness (CCR) Reading Anchor Standard 1 is to ensure that students can read and comprehend the author's message in texts. Readers need to be able to draw conclusions about what they read and make inferences that make sense, even when the text is challenging. Being able to cite specific textual evidence from the text in discussion or writing is an indication that the student can support a thoughtful and logical conclusion when reading literary or informational text. CCR Reading Standard 1 complements CCR Reading Standard 10, which focuses on text complexity and the need for students to be able to read more challenging texts independently.

Reading Anchor Standard 1 focuses on several reading skills:

- The ability to read closely to determine what the text says explicitly
- The ability to make logical inferences from the text when writing or speaking
- The ability to cite specific textual evidence to support conclusions

Reading Closely

The term *close reading* can be likened to reading like a detective. Just like Sherlock Holmes, when students read closely, they need to examine the evidence and draw logical conclusions to support their ideas and interpret those of the author.

Close reading is an actual method in many college-level English classes. In the close reading method of literary analysis, students are expected to observe carefully as they read, looking for facts and details. In a close reading of literature, readers discover and interpret aspects of a narrative or poetic text, such as theme, interactions among characters, and events. Students take note of literacy devices, such as irony, tone, and the author's specific word choice. In informational text, readers analyze an author's use of evidence to make his point, looking for claims the author makes and reasons used to support these claims. Then, in both literature and informational text, students are asked to interpret their observations to make inferences or to support an opinion about the text, most often in a written analysis. Close reading is only one method of achieving CCR Anchor Standard 1, but it is the method that is most widely discussed to date. Common Core Reading Standard 1 for grades K–5 build to CCR Standard 1 with the expectation that students do the fundamental tasks required to "read closely to determine what the text says explicitly" (NGA Center & CCSSO, 2010a, p. 10). (Recommendations for how to teach a close reading lesson in grades 3–5 appear later in this chapter.)

Making Logical Inferences

An author does not include every literal idea in a text. When readers comprehend, they are constantly making inferences. Students must look for clues in the text to help them understand the passage. The clues in the text, along with the reader's background knowledge of the topic, the author, or the context, help the reader make logical leaps in understanding to something that makes sense. Students continually encounter text in which they are required to make inferences to understand the author's intent.

Citing Textual Evidence

Students are expected to be able to draw inferences from challenging text and be credible when talking or writing about the text. Citing text as the source of evidence involves being able to extract words verbatim to prove a point. Students must be able to read a text, determine the main idea or key details, and explain their reasoning using the explicit examples in a text that helped them make decisions about what the text means. Citing textual evidence means being able to quote the author accurately to make a point.

Table 7.1 Common Core State Standard 1 for Reading Literature in Grades K–5

Grade	Standard
K	With prompting and support, ask and answer questions about key details in a text.
1	Ask and answer questions about key details in a text.
2	Ask and answer such questions as *who, what, where, when, why,* and *how* to demonstrate understanding of key details in a text.
3	Ask and answer questions to demonstrate understanding of a text, referring explicitly to the text as the basis for the answers.
4	Refer to details and examples in a text when explaining what the text says explicitly and when drawing inferences from the text.
5	Quote accurately from a text when explaining what the text says explicitly and when drawing inferences from the text.

Note. The standards are from *Common Core State Standards for English Language Arts and Literacy in History/Social Studies, Science, and Technical Subjects* (pp. 11 and 12), by National Governors Association Center for Best Practices and Council of Chief State School Officers, 2010, Washington, DC: Authors.

How Do the CCSS Build to CCR Reading Anchor Standard 1?

Common Core Reading Standard 1 is worded exactly in the same way in both the Reading Literature and Reading Informational Text Standards at every grade level (see Tables 7.1 and 7.2). In grades K–2, the emphasis is on learning how to ask and answer questions about key details in a text. At grade 3, the standard shifts: By the end of grade 3, students should be able to not only ask and answer questions about key details but also refer to the text to support their questions and answers. By the end of grade 4, students should not only refer to the text when asking and answering questions but draw inferences from the text as well. At grade 5, the emphasis shifts again to being able to quote the text accurately when asking and answering questions, drawing conclusions, and making inferences.

There are four main skill areas to teach for Common Core Reading Standard 1 by the end of fifth grade for students to be on track for middle school and the higher expectations of the Standards at grades 6–12:

1. Identifying key details

2. Asking and answering questions

3. Making logical inferences

4. Citing textual evidence

The instructional shift from a focus on literature to more of a balance between literature and informational text is one of the major differences in the Common Core Standards compared with many previous state standards.

What Literacy Skills and Strategies Support Common Core Reading Standard 1?

Common Core Reading Standard 1, for both literature and informational text, is associated with Reading Standard 10, which focuses on complex text. We can introduce reading complex text closely during read-alouds or in a shared reading setting with focused student discussion. Kindergartners should be given prompting and support throughout the kindergarten year, whereas first-grade students should be given prompting and support as necessary at the beginning of the year, scaffolding to independence by the end of the year. We can scaffold students as they approach and read more complex passages closely on their own by grade 3. The supporting skills and strategies for Common Core Reading Literature Standard 1 are featured in Table 7.3.

Table 7.2 Common Core State Standard 1 for Reading Informational Text in Grades K–5

Grade	Standard
K	With prompting and support, ask and answer questions about key details in a text.
1	Ask and answer questions about key details in a text.
2	Ask and answer such questions as *who, what, where, when, why,* and *how* to demonstrate understanding of key details in a text.
3	Ask and answer questions to demonstrate understanding of a text, referring explicitly to the text as the basis for the answers.
4	Refer to details and examples in a text when explaining what the text says explicitly and when drawing inferences from the text.
5	Quote accurately from a text when explaining what the text says explicitly and when drawing inferences from the text.

Note. The standards are from *Common Core State Standards for English Language Arts and Literacy in History/Social Studies, Science, and Technical Subjects* (pp. 13 and 14), by National Governors Association Center for Best Practices and Council of Chief State School Officers, 2010, Washington, DC: Authors.

Table 7.3 Common Core State Standard 1 for Reading Literature: Supporting Skills and Strategies

Grade	Skills and Strategies
K	• Ask questions about stories, poems, and plays. • Answer questions about stories, poems, and plays. • Identify the characters, setting, and sequence of events (key details in a literary text).
1	• Ask questions about stories, poems, and plays. • Answer questions about stories, poems, and plays. • Identify the characters, setting, and sequence of events (key details in a literary text).
2	• Ask and answer questions about stories, poems, and plays. • Identify key details in a literary text (who: characters; what: events; when: time of events; where: setting; why: character's motivation and problem; how: sequence of events and problem resolution).
3	• Ask and answer questions about a literary text. • Refer to details in a literary text to create and answer questions.
4	• Explain what a literary text says explicitly. • Refer to details in a literary text to explain the text. • Draw inferences from a literary text.
5	• Explain a literary text. • Draw inferences from a literary text. • Quote a literary text accurately when explaining inferences. • Use quotation marks for direct quotes when writing about a literary text.

To teach Reading Literature Standard 1, we need to choose stories, dramas, and poetry with rich language, varied sentence structures, and more complex ideas in which students need to make inferences to comprehend the author's meaning. See Appendix B of the Common Core State Standards for a list of exemplar texts in literature for grades K and 1, 2 and 3, and 4 and 5 (NGA Center & CCSSO, 2010b). A glance through these text exemplars should guide teachers to choose a balance of more complex literary texts to be read aloud and texts that students read independently. Texts that are appropriate for differentiated reading instruction, such as leveled texts, should still be part of every elementary classroom reading plan as students learn to decode and comprehend as well as analyze text. Teachers should use children's literature that is engaging and motivating for students when they teach supporting skills and strategies.

To teach Reading Informational Text Standard 1, we can use high-quality informational books, articles, and websites that are relevant to the students and the content to be taught. In informational texts, key details are often important facts. We can teach students to identify key details in an informational book, article, or webpage, using the text and its text features, such as illustrations, maps, graphs, or charts. To accomplish this, we can teach students the supporting skills and strategies outlined in Table 7.4.

Table 7.4 Common Core State Standard 1 for Reading Informational Text: Supporting Skills and Strategies

Grade	Skills and Strategies
K	• Ask questions about an informational text. • Answer questions about an informational text. • Identify facts (key details in an informational text).
1	• Ask questions about an informational text. • Answer questions about an informational text. • Identify facts (key details in an informational text).
2	• Ask and answer questions about an informational text. • Identify key details in an informational text (facts that tell who, what, where, when, why, and how).
3	• Ask and answer questions about an informational text. • Refer to details in an informational text to create and answer questions.
4	• Explain what an informational text says explicitly. • Refer to details in an informational text to explain the text. • Draw inferences from an informational text.
5	• Explain an informational text. • Draw inferences from an informational text. • Quote an informational text accurately when explaining inferences. • Use quotation marks for direct quotes when writing about an informational text.

How Can We Teach Reading Standard 1 to Ensure That Our Students Achieve?

In this section, we discuss the Standards tasks required of students at various grade levels. For example, the first Common Core College and Career Readiness Anchor Standard for Reading requires that students be able to identify key details, ask and answer questions, make inferences, cite textual evidence, and demonstrate understanding of the text. Because technology should be integrated into the curriculum along with the Standards, we also provide an example of how to make that connection. We begin by describing the teaching idea. Next, we discuss how it supports the Standards. Finally, we conclude by sharing a completed example of student work that relates to the standard.

Identifying Key Details

In the first Reading Anchor Standard for grades K–5, one of our tasks is to teach students to identify key details. The key details in a narrative text are the characters, setting, problem, attempts to resolve the problem, and resolution. The Story Map is a widely used graphic organizer designed to promote student understanding of the key details of narrative texts. This organizer provides an alternative format for summarizing stories. When a Story Map is completed, the student can use the information to create an oral summary of the narrative text. Figure 7.1 shows an example of a Story Map based on the book *Click, Clack, Moo: Cows That Type* by Doreen Cronin (2000).

Asking and Answering Questions

Asking and answering questions is another student focus in the first Anchor Standard for Reading for grades K–5. Thick and Thin Questions (Lewin & Shoemaker, 1998) is a teaching idea designed to help students to create questions pertaining to a text. It also helps students discern the depth of the questions they ask. Students use the questions they generate and to which they respond to facilitate their understanding of a text. Thin Questions are created at the literal level, and answers

Figure 7.1 Example of a Story Map

Example Text: Cronin, D. (2000). *Click, clack, moo: Cows that type.* New York: Simon & Schuster Books for Young Readers.

Title:
Click, Clack, Moo: Cows That Type

Setting:
A farm

Characters:
Farmer Brown, the cows, the hens, the ducks

Problem:
The cows on Farmer Brown's farm have learned to type and are making unusual demands on Farmer Brown.

Attempts to Resolve the Problem:

Event 1:
The cows refuse to produce milk unless they get electric blankets.

Event 2:
The hens refuse to produce eggs unless they get electric blankets.

Event 3:
Farmer Brown types his own note and sends Duck to make a deal with the cows and hens.

Event 4:
The cows and hens get electric blankets and give the typewriter to Duck.

Event 5:
Duck gets the typewriter and writes a note demanding a diving board for the pond.

Resolution:
Duck gets a diving board, Farmer Brown gets the typewriter, and everyone is happy.

Figure 7.2 Example of Thick and Thin Questions

Example Text: Osborne, M.P., & Boyce, N.P. (2007). *Polar bears and the Arctic*. New York: Scholastic.

Thick Question: <u>Why do scientists call polar bears "sea bears"?</u>

Thin Question: <u>How wide are polar bear paws?</u>

may easily be found in the text. Thick Questions are queries in which the answer may not be as noticeable in the text or may need to be inferred. Figure 7.2 shows an example of Thick and Thin Questions based on the book *Polar Bears and the Arctic* by Mary Pope Osborne and Natalie Pope Boyce (2007).

Making Inferences

To achieve Reading Standard 1, students must refer to the text to make logical inferences. Primary-grade students can learn to make inferences using concrete objects. For example, McGregor (2007) taught primary-grade students about the concept of inference by asking them to infer about an old shoe and creating an Inference/Evidence chart. In Reading Standard 1, intermediate-grade students are expected to refer to details and examples in a text when explaining what the text says explicitly and when drawing inferences from the text. The teaching idea that we have selected for teaching this skill is the Inferring Equation (Harvey & Goudvis, 2007).

The Inferring Equation, "Background Knowledge + Text Clues = Inference" (Harvey & Goudvis, 2007, p. 141), can be used with any text. Harvey and Goudvis explain that when readers infer, they merge "background knowledge with clues in the text to come up with an idea that is not explicitly stated by the author. Reasonable inferences need to be tied to the text" (p. 132). Students can use the words on the page and any illustrations, charts, graphs, or photographs as text clues. As they see the text clues, the students think about what they already know about the topic (background knowledge). Using background knowledge plus the text clues, the students arrive at a conclusion, or inference, about what is happening in the story or what the author is saying about the topic. Harvey and Goudvis suggest creating an anchor chart with the Inferring Equation written at the top and completing the chart as students read and discuss the text.

Citing Textual Evidence

In Reading Standard 1, students are responsible for making logical inferences and citing textual evidence by the end of fifth grade. A useful idea to teach this is the Read–Head–Said graphic organizer; Figure 7.3 shows an example using the text *Starry Messenger: Galileo Galilei* by Peter Sís (1996). As students read, they can use the graphic organizer to keep track of their inferences and textual evidence for those inferences. In the "What I Read" column, students summarize in a sentence or phrase what the text passage says. In the "What Is in My Head" column, students record their

Figure 7.3 Example of Citing Textual Evidence

Example Text: Sís, P. (1996). *Starry messenger: Galileo Galilei*. New York: Frances Foster.

What I Read (summary of passage)	What Is in My Head (inference)	What the Text Said (evidence from the text)
Galileo was tried for saying Earth was not the center of the universe.	Galileo was unhappy.	p. 16: "…everyone could see that the stars had left his eyes."

inference. In the "What the Text Said" column, students write the word or phrase included in the text that explicitly caused them to develop the inference. In this last column, words or phrases from the text are direct quotes and should be enclosed in quotation marks.

Understanding Text

The goal of Reading Standard 1 is for students to use skills such as asking and answering questions, referring to details and examples in a text when explaining what the text says explicitly, drawing inferences from the text, and quoting accurately when explaining what the text says explicitly. One way to facilitate the integration of these skills and help students better understand text is for students to engage in peer discussion of the text. Literature Circles (narrative text) and Discussion Circles (informational text) are teaching ideas that provide students with opportunities to discuss the ideas in the text.

Engaging students in Literature Circles when reading literary text or in Discussion Circles when reading informational texts provides a means for students to engage in small-group, text-based conversations in which they share meaningful ideas about texts as they read them (McLaughlin, 2010). Ketch (2005) notes, "Conversation helps individuals make sense of their world. It helps to build empathy, understanding, respect for different opinions, and ownership of the learning process" (p. 8). Researchers also report that small-group conversations motivate students, foster higher order thinking, and promote reading comprehension (Berne & Clark, 2008; Gambrell, 2004; Ketch, 2005; Kucan & Beck, 2003). Blanton, Pilonieta, and Wood (2007) further note that students of diverse linguistic and cultural backgrounds benefit from participating in such discussions.

It is important to remember that both the text and students' personal interpretations drive these discussions. There is not a list of questions to be answered, but rather a focus on students' inquiries, connections, and interpretations concerning the text that they are reading. The time spent in Literature or Discussion Circles varies by length of text, but usually 10–20 minutes is sufficient. We can, on occasion, use a minilesson to demonstrate a particular literary element (e.g., plot, theme, characterization) or comprehension strategies (e.g., making connections, visualizing, summarizing) on which the students may focus their discussion, but it is critical that we allow each group's conversation to evolve on its own.

Literary or informational texts can be the source of these discussions. Students typically self-select what they read from choices we provide. To learn more about Literature Circles, visit the Literature Circle Resource Center online (www.litcircles.org) and "Literature Circles: Getting Started" on ReadWriteThink's website (www.readwritethink.org/classroom-resources/lesson -plans/literature-circles-getting-started-19.html).

Technology Connections to Standard 1

We can use the Acrostic Poems interactive tool on ReadWriteThink's website (www.readwritethink .org/classroom-resources/student-interactives/acrostic-poems-30045.html) to write an acrostic poem about key details in a text. Students can write about the topic of the informational text (or character, setting, or events in a literary text) in the designated box, then record key details from the text about the topic. Finally, they can use the interactive organizer to create and print an acrostic poem based on key details in the text.

How Can We Integrate Other ELA Standards With Reading Standard 1?

When planning to teach CCR Reading Anchor Standard 1, we can integrate several other ELA standards to design rich instructional tasks. Examples of ideas to include when creating these tasks follow.

Integrating Other ELA Standards With Reading Literature Standard 1

- Reading Literature Standard 2 focuses on the ability to retell a literary text and determine the author's message or theme. *Example:* Engage students in inferring the theme of a literary text by exploring the characters' actions, dialogue, and thoughts and feelings.

- Reading Literature Standard 3 focuses on being able to describe characters, settings, or events in a story or drama, drawing on specific details in the text. *Example:* During close reading of literature, encourage students to carefully describe and discuss the traits of the characters, the significance of the setting, and the manner in which the events in a literary text take place.

- Reading Literature Standard 4 refers to the author's choice and use of words in a literary text. *Example:* Discuss the author's use of particular words and phrases in writing or discussion, including examples of figurative language. Explicitly teach students how to create examples of figurative language to include in their writing.

- Reading Literature Standard 5 refers to terms that are germane to literary texts, such as *chapter*, *scene*, and *stanza*. *Example:* Ask students to refer to the structural elements of stories, dramas, and poems when discussing or writing about a literary text.

- Reading Literature Standard 6 refers to point of view. *Example:* Encourage students to explain an author's or character's point of view when engaging in close reading of a literary text.

- Reading Literature Standard 7 focuses on how the illustrations in a text or multimedia versions of the text can help establish mood, tone, and meaning. *Example:* Explicitly teach students how to carefully study and analyze illustrations in a text for clues and key details about the author's intent.

- Writing Standard 1 provides the expectations for writing opinions about a topic or text. *Example:* Explicitly teach students to write or discuss opinions about the text and justify their thinking by providing supporting information.

- Speaking and Listening Standard 1 describes the expectation that students engage in a range of collaborative discussions, with specific indicators to demonstrate how to participate in an effective academic conversation. *Example:* Engage students in whole-group and small-group collaborative conversations when reading stories, dramas, and poems closely.

- Language Standard 5 is the vocabulary standard that refers to descriptive use of language. *Example:* When students engage in close reading of a literary text, teach them to identify or analyze the way authors use adjectives, shades of word meaning, and figurative language. Then, encourage students to add adjectives and figurative language to a piece that they have already written.

Integrating Other ELA Standards With Reading Informational Text Standard 1

- Reading Informational Text Standard 2 focuses on the ability to summarize the main idea and supporting details of in informational text. *Example:* When students read an informational text closely, encourage discussion of the main idea and teach them to support the main idea with facts. (See Chapter 8, Main Idea Chart, p. 98.)

- Reading Informational Text Standard 3 focuses on describing the connections and relationships among people, events, ideas, or pieces of information in a text. *Example:* During close reading, teach students to use the clues (connections and relationships among people, events, ideas, or pieces of information) in the text to better understand historical events, scientific ideas or concepts, or steps in technical procedures.

- Reading Informational Text Standard 4 focuses on the use of words and phrases in an informational text. *Example:* When reading informational text closely, teach students to identify and use the domain-specific words and phrases included in the author's discussion of the topic.

- Reading Informational Text Standard 5 refers to the use of text features (e.g., headings, captions, tables of contents) and text structures (e.g., chronology, comparison, cause/effect). *Example:* When engaging in close reading, whether in print or digital form, teach students to use text features and structures as clues for understanding (see Chapter 11).

- Reading Informational Text Standard 6 is point of view. When reading informational text closely, students identify or analyze the author's point of view. *Example:* When engaging in close reading of informational text, encourage students to think about the author's point of view and how the text would be different if it were written from another point of view.

- Reading Informational Text Standard 7 focuses on how the illustrations in a text or multimedia versions of the text can help establish the key ideas. *Example:* Teach students to use the illustrations in a text as supports when attempting to clarify the main idea and key details.

- Reading Informational Text Standard 8 addresses the reasons and evidence the author provides to support various points in the text. *Example:* When students are engaged in a close reading in which the author has stated an opinion, teach them how to identify and discuss the reasons and evidence provided to support the author's thinking.

- Reading Informational Text Standard 10 refers to the expectation that students be able to read more challenging text. *Example:* Teach students to read increasingly complex texts over time.

- Writing Standard 1 addresses the expectations for writing opinions. *Example:* Explicitly teach students to write an opinion about a topic or text and support their point of view with reasons and evidence.

- Speaking and Listening Standard 1 describes the expectation that students engage effectively in a range of collaborative discussions, with specific indicators to demonstrate how to participate in an effective academic conversation. *Example:* Engage students in collaborative academic conversations about disciplinary texts on a regular basis.

THE COMMON CORE IN ACTION

In this section of Chapters 7–16, we examine one of the foundational ideas that underpin each of the Common Core Anchor Standards for Reading. For the first Standard, "Read closely to determine what the text says explicitly and to make logical inferences from it; cite specific textual evidence when writing or speaking to support conclusions drawn from the text" (NGA Center & CCSSO, 2010a, p. 10), we have elected to share more detailed information about the process of close reading, which is an explicit part of the standard for grades 3–5.

Common Core Literacy Task: Close Reading

Beginning in grade 3, students are expected to begin closer analysis of complex text. Close reading exemplars, beginning at grade 3, have been posted on websites such as that of Student Achievement Partners (achievethecore.org). One of the hallmarks of the close reading exemplars is that students approach challenging texts with no support from the teacher; in fact, students should read and interpret complex text cold, without the teacher building background for the passage, engaging students in prereading strategies, or teaching reading comprehension minilessons for the text to be closely read. Although we teach comprehension strategies, such as activating prior knowledge to make connections, asking questions, visualizing and inferring, determining importance, and synthesizing, in other lessons, in a close reading lesson, students apply what they have learned. During the close reading lesson, the teacher leads students through a step-by-step process, facilitating student discussion and asking text-dependent questions—that is, questions in which students must use or quote the text to provide evidence for their answers. This process prepares students for engaging in close reading on their own, as well as building their ability to analyze complex text as a college and career readiness skill.

The expectation is that students build the ability to read challenging texts with no support from others. (See Student Achievement Partners, 2012a, for examples of close reading lessons.) In the following example, we describe how Suzanne, a fifth-grade teacher, prepares to teach a close reading lesson.

Suzanne is planning a reading lesson to focus on Reading Standard 1 for fifth grade. Although she wants to ensure that she teaches her students to focus on reading a text closely, she knows that she also needs to integrate several other ELA standards to create a rich instructional task. Suzanne knows that she needs to emphasize complex texts (Reading Standard 10), so she reviews the text exemplars for grades 4 and 5 found in Appendix B of the Common Core State Standards (NGA Center & CCSSO, 2010b). She thinks about her students and their abilities and interests before she chooses a text that correlates with the level and complexity of the text exemplars for grades 4 and 5.

Suzanne has learned about close reading exemplars for complex text and how to write text-dependent questions (e.g., see Student Achievement Partners, 2012c). She knows the basic steps for a close reading lesson, which is conducted in a whole-group setting and can take several days to complete:

1. Introduce the text with little or no prereading discussion.

2. *First reading*—Students read the entire text independently without assistance.

3. *Second reading*—The teacher reads the entire text aloud so all students experience a model of fluent reading. The teacher may stop at points for a discussion of domain-specific vocabulary, the social or historical context of the passage, or a more challenging sentence structure. The teacher does not explain the characters, ideas, or events of the text. Then, the students discuss the text.

4. The teacher poses text-dependent question(s), which can only be answered by reading the text. No questions should be included that have answers based on personal student experience.

5. *Third reading*—The students read the text and find evidence to answer the text-dependent questions.

6. In some lesson models, the students engage in art, music, or drama or use graphic organizers to better visualize and understand the text.

7. The students develop a single, concise sentence to answer each text-dependent question.

8. The students write or state orally an analysis of the text and support their analysis with text-based evidence.

Suzanne has already taught supporting lessons on comprehension strategies, how to use key details to find evidence in the text, how to quote accurately when citing evidence from the text, and how to write a text-based answer to a question. She begins her current task by reviewing the text for vocabulary that students need to discuss in the course of the lesson to ensure that key vocabulary is part of the class discussion. She creates text-dependent questions to ask about the text. To create these questions, Suzanne reviews the expectations of ELA Reading Standards 2–9 to ensure that she includes some of these concepts (for guidelines and free professional development modules about creating text-dependent questions, see Student Achievement Partners, 2012b). Next, she creates a series of questions that her students will need to use the text to answer. After planning the lesson thoroughly, Suzanne leads her fifth graders through the steps of the lesson.

Reading Standard 1 focuses on ensuring that students can read and comprehend the author's message in texts. It requires students to read closely, make logical inferences, and cite specific textual evidence to support conclusions. When students read like a detective, they read closely.

References

Berne, J.I., & Clark, K.F. (2008). Focusing literature discussion groups on comprehension strategies. *The Reading Teacher, 62*(1), 74–79.

Blanton, W.E., Pilonieta, P., & Wood, K.D. (2007). Promoting meaningful adolescent reading instruction through integrated literacy circles. In J. Lewis & G. Moorman (Eds.), *Adolescent literacy instruction: Policies and promising practices* (pp. 212–237). Newark, DE: International Reading Association.

Gambrell, L.B. (2004). Shifts in the conversation: Teacher-led, peer-led, and computer-mediated discussions. *The Reading Teacher, 58*(2), 212–215.

Harvey, S., & Goudvis, A. (2007). *Strategies that work: Teaching comprehension for understanding and engagement* (2nd ed.). Portland, ME: Stenhouse.

Ketch, A. (2005). Conversation: The comprehension connection. *The Reading Teacher, 59*(1), 8–13.

Kucan, L., & Beck, I.L. (2003). Inviting students to talk about expository texts: A comparison of two discourse environments and their effects on comprehension. *Reading Research and Instruction, 42*(3), 1–31.

Lewin, L., & Shoemaker, B.J. (1998). *Great performances: Creating classroom-based assessment tasks.* Alexandria, VA: Association for Supervision and Curriculum Development.

McGregor, T. (2007). *Comprehension connections: Bridges to strategic reading.* Portsmouth, NH: Heinemann.

McLaughlin, M. (2010). *Content area reading: Teaching and learning in an age of multiple literacies.* Boston: Allyn & Bacon.

National Governors Association Center for Best Practices & Council of Chief State School Officers. (2010a). *Common Core State Standards for English language arts and literacy in history/social studies, science, and technical subjects.* Washington, DC: Authors. Retrieved August 3, 2012, from www.corestandards.org/assets/CCSSI _ELA%20Standards.pdf

National Governors Association Center for Best Practices & Council of Chief State School Officers. (2010b). *Common Core State Standards for English language arts and literacy in history/social studies, science, and technical subjects: Appendix B: Text exemplars and sample performance tasks.* Washington, DC: Authors. Retrieved August 3, 2012, from www.corestandards.org/assets/Appendix_B.pdf

Student Achievement Partners. (2012a). *Close reading exemplars.* Retrieved June 27, 2012, from www.achievethe core.org/steal-these-tools/close-reading-exemplars

Student Achievement Partners. (2012b). *Professional development modules.* Retrieved July 15, 2012, from www .achievethecore.org/steal-these-tools/professional-development-modules

Student Achievement Partners. (2012c). *Text dependent questions.* Retrieved July 15, 2012, from www.achievethe core.org/steal-these-tools/text-dependent-questions

Children's Literature Cited

Cronin, D. (2000). *Click, clack, moo: Cows that type.* New York: Simon & Schuster Books for Young Readers.

Osborne, M.P., & Boyce, N.P. (2007). *Polar bears and the Arctic.* New York: Scholastic.

Sís, P. (1996). *Starry messenger: Galileo Galilei.* New York: Frances Foster.

CHAPTER 8

CCR Reading Anchor Standard 2: Determining Central Ideas and Themes

Getting to the Point

College and Career Readiness Reading Anchor Standard 2
Determine central ideas or themes of a text and analyze their development; summarize the key supporting details and ideas. (NGA Center & CCSSO, 2010a, p. 10)

What Does CCR Reading Anchor Standard 2 Mean?

For readers to understand the author's message, they must be able to determine the point of the text—the main idea. Being able to "identify clear main ideas or purposes of complex passages or their paragraphs" (ACT, 2006, p. 36) has been identified as a college and career readiness requirement for academic success. In College and Career Readiness (CCR) Reading Anchor Standard 2, students are expected to know how to get to the point by determining the central idea of a text and summarizing the key details that support it.

Students encounter the expectations of CCR Reading Anchor Standard 2 every day. They need to be able to determine the main idea of texts in order to learn the content of the course. Being able to determine the central idea and summarize a text is a key comprehension skill used across all content areas.

Reading Anchor Standard 2 focuses on three reading skills:

1. The ability to determine the central idea or theme of a text
2. The ability to analyze the development of ideas or themes in a text
3. The ability to summarize the key details and ideas in a text

Central Ideas in Informational Text

Determining the central idea of an informational text means understanding the message that the author is trying to convey. Because students are asked to read a variety of types of materials, they should prepare to determine the central idea in an array of informational texts: magazine articles, newspapers, textbooks, websites, technical materials, and so forth. Being able to analyze the development of ideas in a text is a component of logical thinking. If students can explain how key details can be arranged under main ideas, they are more likely to be able to write a logical, coherent essay or thoughtful, organized answer to a question.

Themes in Literature

In English language arts classes, students read and analyze text, including books, short stories, plays, and poetry. One of the concepts in literary analysis is that of theme. The theme of a literary text is the author's message to the reader—what the author wants the reader to remember or take away after reading the text. The theme is often a value judgment by the author about aspects of life and can often be expressed in a proverb such as "money can't buy happiness." Short stories usually have one theme, whereas a novel can have several themes at the same time.

Authors express themes in several different ways: through the title of the text, how the characters feel, what the characters think or say, what the characters learn, and the conflict, events, or actions in the story. Students must infer to make the logical conclusion about the author's intent. A more sophisticated way that authors help establish a theme is by making allusions to history, mythology, culture, art, music, or other literary works. For example, many of the names in A Series of Unfortunate Events, the children's book series by Lemony Snicket, are allusions to literary or historical villains, orphans, or authors of tragedy. Only readers with outside knowledge of classic literature or history would understand the allusion to Mr. Poe, the banker (whose sons are named Edgar and Allen), or Vice Principal Nero, who makes the children sit through six-hour concerts while he plays the violin (clearly a reference to the Roman Emperor Nero, who allegedly fiddled while Rome burned). In this instance, the reader may comprehend the story but must have particular background knowledge to truly understand the references. Many short stories and novels that are considered classics use such allusions to help establish the theme.

Other complex ways that authors give clues to the themes in literary texts are through the use of archetypes and motifs. An archetype is a character, action, or situation with fairly stereotypical traits. This helps the reader understand how he or she is supposed to feel and adds to the establishment of the theme. For example, in the classic fairy tale Snow White and the Seven Dwarfs, Snow White always acts in a way that is sweet and kind, whereas the Queen is consistent in her evil behavior. Snow White represents good, while the Queen represents evil. A motif is any element that is repeated throughout the literary work, and can be an image, sound, phrase, or idea. A motif is symbolic of the theme and helps establish the theme by repetition.

Summarizing Key Supporting Details and Ideas

Summarizing is extracting the most important ideas from a text. In content area classes, students are often expected to extract the most important information from the text and write a brief synopsis of the information in the text.

How Do the Common Core Standards Build to CCR Anchor Standard 2?

When considering the importance of the big ideas in texts, Walmsley (2006) states,

> Encouraging children to focus on the big ideas of a text promotes understanding of not only big ideas but also smaller details. In fact, stronger readers routinely use their knowledge of the big ideas to work through and understand the text at sentence and paragraph levels. (p. 282)

Walmsley further urges us to teach in such a way that by the middle of first grade, after reading a story, we could "simply pose the question, So, what's the big idea?" (p. 284). CCR Anchor Standard 2 is the standard that focuses on the big ideas in texts. It is up to us to teach in such a way that our students can meet the standard and be able to discuss the big ideas in a variety of texts across the curriculum.

There are four main skill areas to teach in Anchor Standard 2 by the end of fifth grade for students to be on track for middle school and the higher expectations of the Standards in grades 6–12:

1. Retelling and recounting

2. Determining themes in literary text (with a focus on fables and folk tales in grades 2 and 3)

3. Determining main ideas and key details in informational text

4. Summarizing

In Reading Literature Standard 2, early primary students learn to retell stories, including key details and understanding of the central message, by the end of first grade. Students in grades 2 and 3 focus on determining the lesson or moral of fables, folk tales, and simple myths from diverse cultures. Fourth and fifth graders focus on determining themes and summarizing texts. Reading Standard 2 for Literature is featured in Table 8.1.

For Reading Standard 2 for Informational Text, early primary students are expected to identify the main topic and retell key details of an informational text. In second grade, students expand their learning to be able to identify the main topics of paragraphs within the text. Third graders determine a main idea of a text and discuss key details, and fourth graders also learn to summarize the text. In fifth grade, students determine more than one main idea in a text, explain how each main idea is supported by key details, and summarize the text. Reading Standard 2 for Informational Text is detailed in Table 8.2.

Table 8.1 Common Core State Standard 2 for Reading Literature in Grades K–5

Grade	Standard
K	With prompting and support, retell familiar stories, including key details.
1	Retell stories, including key details, and demonstrate understanding of their central message or lesson.
2	Recount stories, including fables and folktales from diverse cultures, and determine their central message, lesson, or moral.
3	Recount stories, including fables, folktales, and myths from diverse cultures; determine the central message, lesson, or moral and explain how it is conveyed through key details in the text.
4	Determine a theme of a story, drama, or poem from details in the text; summarize the text.
5	Determine a theme of a story, drama, or poem from details in the text, including how characters in a story or drama respond to challenges or how the speaker in a poem reflects upon a topic; summarize the text.

Note. The standards are from *Common Core State Standards for English Language Arts and Literacy in History/Social Studies, Science, and Technical Subjects* (pp. 11 and 12), by National Governors Association Center for Best Practices and Council of Chief State School Officers, 2010, Washington, DC: Authors.

Table 8.2 Common Core State Standard 2 for Reading Informational Text in Grades K–5

Grade	Standard
K	With prompting and support, identify the main topic and retell key details of a text.
1	Identify the main topic and retell key details of a text.
2	Identify the main topic of a multiparagraph text as well as the focus of specific paragraphs within the text.
3	Determine the main idea of a text; recount the key details and explain how they support the main idea.
4	Determine the main idea of a text and explain how it is supported by key details; summarize the text.
5	Determine two or more main ideas of a text and explain how they are supported by key details; summarize the text.

Note. The standards are from *Common Core State Standards for English Language Arts and Literacy in History/Social Studies, Science, and Technical Subjects* (pp. 13 and 14), by National Governors Association Center for Best Practices and Council of Chief State School Officers, 2010, Washington, DC: Authors.

What Literacy Skills and Strategies Support Reading Anchor Standard 2?

To teach Reading Anchor Standard 2 in literature, teachers need to use a variety of literary materials, such as stories, dramas, and poetry. Choose literature with an obvious theme for younger students, but for intermediate students, the theme of a selected text may be a bit more subtle. Popular themes in children's literature are friendship or love, honesty and deception, family, prejudice, growing up, the environment, the great battle for good and evil (fantasy and science fiction), or the long journey home. Second and third graders will need to read a number of fables, folk tales, and myths to meet the expectations of this standard. See Appendix B of the Common Core State Standards for a list of exemplar texts in literature for grades K and 1, 2 and 3, and 4 and 5 (NGA Center & CCSSO, 2010b). The supporting skills and strategies for Reading Standard 2 for Literature appear in Table 8.3.

Reading Standard 2 for Informational Text should be integrated with content area instruction, and students should be engaged in texts that support content area concepts. For example, if the class is engaged in a unit on sea life, an engaging article about sharks could be the foundation to teach main idea, key details, and summarizing. See Appendix B of the Common Core State Standards for a list of exemplar informational texts at the elementary text complexity

Table 8.3 Common Core State Standard 2 for Reading Literature: Supporting Skills and Strategies

Grade	Skills and Strategies
K	• Identify the beginning, middle, and end of a story • Retell a story with details
1	• Understand story grammar • Retell a story with details • Determine an author's message
2	• Understand story grammar • Understand structure of fables and folk tales • Understand stories from diverse cultures • Recount a story with key details • Determine the message, lesson, or moral of a story
3	• Understand story grammar • Understand structure of fables, folktales, and myths • Understand stories from diverse cultures • Recount a story with key details • Determine the moral of a fable, the lesson of a folk tale, and the central message of a myth • Identify key details that help the reader determine the author's message
4	• Determine a theme of a story, drama, or poem • Determine which key details decide the theme • Summarize a story, drama, or poem
5	• Determine a theme of a story, drama, or poem • Summarize a text using details • Identify challenges that characters face in a story, drama, or poem • Explain how the characters respond to challenges • Identify the topic of a poem • Explain how the speaker in a poem reflects on the topic

bands (NGA Center & CCSSO, 2010b). The supporting skills and strategies for Reading Informational Text Standard 2 are outlined in Table 8.4.

How Can We Teach Reading Standard 2 So Our Students Achieve?

To teach Reading Standard 2 so our students achieve, teachers need to engage students, at the appropriate grade level, in lessons focused on story structure, retelling, and determining theme in stories, plays, or poems. To teach Standard 2 with informational texts such as magazine articles, nonfiction books, newspaper articles, and websites, teachers need to engage students in lessons focused on main idea and supporting details. Fourth and fifth graders will need instruction in how to summarize both literary and informational texts.

In this section, we discuss the Standards tasks required of students at various grade levels. For example, CCR Anchor Standard 2 is "Determine central ideas or themes of a text and analyze their development; summarize the key supporting details and ideas" (NGA Center & CCSSO, 2010a, p. 10). This standard requires students to demonstrate knowledge of story structure, engage in retelling, determine message or theme, recognize main idea and supporting details, and summarize text. In addition, because technology should be interwoven into the curriculum along with the Standards, we also provide information about Digital Storytelling. We begin by describing the teaching idea. Next, we discuss how it supports the Standards. Then, we provide a teaching example.

Table 8.4 Common Core State Standard 2 for Reading Informational Text: Supporting Skills and Strategies

Grade	Skills and Strategies
K	• Identify the main topic of an informational text • Identify key details in the text • Retell with key details
1	• Identify the main topic of an informational text • Identify key details in the text • Retell with key details
2	• Recognize paragraph structure • Recognize the main topic of a paragraph • Recognize the main topic in a text with several paragraphs
3	• Determine the main idea of a text • Recount key details in the text • Explain how key details in a text support the main idea
4	• Identify supporting details in a text • Explaining how details in a text support the main idea • Summarize a text with key details
5	• Explain which supporting details support a main idea in a text • Determine two or more main ideas in a text • Explaining how each main idea in a text is supported by key details • Summarize multiple ideas of a text with key details

Story Structure: S-T-O-R-Y

In the second Reading Anchor Standard for grades K–5, one of our tasks is to teach students about story structure. In narrative text, the story structure involves the five elements of story grammar: characters, setting, problem, attempts to resolve the problem, and resolution. A great way to teach story structure is with Picture It! (Naughton, 2008). This teaching idea uses visualization to help students comprehend stories. It is based on the five elements of story grammar. This strategy uses the acronym STORY to help students visualize the parts of a story:

S—setting

T—talking characters

O—oops, a problem!

R—attempts to resolve the problem

Y—yes, the problem is solved (p. 65)

Students read or listen to a story with the five elements of story grammar in mind. After the story has been read and discussed, students create an illustration that incorporates all five parts of the story into a drawing. Specific vocabulary and key details can be added to the picture. Although the Picture It! strategy was created to help students visualize the parts of the story, it can also be used as a mnemonic device to help students retell a story using the correct sequence. The illustration could be done in the style of a five-part storyboard to help students remember the important parts of the story for retelling.

Retelling: Draw and Label Retelling

Retelling (Morrow, 1985), which involves summarizing the narrative elements, is a very flexible teaching idea. It can be completed orally, in writing, by sketching, or through dramatization. The Draw and Label Retelling (McLaughlin, 2010) for *Giraffes Can't Dance* by Giles Andreae (2001), which appears in Figure 8.1, focuses on four points: Who? Where? What happened? and How did it end? These parallel the narrative elements: characters, setting, problem, and resolution.

Figure 8.1 Example of a Draw and Label Retelling

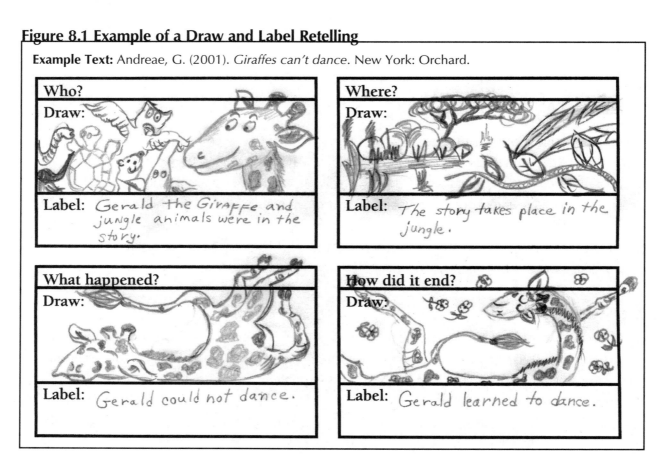

Example Text: Andreae, G. (2001). *Giraffes can't dance*. New York: Orchard.

Who?

Draw:

Label: Gerald the Giraffe and jungle animals were in the story.

Where?

Draw:

Label: The story takes place in the jungle.

What happened?

Draw:

Label: Gerald could not dance.

How did it end?

Draw:

Label: Gerald learned to dance.

Determining Message, Lesson, or Moral

The ability to retell fables or folk tales and determine the central message, lesson, or moral is an expectation in Reading Literature Standard 2 beginning at grade 2. One way to do this is to share Aesop's fables, which are very short stories about animals that learn a lesson, and the lesson or moral is usually written at the end of the story. Examples of Aesop's fables are "The Ant and the Grasshopper," "The Wolf in Sheep's Clothing," and "The Town Mouse and the Country Mouse." A number of picture book versions of Aesop's fables are available, and they are also readily found on the Internet (e.g., www.aesopfables.com/aesopsel.html).

It is important that students understand that a fable teaches a lesson. Read aloud a few of Aesop's fables that are appropriate for the class. After reading each fable, hold up a large card with the moral of that particular story. Lead students in a discussion of the message of the fable, relating it to the students' lives. For example, when discussing "The Ant and the Grasshopper," say, "Tell us about a time when you were like the grasshopper and played instead of planning ahead."

We can also divide students into small groups and give each group an Aesop's fable written in student-friendly language, but with the moral missing. Then, we can provide each group with three strips of paper, each with a moral written on it. Students read the fable and decide together which moral matches the fable. In a follow-up class discussion, students can explain why they chose that moral.

Main Idea and Supporting Details

The Main Idea Table (McLaughlin & Allen, 2009) is designed to provide students with opportunities to record the main idea and three supporting details from a text. In the example included in Figure 8.2, the main idea is about the triceratops's frill. Three details about the frill are also listed.

Summarizing: The Bio-Pyramid

The Bio-Pyramid is an alternative way to summarize facts about a person's life (Macon, 1991). It contains eight lines to be filled in with specific details. The pyramid begins with one word and expands to eight. A Bio-Pyramid about Dr. Martin Luther King Jr. is featured in Figure 8.3.

Technology Connections

We can use Digital Storytelling to integrate technology into teaching narrative text structure at the elementary level. Digital stories are digitally recorded pictures with a soundtrack of the narration and music. For example, Lotherington and Chow (2006) helped urban second-grade students create digital stories of new versions of Goldilocks and the Three Bears. After learning about the elements of narrative text structure—characters, setting, problem, attempts to resolve the problem, and resolution—students can rewrite classic fairy tales or familiar stories and then illustrate a series of pictures representing the parts of their new story.

Students can use digital cameras to take pictures of their artwork and import them into a technology tool to make digital stories. Two familiar tools that can be used to make digital stories are iMovie and Movie Maker (found on all Macs and PCs, respectively). Another is Photo Story, which is a free, downloadable software program from Microsoft that provides an easy step-by-step tool for elementary students, resulting in a professional-looking digital story. PowerPoint is a more

Figure 8.2 Main Idea and Supporting Details

Main Idea Chart

Main Idea   A frill is a large fan-shaped plate of bone that circled the back of the triceratops's head.

#1 On an adult Triceratops, the frill might be 7 feet wide.	#2 Along the frill's outer edge was usually a row of small, pointed, knob-shaped bones.	# 3 Triceratops used its bony frill as a weapon or shield.

Supporting Details

Adapted for the primary grades from *Guided Comprehension: A Teaching Model for Grades 3–8* by Maureen McLaughlin and Mary Beth Allen ©2002. Newark, DE: International Reading Association. May be copied for classroom use.

Figure 8.3 Example of a Bio-Pyramid About Dr. Martin Luther King Jr.

__King__
Person's name

__educated,__ __dedicated__
Two words describing the person

__brother,__ __son,__ __grandson__
Three words describing the person's childhood

__prejudice__ __in__ __United__ __States__
Four words indicating a problem the person had to overcome

__He__ __was__ __a__ __Baptist__ __Minister.__
Five words stating one of his or her accomplishments

__He__ __worked__ __for__ __American__ __civil__ __rights.__
Six words stating a second accomplishment

__gave__ __the__ __"I__ __Have__ __a__ __Dream"__ __speech__
Seven words stating a third accomplishment

__We__ __learned__ __to__ __celebrate__ __the__ __equality__ __of__ __all.__
Eight words stating how mankind benefited from his or her accomplishments

rudimentary tool that can be used by importing pictures into the slides and recording the narration under "Record Slide Show."

Digital Storytelling can also be used to show the main idea and key details of a text. Students create illustrations or take photographs that represent the main idea and key details of an informational text, import them into a digital storytelling tool, and add narration. Digital Storytelling has been suggested as an excellent way to motivate struggling writers and English learners.

How Can We Integrate Other ELA Standards With Reading Standard 2?

When planning to teach College and Career Readiness Reading Anchor Standard 2, we can integrate several other ELA standards to design rich instructional tasks. Examples of ideas to include when creating rich instructional tasks follow.

Integrating Other ELA Standards With Reading Literature Standard 1

- Reading Literature Standard 1 focuses on reading a narrative text closely. *Example:* During a close reading, encourage students to ask and answer questions about key details, refer to the text, and draw inferences to determine the central theme.

- Reading Literature Standard 3 focuses on being able to describe characters, settings, or events in a story or drama, drawing on specific details in the text. *Example:* As students are retelling or determining the theme of a literary text, encourage them to describe the story elements.

- Reading Literature Standard 5 refers to terms that are germane to literary texts, such as *chapter*, *scene*, or *stanza*. Fifth graders begin to examine the structure of literary texts. *Example:* Encourage students to use specific language when discussing various components of literary texts.

- Reading Literature Standard 7 focuses on how the illustrations in a text or multimedia versions of the text can help establish mood, tone, and meaning. *Example:* Teach students to refer to the illustrations in a text when attempting to determine the author's message or theme.

- Reading Literature Standard 9 focuses on comparing and contrasting aspects of literary text, such as the adventures of characters, two or more versions of the same story, and similar themes and topics. *Example:* Encourage students to compare and contrast the themes of two stories.

- Writing Standard 3 describes expectations for young children to tell or retell stories. Students in grades 3–6 write narratives to develop real or imagined experiences or events using effective techniques, descriptive details, and clear event sequences. *Example:* Involve students in writing narratives as they learn about the author's message or theme.

- Speaking and Listening Standard 1 describes the expectation that students engage effectively in a range of collaborative discussions, with specific indicators to demonstrate how to participate in an effective academic conversation. *Example:* Engage students in a number of collaborative discussions, such as Literature Circles and whole-class discussions, when exploring ideas in literature.

- Speaking and Listening Standard 5 refers to creating audio recordings, visual displays, or multimedia presentations of main ideas or themes. *Example:* Encourage students to create visual displays that focus on the narrative elements of a book that they have read.

- Language Standard 5 is the vocabulary standard that refers to the descriptive use of language. *Example:* Focus students' attention on preselected descriptive adjectives, shades of word meaning, and figurative language while reading literary text.

Integrating Other ELA Standards With Reading Informational Text Standard 2

- Reading Informational Text Standard 1 refers to closely reading an informational text. *Example:* When engaging in close reading of an informational text, guide students to refer to the text while asking and answering questions about key details to determine the central idea and supporting details in the text.

- Reading Informational Text Standard 3 focuses on describing the connections and relationships among people, events, ideas, or pieces of information in a text. *Example:* Encourage students to make connections between and among ideas to determine the main idea and supporting details of an informational text.

- Reading Informational Text Standard 7 focuses on how the illustrations in a text or multimedia versions of the text can help establish the key ideas. *Example:* Teach students how to refer to the illustrations in a text when attempting to determine the main idea.

- Writing Standard 2 describes expectations for informative/explanatory writing. K–2 students introduce the topic, supply some facts, and provide closure. Students in grades 3–5 write informative/explanatory texts to examine a topic and convey ideas and information clearly. *Example:* Encourage students to write informative/explanatory texts as they learn what makes such texts effective.

- Speaking and Listening Standard 1 describes the expectation that students will engage effectively in a range of collaborative discussions, with specific indicators to demonstrate how to participate in an effective academic conversation. *Example:* Engage students in a number of collaborative academic conversations about content area concepts in a variety of settings (paired, small group, whole group).

- Speaking and Listening Standard 5 refers to creating audio recordings, visual displays, or multimedia presentations of main ideas or themes. *Example:* Invite students to create multimedia presentations about concepts in various disciplines.

- Language Standard 6 is the vocabulary standard that refers to general academic and domain-specific words and phrases. *Example:* Teach students to become word conscious by learning and using meaningful new vocabulary related to various disciplines.

THE COMMON CORE IN ACTION

Every text has a central idea, message, or theme. Students need to learn to ask themselves, What is the big idea? when reading a text to determine the central idea. In the example that follows, we describe how a second-grade teacher, Jerome, teaches his students about main idea.

Common Core Literacy Task: Determining the Central Idea in a Literary Text

Jerome is planning to teach his second-grade students about determining an author's central message in a literary text (Reading Standard 2). He knows he needs to emphasize complex texts

(Reading Standard 10), so after reviewing Appendix B in the Common Core Standards, he sees that there is an emphasis on fables and folk tales from diverse cultures in second and third grade. He also sees that Janet Stevens's picture book *Tops and Bottoms* (1995) is recommended as the type of exemplar text that would be appropriate for second and third grades. Jerome remembers reading that *Tops and Bottoms* is a trickster tale based on the structure of European folk tales and slave stories of the American South. According to the National Endowment for the Humanities (2010), a trickster tale is a fable with animals that have human characteristics that was told to convey folk wisdom and teach us about human characteristics and behavior. Fables and folk tales were often first told orally and then passed down to the next generation. In a trickster tale, a smaller animal usually tricks a bigger animal into doing something that the smaller animal wants. Jerome has always liked the book *Tops and Bottoms* and thinks his diverse students could relate to this story before moving on to more traditional fables and folk tales. His second graders will need scaffolding, so he plans to do this lesson as a read-aloud with discussion on the carpet.

Jerome teaches comprehension every day in small-group instruction, so his students are familiar with concepts such as making connections and visualizing. Although he wants to make sure that he leads his students to focus on the central idea of the text, he knows he also needs to integrate several other ELA standards in order to create a rich instructional task. After reviewing all the Reading Standards for Literature for grade 2, he sees that he can integrate a number of standards to focus on the central idea of the story:

- Who, what, where, why, and how questions about key details (RL.2.1)
- How characters respond to events and challenges in a story (RL.2.3)
- Structure of a folktale (RL.2.5)
- Differences in point of view of the characters (RL.2.6)
- Using the illustrations to help understand the story (RL.2.7)

Jerome gathers his students on the carpet and prepares them for the reading by telling them that he wants them to listen for the big idea of the story. He writes, "What's the big idea?" on the chart propped on the easel next to his chair. He then reads the book aloud, stopping occasionally so the students can react to the story and illustrations.

Jerome leads his students to discuss the story by first asking, "So, what's the big idea of this story?" He listens carefully to student responses and builds comments and questions from the students' answers. He facilitates deeper understanding by asking questions (weaving in the ELA Standards), such as, "What happened first in the story?" "What happened next?" "What did Hare do? Why?" and "How did Bear react? Why?"

After a discussion of the purpose of folk tales (to teach a lesson), Jerome divides the story into five parts: (1) Hare makes a plan; (2) Bear gets the tops of the carrots, radishes, and beets; (3) Bear gets the bottoms of the lettuce, broccoli, and celery; (4) Bear gets the tops and bottoms of the corn; and (5) Bear learns his lesson. Jerome has students act out each part, with different students playing the parts of Bear, Hare, and Hare's family. After students dramatize the story, Jerome asks again, "What does the author want you to learn? What is the big idea?" By asking questions, Jerome guides his students to understand that the author expects the reader to learn the lesson that everyone must do his part. He emphasizes that every story has a big idea.

Reading Anchor Standard 2 focuses on determining the central idea, message, or theme of a literary text. It requires students to determine the main idea and summarize informational text. When students get to the point, they think about the big idea of the text—an important college and career readiness skill.

References

ACT. (2006). *Reading between the lines: What the ACT reveals about college readiness in reading.* Iowa City, IA: Author. Retrieved August 22, 2012, from www.act.org/research/policymakers/pdf/reading_report.pdf

Lotherington, H., & Chow, S. (2006). Rewriting "Goldilocks" in the urban, multicultural elementary school. *The Reading Teacher, 60*(3), 242–252.

Macon, J.M. (1991). *Literature response.* Paper presented at the Annual Literacy Workshop, Anaheim, CA.

McLaughlin, M. (2010). *Guided Comprehension in the primary grades* (2nd ed.). Newark, DE: International Reading Association.

McLaughlin, M., & Allen, M.B. (2009). *Guided Comprehension in grades 3–8* (Combined 2nd ed.). Newark, DE: International Reading Association.

Morrow, L.M. (1985). Retelling stories: A strategy for improving young children's comprehension, concept of story structure, and oral language complexity. *The Elementary School Journal, 85*(5), 647–661.

National Endowment for the Humanities. (2010). *Fables and trickster tales around the world* [Lesson]. Retrieved July 14, 2012, from edsitement.neh.gov/lesson-plan/fables-and-trickster-tales-around-world

National Governors Association Center for Best Practices & Council of Chief State School Officers. (2010a). *Common Core State Standards for English language arts and literacy in history/social studies, science, and technical subjects.* Washington, DC: Authors. Retrieved August 3, 2012, from www.corestandards.org/assets/CCSSI_ELA%20Standards.pdf

National Governors Association Center for Best Practices & Council of Chief State School Officers. (2010b). *Common Core State Standards for English language arts and literacy in history/social studies, science, and technical subjects: Appendix B: Text exemplars and sample performance tasks.* Washington, DC: Authors. Retrieved August 3, 2012, from www.corestandards.org/assets/Appendix_B.pdf

Naughton, V. M. (2008). Picture it! *The Reading Teacher, 62*(1), 65–68.

Walmsley, S.A. (2006). Getting the big idea: A neglected goal for reading comprehension. *The Reading Teacher, 60*(3), 281–285.

Children's Literature Cited

Andreae, G. (2001). *Giraffes can't dance.* New York: Orchard.

Stevens, J. (1995). *Tops and bottoms.* San Diego, CA: Harcourt.

CHAPTER 9

CCR Reading Anchor Standard 3: Individual, Event, and Idea Development

Following the Thread

College and Career Readiness Reading Anchor Standard 3
Analyze how and why individuals, events, and ideas develop and interact over the course of a text. (NGA Center & CCSSO, 2010, p. 10)

What Does CCR Reading Anchor Standard 3 Mean?

Students need to read and comprehend text that is not always explicit. According to ACT (2006), one of the characteristics of complex text is that of relationships in the text. Relationships in a complex text have been defined as "interactions among ideas or characters in the text [that] are subtle, involved, or deeply embedded" (ACT, 2006, p. 17). College and Career Readiness (CCR) Reading Anchor Standard 3 is related to the author's development of relationships in a text and is highly connected with Reading Standard 1 (read closely) and Reading Standard 10 (text complexity). Students must be able to follow the thread that the author establishes for character and idea development.

Reading Anchor Standard 3 focuses on four college reading skills:

1. The ability to analyze how individuals develop and interact

2. The ability to analyze how events develop and interact

3. The ability to analyze how ideas develop and interact

4. The ability to recognize how individuals, events, and ideas interact

Authors of literature often show the relationships between and among characters, events, and ideas in an understated way, using literary devices to help build the relationships. The way the author describes characters, the dialogue among them, and their actions toward one another help the reader get a deeper sense of the story or poem. The structure of a literary text (characters, setting, problem, attempts to solve the problem, resolution) helps build relationships over the course of events in the text.

In informational text, readers understand how ideas are related and build to the main idea. If students can explain the relationships or interactions among ideas in a text, they better understand the concepts in the text and are better prepared to write coherently.

Table 9.1 Common Core State Standard 3 for Reading Literature in Grades K–5

Grade	Standard
K	With prompting and support, identify characters, settings, and major events in a story.
1	Describe characters, settings, and major events in a story, using key details.
2	Describe how characters in a story respond to major events and challenges.
3	Describe characters in a story (e.g., their traits, motivations, or feelings) and explain how their actions contribute to the sequence of events.
4	Describe in depth a character, setting, or event in a story or drama, drawing on specific details in the text (e.g., a character's thoughts, words, or actions).
5	Compare and contrast two or more characters, settings, or events in a story or drama, drawing on specific details in the text (e.g., how characters interact).

Note. The standards are from *Common Core State Standards for English Language Arts and Literacy in History/Social Studies, Science, and Technical Subjects* (pp. 11 and 12), by National Governors Association Center for Best Practices and Council of Chief State School Officers, 2010, Washington, DC: Authors.

Table 9.2 Common Core State Standard 3 for Reading Informational Text in Grades K–5

Grade	Standard
K	With prompting and support, describe the connection between two individuals, events, ideas, or pieces of information in a text.
1	Describe the connection between two individuals, events, ideas, or pieces of information in a text.
2	Describe the connection between a series of historical events, scientific ideas or concepts, or steps in technical procedures in text.
3	Describe the relationship between a series of historical events, scientific ideas or concepts, or steps in technical procedures in a text, using language that pertains to time, sequence, and cause/effect.
4	Explain events, procedures, ideas, or concepts in a historical, scientific, or technical text, including what happened and why, based on specific information in the text.
5	Explain the relationships or interactions between two or more individuals, events, ideas, or concepts in a historical, scientific, or technical text based on specific information in the text.

Note. The standards are from *Common Core State Standards for English Language Arts and Literacy in History/Social Studies, Science, and Technical Subjects* (pp. 13 and 14), by National Governors Association Center for Best Practices and Council of Chief State School Officers, 2010, Washington, DC: Authors.

How Do the Common Core Standards Build to CCR Anchor Standard 3?

The CCSS build to Anchor Standard 3 by focusing on students' beginning understanding of the relationships between and among characters and story elements in literature, and connections between and among ideas and historical and scientific texts.

For literature, kindergartners and first-grade students learn to first identify and then describe characters, settings, and major events in a story. In second grade, students begin to respond to events and the challenges that characters face in a text. Fourth-grade students are expected to describe characters, setting, and events in depth. By fifth grade, students are expected to compare and contrast characters, settings, and events. The expectations for Anchor Standard 3 for Reading Literature are delineated in Table 9.1.

For informational text, kindergartners and first-grade students are expected to be able to describe the connection between two people, events, ideas, or information in a text. By the end of the second grade, students are expected to describe the connection between two series of events, ideas, or steps in a procedure. By fourth grade, students should be able to describe the relationship among a series of events, ideas, or steps in a procedure by adding more details. By the end of fifth grade, students should be able to explain the relationships among people, events, ideas, or concepts in disciplinary texts by citing specific information found in the text. The expectations for Reading Informational Text Standard 3 appear in Table 9.2.

There are five main skill areas to teach in Reading Standard 3 by the end of fifth grade for students to be on track for middle school and the higher expectations of the Standards in grades 6–12:

1. Characters, settings, and events

2. Characterization

3. Comparing and contrasting characters, settings, and events

4. Connections among individuals, events, and ideas

5. Explaining relationships between two or more individuals, events, ideas, or concepts in content area texts

What Literacy Skills and Strategies Support Reading Standard 3?

Reading Standard 3 is about reading and understanding a text that is rich in detail and idea development. Reading Standard 3 for Literature is about character and story development. To achieve this standard, students need to understand the narrative text structure of stories, poems, and dramas. Students learn how authors develop the characters over the course of a literary text. They also learn how the ideas and events develop as the author unfolds the story. To teach Reading Standard 3 for literature, teachers need to engage students with a wide variety of literary genres. Table 9.3 is a list of skills and strategies for Reading Literature Standard 3.

Reading Standard 3 for informational text is about how authors develop ideas in historical, scientific, and technical texts. Students need to learn how individuals interact in an informational text. They need to learn how events unfold in a historical or scientific text. They also need to learn how authors demonstrate steps in a technical procedure, such as a how-to book or article. To teach Reading Standard 3, teachers need to engage students with a wide variety of informational texts about social studies, science, and procedures. The supporting skills and strategies for Reading Standard 3 are featured in Table 9.4.

Table 9.3 Common Core State Standard 3 for Reading Literature: Supporting Skills and Strategies

Grade	Skills and Strategies
K	• Define *character* • Define *setting* • Define *event* • Identify characters in a story, poem, or drama • Identify settings in a story, poem, or drama • Identify events in a story, poem, or drama
1	• Define *character* • Define *setting* • Define *major event* • Define *details* • Identify characters using key details in a story, poem, or drama • Identify settings using key details in a story, poem, or drama • Identify events using key details in a story, poem, or drama
2	• Identify characters • Identify major events • Identify challenges • Describe how characters respond to major events and challenges
3	• Infer and describe a character's feelings/emotions based on details in the text • Describe a character's traits/motivations • Retell the sequence of events in a story • Interpret how the character's actions contribute to the sequence of events
4	• Identify characters, settings, and/or events in a story • Describe a character's thoughts • Describe the character's actions • Describe how a character's words tell about the character • Describe the setting using specific details from the text • Describe events using specific details from the text
5	• Compare and contrast characters, settings, and events • Identify similarities and differences in two or more characters • Identify similarities and differences in two or more settings • Identify similarities and differences in two or more events

Table 9.4 Common Core State Standard 3 for Reading Informational Text: Supporting Skills and Strategies

Grade	Skills and Strategies
K	• Identify key details about an individual, event, or idea in an informational text • Describe the connection between two individuals, events, or ideas in the text
1	• Identify key details about an individual, event, or idea in an informational text • Describe the connection between two individuals, events, or ideas in the text
2	• Identify the historical events in a text • Identify scientific ideas in a text • Identify the steps in a procedure in a text • Describe the connection between two historical events, scientific ideas, or steps in a procedure
3	• Define terms that pertain to time • Define terms that pertain to sequence • Define terms that pertain to cause/effect • Describe the relationship among historical events • Describe the relationship among scientific ideas and procedures • Describe the relationship among steps in a procedure
4	• Identify events, procedures, ideas, and concepts in a text • Explain why events, procedures, ideas, or concepts appeared in a text • Use specific information in the text to support an explanation
5	• Define *relationships* and *interactions* • Explain the relationships or interactions between two or more individuals, events, ideas, or concepts in multiple informational texts • Use specific information in texts to support an explanation

How Can We Teach Reading Standard 3 So Our Students Achieve?

In this section, we discuss the Standards tasks required of students at various grade levels. For example, the third College and Career Readiness Anchor Standard requires students to identify characters, settings, and events; describe characters and their traits; compare and contrast characters, settings, and events; describe the connection among individuals, events, and ideas; and explain relationships between two or more individuals, events, ideas, or concepts in content area texts. We begin by describing the teaching idea. Next, we discuss how it supports the Standards. Finally, we conclude by sharing a completed example of student work that relates to the standard.

Development of Characters, Settings, and Events: Story Impression

Story Impressions were developed by McGinley and Denner (1987) to encourage students to make predictions about stories, acquaint students with story vocabulary, and provide a framework for narrative writing. We begin by selecting a published story on which we will base the Story Impression. Next, we provide students with a list of words that relate to the literary elements: characters, setting, problem, attempts to resolve, and resolution. These are the clues for the Story Impression. When we give the list to the students, the words are connected by downward arrows to show the sequence in which they appear in the story. Next, the students work in small groups to create a story based on the clues provided. Then, each group reads its story aloud. After each group has shared its story, we read the published story. Finally, we discuss by comparing and contrasting the stories that the students have written and the original. Our example clues for a Story Impression based on Patricia Polacco's book (1978) *Meteor!* appear in Figure 9.1.

Characterization: Character, Trait, and Quote Map

To teach characterization, we created the Character, Trait, and Quote Map. The character's name is written in an oval in the center. Then, students can list characteristics related to the focus character in circles around the oval. Under each trait, students also include a quote from the text that supports the characteristic. For example, Figure 9.2 is based on *Superdog: The Heart of a Hero* by Caralyn Buehner (2004). Dexter the dachshund is the focus character. Traits include dreamer, superhero, and superhero partner. Each is supported by a quote that students took directly from the text.

Comparing and Contrasting Story Elements: Comparison/Contrast Story Map

To help students compare and contrast story elements, we created the Comparison/Contrast Story Map. The information presented in the graphic organizer includes the five narrative elements (characters, setting, problem, attempts to resolve the problem, and resolution) and two book titles, all for students to fill in. The books that are compared and contrasted in Figure 9.3 are "The Three Little Pigs" (original story) and *Alaska's Three Pigs* by Arlene Laverde (2000).

Connections Among Individuals, Events, and Ideas

We provide three examples in this section to accommodate the wording of Reading Standard 3 for Informational Text for grades 3, 4, and 5.

For a third-grade example of steps in a procedure, using language that pertains to time, sequence, and cause/effect, see the Sequence Chain in Chapter 11 (Figure 11.3). The scientific method is the topic of this sample graphic organizer.

A fourth-grade example of events in history, including what happened and why based on specific information in the text, can be found in Chapter 11 (Figure 11.5). The Cherokee Trail of Tears and the political move that caused it are the focus of this sample Cause and Effect Text Organizer.

For an example of the relationships between two concepts in a scientific text for grade 5, see the Venn Diagram in Chapter 11 (Figure 11.4). Sharks and dolphins are compared and contrasted in this sample graphic organizer. Similarities appear in the overlapping part of the circles, and differences appear in the outer parts of each circle.

Explaining Relationships Between Two or More Individuals, Events, Ideas, or Concepts in Informational Texts

To show the relations between two concepts in an informational text, we use a Contrast Chart (McLaughlin & Allen, 2009) to focus on the differences between hurricanes and tornadoes. The Contrast Chart is featured in Figure 9.4.

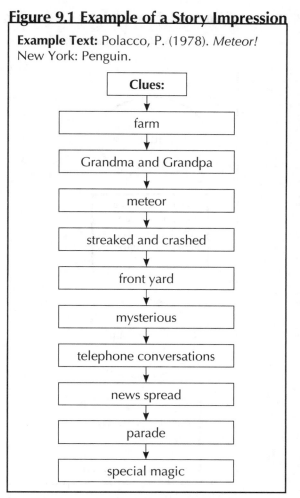

Figure 9.1 Example of a Story Impression

Example Text: Polacco, P. (1978). *Meteor!* New York: Penguin.

Clues:
- farm
- Grandma and Grandpa
- meteor
- streaked and crashed
- front yard
- mysterious
- telephone conversations
- news spread
- parade
- special magic

Note. Story Impressions from McGinley, W.J., & Denner, P.R. (1987). Story impressions: A prereading/writing activity. *Journal of Reading*, 31(3), 248–253.

Figure 9.2 Example of a Character, Trait, and Quote Map

Example Text: Buehner, C. (2004). *Superdog: The heart of a hero*. New York: HarperCollins.

Title: *Superdog: The Heart of a Hero*

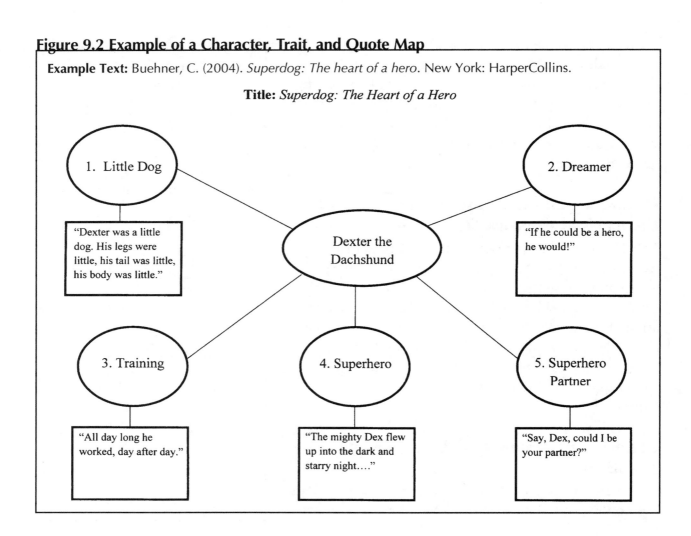

Figure 9.3 Example of a Comparison/Contrast Story Map

Example Texts: "The Three Little Pigs"
Laverde, A. (2000). *Alaska's three pigs*. Seattle, WA: Sasquatch.

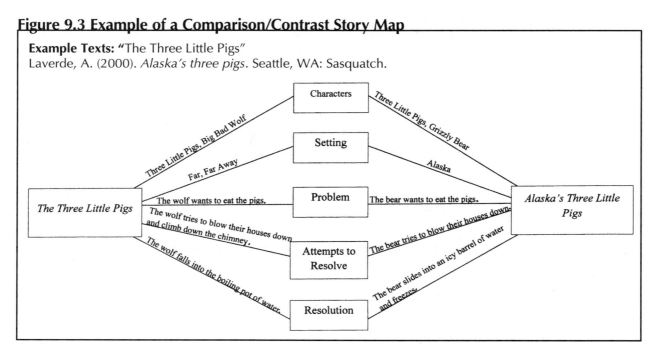

Figure 9.4 Example of a Contrast Chart

Contrast Chart	
Hurricanes	**Tornadoes**
1. A hurricane is a spiraling tropical storm.	1. A tornado is a violent windstorm characterized by a twisting, funnel-shaped cloud.
2. Hurricanes can have speeds of over 160 miles per hour.	2. Violent tornadoes can develop winds of over 200 miles per hour.
3. Hurricanes usually last for several hours and can last for more than two weeks over open water.	3. Most tornadoes last less than 10 minutes, but some last for an hour.
4. The Saffir-Simpson scale rates the severity of hurricanes.	4. The Fujita Scale rates the intensity of a tornado.

Technology Connections

The Story Map interactive tool (grades K–12) on ReadWriteThink's website (www.readwrforethink .org/classroom-resources/student-interactives/story-30008.html) can be used during prewriting to help students plan a story or can be used to describe the idea development of a published story. This tool includes a set of graphic organizers that students can complete with details about parts of a narrative story: characters, setting, conflict, and resolution.

The Cube Creator interactive tool (grades 3–12) on ReadWriteThink's website (www .readwrforethink.org/classroom-resources/student-interactives/cube-creator-30850.html) helps students think about how to summarize a text using a Summary Cube (McLaughlin & Allen, 2009). Students compete a Bio Cube (biography elements), Mystery Cube (mystery elements), or Story Cube (story elements) planning sheet in which they summarize key components of the text. A fourth planning sheet can be customized by the teacher or students for a research project or another genre. After completing the planning sheets, students complete the chosen Summary Cube on the computer. They also answer questions on each side of a 3-D cube based on the summaries that they have written on their planning sheets. The printed product is a template for a cube that students can cut out and tape together. Each side of the cube summarizes part of the text according to the questions that the students answered.

How Can We Integrate Other ELA Standards With Reading Standard 3?

When planning to teach College and Career Readiness Reading Anchor Standard 3, we can integrate several other ELA standards to design rich instructional tasks. Examples of ideas to include when creating rich instructional tasks follow.

Integrating Other ELA Standards With Reading Literature Standard 3

- Reading Literature Standard 1 focuses on reading a literary text closely. *Example:* When reading a literary text, ask students to describe the characters, settings, or events of the text in detail.

- Reading Literature Standard 5 refers to terms that are germane to literary texts, such as *chapter*, *scene*, or *stanza*. *Example:* When discussing the development of characters, settings, or ideas in a story or drama, encourage students to use terms that describe literary texts.

- Reading Literature Standard 6 refers to point of view. *Example:* Teach students to refer to a character's or the author's point of view when writing or speaking about a text.

- Reading Literature Standard 9 focuses on comparing and contrasting elements or versions of literary texts. *Example:* Teach students to compare and contrast two or more versions of the same story or the themes, settings, or plots in different stories.

- Writing Standard 3 lays out the expectations for narrative writing. *Example:* Teach students to write a story with descriptive characters, settings, and event sequences following the criteria in Writing Standard 3.

- Speaking and Listening Standard 1 describes the expectation that students will engage effectively in a range of collaborative discussions, with specific indicators to demonstrate how to participate in an effective academic conversation. *Example:* When reading stories, dramas, and poetry, engage students in whole-group discussions and small-group Literature Circles.

- Language Standard 5 is the vocabulary standard that refers to descriptive use of language. *Example:* Ask students to describe characters, settings, or events in a story or drama by using descriptive language.

Integrating Other ELA Standards With Reading Informational Text Standard 3

When planning to teach College and Career Readiness Reading Anchor Standard 3, we can integrate several other ELA standards to design rich instructional tasks. Examples of ideas to include when creating rich instructional tasks follow.

- Reading Informational Text Standard 1 refers to closely reading an informational text. *Example:* Ask students to read closely to find connections between individuals, events, ideas, or concepts in historical, scientific, or technical texts.

- Reading Informational Text Standard 2 focuses on the ability to summarize the main idea and supporting details of an informational text. *Example:* Teach students to summarize the main idea and supporting details when discussing the connection between individuals, events, ideas, or concepts in a historical, scientific, or technical text.

- Reading Informational Text Standard 5 refers to the use of text features (e.g., headings, captions, tables of contents) and text structures (e.g., chronology, comparison, cause/effect). *Example:* Explicitly teach students to use text features and structures when reading informational text.

- Reading Informational Text Standard 6 is point of view. *Example:* When reading an informational text, teach students to determine and consider the author's point of view.

- Writing Standard 2 lays out the expectations for informative/explanatory writing. *Example:* Teach students to write an informative/explanatory paragraph or essay to explain what they learned about individuals, events, ideas, or concepts in an informational text, following the criteria found in Writing Standard 2.

- Writing Standard 7 refers to participating in brief shared or individual research projects that build knowledge about a topic. *Example:* Create situations in which students engage in authentic research to build knowledge about individuals, events, ideas, or concepts.

- Writing Standard 8 focuses on recalling information from experiences or gathering information from sources to answer questions about a topic. *Example:* While engaged in research, encourage students to explore a variety of informational texts to determine answers to questions and connections between individuals, events, ideas, or concepts.

- Speaking and Listening Standard 1 describes the expectation that students will engage effectively in a range of collaborative discussions, with specific indicators to demonstrate how to participate in an effective academic conversation. *Example:* Engage students in collaborative academic conversations on a regular basis about the individuals, events, ideas, or concepts in informational text.

- Language Standard 6 is the vocabulary standard that refers to general academic and domain-specific words and phrases. *Example:* Ask students to use vocabulary specific to informational text when writing or speaking about disciplinary concepts.

THE COMMON CORE IN ACTION

In this section, we examine one of the foundational ideas that underpins each of the Common Core's Anchor Standards for Reading. For the third standard, "Analyze how and why individuals, events, and ideas develop and interact over the course of the text" (NGA Center & CCSSO, 2010, p. 10), we have elected to share more detailed information about characterization, which is an explicit part of the standard for grades K–5.

Common Core Literacy Task: Characterization

Frieda is a third-grade teacher. She and her team have studied the Standards and are planning a lesson on Reading Literature Standard 3: "Describe characters in a story (e.g., their traits, motivations, or feelings) and explain how their actions contribute to the sequence of events" (NGA Center & CCSSO, 2010, p. 12). Frieda has been involved in a professional development task in which the teachers in her school have reviewed the K–5 Standards. She knows that in kindergarten and first grade, students should identify and describe characters as part of Reading Literature Standard 3. She also knows that in second grade last year, students were expected to describe how characters in a story respond to major events and challenges. Frieda wants to make sure that her students are prepared to address Reading Literature Standard 3 by teaching a lesson on characterization.

Frieda decides to use the Subtext Strategy (Clyde, 2003) to have her students experience what might motivate characters and make them respond to events and challenges in certain ways. Clyde discusses research that suggests that young children have difficulty identifying with different characters in a book and that preadolescents have a tendency to believe that characters think and feel the way that they, as students, do. Clyde created the Subtext Strategy as a way for students to identify with the characters. In this strategy, students listen to a story read aloud, think about the descriptions of the characters in the story, study the pictures in the text, and dramatize the story, taking the role of different characters. As the events unfold, the teacher asks students to pretend to be the character and explain the character's thoughts and feelings based on evidence in the book. By providing copies of the story, students can work in small groups to plan how to respond when they dramatize each character.

To begin the class study on characterization, Frieda decides to use the book *Yo! Yes?* by Chris Raschka (1993). In this deceptively simple Caldecott Honor book, two boys who are just getting to know each other communicate in very brief language. Students infer the characters' thoughts and feelings mostly from the pictures and punctuation.

Frieda plans to use this lesson sequence:

1. Introduce the book *Yo! Yes?* Students ask and answer questions about the cover. (RL.3.1)

2. Read the book aloud without discussing the meaning. (Frieda will practice reading aloud to make sure her reading is very expressive and helps tell the story with such few words.) Students will listen to the story and then ask and answer questions to clarify the meaning of the story. (SL.3.2)

3. Students will do a choral reading of the story, using expression. (RF.3.4b)

4. Frieda will divide the students into small groups and give each group a copy of the story. With her guidance for the directions and pacing, students will work together to decide what each character might be thinking. They will write the character's thoughts on sticky notes and place them on each page above the character's head. (W.3.8)

5. Students will take turns dramatizing the pages. After they dramatize the actions and facial expressions of the character, they will pretend to be the character and describe what he is thinking. (SL.3.4)

6. Frieda will explain that characters in stories have a point of view that helps the reader understand more about the character. (RL.3.6) Students ask and answer questions about the point of view of the two boys in the story. (RL.3.1)

7. Students will choose one of the two characters. They will write an explanatory paragraph with an introductory sentence that includes the name of the story and at least three sentences describing the character's traits (what he is like), motivations (why he acts the way he does), or feelings (how he feels). Students should end their paragraphs with a concluding sentence that tells why this character is important in the story. (RL.3.3, W.3.2)

After this initial lesson on characterization, Frieda will use this format again with longer and more complex texts as the year progresses.

Reading Standard 3 focuses on ensuring that students can analyze the development of characters, events, and ideas in texts. It requires students to describe and explain the changes in a story line, the motivations of characters, and the connections and relationships between and among individuals, ideas, and events. When students can follow the thread, they better understand how to comprehend the text.

References

ACT. (2006). *Reading between the lines: What the ACT reveals about college readiness in reading.* Iowa City, IA: Author. Retrieved August 22, 2012, from www.act.org/research/policymakers/pdf/reading_report.pdf

Clyde, J. (2003). Stepping inside the story world: The Subtext Strategy—a tool for connecting and comprehending. *The Reading Teacher, 57*(2), 150–160.

McGinley, W.J., & Denner, P.R. (1987). Story impressions: A prereading/writing activity. *Journal of Reading, 31*(3), 248–253.

McLaughlin, M., & Allen, M.B. (2009). *Guided Comprehension in grades 3–8* (Combined 2nd ed.). Newark, DE: International Reading Association.

National Governors Association Center for Best Practices & Council of Chief State School Officers. (2010). *Common Core State Standards for English language arts and literacy in history/social studies, science, and technical subjects.* Washington, DC: Authors. Retrieved August 3, 2012, from www.corestandards.org/assets/CCSSI_ELA%20 Standards.pdf

Children's Literature Cited

Buehner, C. (2004). *Superdog: The heart of a hero.* New York: HarperCollins.

Laverde, A. (2000). *Alaska's three pigs.* Seattle, WA: Sasquatch.

Polacco, P. (1978). *Meteor!* New York: Penguin.

Raschka, C. (1993). *Yo! Yes?* New York: Orchard.

CHAPTER 10

CCR Reading Anchor Standard 4: Meanings of Words and Phrases

Knowing the Word

| **College and Career Readiness Reading Anchor Standard 4** |
| Interpret words and phrases as they are used in a text, including determining technical, connotative, and figurative meanings, and analyze how specific word choices shape meaning or tone. (NGA Center & CCSSO, 2010, p. 10) |

What Does CCR Reading Anchor Standard 4 Mean?

College and Career Readiness (CCR) Reading Anchor Standard 4 focuses on the words and phrases that authors use in their writing. In a report on college and career readiness, ACT (2006) reports that a characteristic of complex text is the author's use of language, which is often intricate. In Reading Standard 4, students are expected to be able to interpret and analyze the words an author uses in a text and the way the author uses words and phrases to bring meaning to the text. This standard helps fulfill expectations that students be able to "determine, even when the language is richly figurative and the vocabulary is difficult, the appropriate meaning of context-dependent words, phrases, or statements in virtually any passage" (ACT, 2006, p. 37).

CCR Reading Anchor Standard 4 is focused on understanding words in context. It is also focused on the concept of diction. Diction means not only the exact way a person pronounces words but also an author's word choice and style of expression. An author's diction helps determine the message of the text. When students analyze a text for diction, they identify the diction devices the author used and try to interpret why the author chose those words for the text. Examples of diction devices are denotation (technical meaning of a word), connotation (interpretive meaning of a word or phrase), and figurative language, such as similes and metaphors.

When studying literature, high school English teachers and college English professors may ask students to write a diction analysis about a text. This type of analysis is an essay in which students analyze a piece of text for the author's vocabulary choices, style of expression, type of language (formal, informal, colloquial, or poetic), and tone. The essay focuses on how the text was written to create a certain effect, which then ties back to the purpose of the text.

When reading an informational text, students are expected to determine the meanings of symbols, key terms, and domain-specific words and phrases as they are used in the text in order to comprehend and learn from it. A domain is a content area. Determining the meanings of domain-specific words and phrases will help students learn the content of a text.

Reading Anchor Standard 4 focuses on five college reading skills:

1. The ability to interpret words and phrases as they are used in a text

2. The ability to determine technical meanings

3. The ability to determine connotative meanings

4. The ability to determine figurative meanings

5. The ability to analyze how word choices determine meaning or tone

Interpreting Words and Phrases

Authors choose words and phrases very carefully to create a mood or tone and to help the reader visualize the characters, setting, and events. In poetry especially, just a few words can portray a host of images. The reader is expected to interpret the text, using the words and phrases that the author chose as clues to the meaning. For example, in Carl Sandburg's (1970) poem "Fog" (which is recommended for grades 4 and 5 in the Common Core State Standards), the first two lines are "The fog comes / on little cat feet" (p. 33). The poet creates a metaphor comparing fog to a cat, but also, by his word choice, he creates a mood of quiet and mystery that helps the reader visualize the fog.

Technical Meanings

When students read content area texts, such as textbooks, newspapers, magazine articles, and websites, they will encounter a large number of words that have technical meanings. A technical meaning is the specialized meaning of a particular word from a field of study. For example, when a student in education reads texts about reading instruction, the student may come across words and phrases such as *schema*, *structural analysis*, and *text complexity*. These terms have technical meanings in the field of literacy, and each field has its own specialized vocabulary.

Connotative Meanings

Connotation is the way we interpret the author's words to help paint a picture in our minds. For example, an author may describe a woman as either "slender as a willow tree" or "skinny as a fence post." The connotation of the word *slender* coupled with the simile "as a willow tree" may give us an image of a young, beautiful girl, whereas the connotation of *skinny* along with the simile "as a fence post" may give us quite a different image of a woman who has known hard work. Authors deliberately use words to attempt to influence the reader's connotation—the way the reader might interpret the word or phrase. The opposite of connotation is denotation, which means the literal dictionary definition of a word.

Figurative Meanings

Authors use figurative language to help the reader visualize the text and to add interest to their writing. Readers interpret figurative language to visualize the text and determine the author's message and intent. The following are common examples of figurative language:

Simile—A figure of speech that compares two things that are basically different, often using the words *like* or *as*. *Example:* The race car was like lightning.

Metaphor—A figure of speech that compares two things that are basically unlike, but says the first thing actually is the second thing. *Example:* Coffee was my life preserver that morning.

Personification—A figure of speech in which the author gives an object the qualities of a person. *Example:* The raindrops tiptoed across the window.

Hyperbole—A figure of speech that uses exaggeration and is not meant to be taken literally. *Example:* I'm so hungry that I could eat an elephant.

Onomatopoeia—Words or phrases that sound like the object they are describing. *Example:* The firecrackers popped and crackled in the night sky.

Alliteration—Words that repeat the same letters or sounds. *Example:* Gabby's gainer was as good as gold.

Idiom—A phrase whose meaning is not predictable from the words in the phrase. *Example:* A piece of cake (meaning easy)

Analyzing How Word Choices Shape Meaning or Tone

The ability to analyze the author's word choice in poetry or prose is a college readiness skill. To analyze how the author's word choice shapes meaning or tone, The College Board (College Entrance Examination Board, 2002) suggests using the acronym DIDLS, which stands for diction, imagery, details, language, and sentence structure (or syntax). Diction was discussed previously as the connotation or denotation of a word the author chose to use. Imagery consists of words the author chose to appeal to the senses, and that can sway meaning from positive to negative. When an author uses details for effect, he or she adds (or omits) facts that emphasize certain aspects of characters, settings, or events and focuses the reader's attention on that aspect. Language refers to the overall type of language the author uses: Is the tone formal, clinical, or informal, or does the passage use jargon? Sentence structure (syntax) refers to the author's use of sentence structure for effect, such as the use of short, choppy sentences to be emphatic or longer, more complex sentences to be thoughtful.

How Do the Common Core Standards Build to CCR Anchor Standard 4?

For literature, the focus in Reading Standard 4 builds from asking and answering questions about unknown words in a text in kindergarten to a focus on words and phrases that suggest feelings and meanings in literary texts in grades 1 and 2. In third and fourth grades, students learn to determine the meanings of words and phrases. One of the expectations for fourth graders is that students will be able to determine meanings of words and phrases that allude to significant characters found in mythology. Fourth-grade students need considerable experience with reading and discussing Greek and Roman myths to recognize the origins of words such as *herculean*. Lists of words that come from mythology can be found online. By the end of fifth grade, students should be able to determine the meanings of words, phrases, and the use of figurative language used in a text. Reading Standard 4 for Literature for grades K–5 is delineated in Table 10.1.

For informational text, students learn to ask and answer questions about unknown words in a text. Standard 4 then builds to determining the meanings of words and phrases in grade-appropriate content area texts by the end of fifth grade. Reading Standard 4 for Informational Text for grades K–5 appears in Table 10.2.

There are four main skill areas to teach in Reading Standard 4 by the end of fifth grade for students to be on track for middle school and the higher expectations of the Standards in grades 6–12:

1. Asking and answering questions about words

2. Words and phrases that suggest feelings and appeal to the senses

3. General academic and domain-specific words and phrases

4. Figurative language

However, Reading Standard 4 is also the standard that connects to vocabulary. The standards for vocabulary acquisition and use (Language Standards 4–6) need to be taught across the curriculum in conjunction with the expectations for Reading Standard 4.

What Literacy Skills and Strategies Support Reading Standard 4?

Elementary students need to develop a broad vocabulary base. Research shows that vocabulary development is a key to reading comprehension (Anderson & Nagy, 1991; Stahl & Fairbanks, 1986). To develop a robust vocabulary base, students in grades K–5 need to engage in intentional and varied learning experiences with words. To meet Reading Standard 4, students need to be engaged in regular vocabulary instruction designed to help them learn a host of skills and strategies. Teaching the vocabulary concepts found in the Language Standards for vocabulary acquisition and use supports Reading Standard 4.

There are three major areas of focus for vocabulary instruction to meet the Language (vocabulary) Standards:

Table 10.1 Common Core State Standard 4 for Reading Literature in Grades K–5

Grade	Standard
K	Ask and answer questions about unknown words in a text.
1	Identify words and phrases in stories or poems that suggest feelings or appeal to the senses.
2	Describe how words and phrases (e.g., regular beats, alliteration, rhymes, repeated lines) supply rhythm and meaning in a story, poem, or song.
3	Determine the meaning of words and phrases as they are used in a text, distinguishing literal from nonliteral language.
4	Determine the meaning of words and phrases as they are used in a text, including those that allude to significant characters found in mythology (e.g., Herculean).
5	Determine the meaning of words and phrases as they are used in a text, including figurative language such as metaphors and similes.

Note. The standards are from *Common Core State Standards for English Language Arts and Literacy in History/Social Studies, Science, and Technical Subjects* (pp. 11 and 12), by National Governors Association Center for Best Practices and Council of Chief State School Officers, 2010, Washington, DC: Authors.

Table 10.2 Common Core State Standard 4 for Reading Informational Text in Grades K–5

Grade	Standard
K	With prompting and support, ask and answer questions about unknown words in a text.
1	Ask and answer questions to help determine or clarify the meaning of words and phrases in a text.
2	Determine the meaning of words and phrases in a text relevant to a *grade 2 topic or subject area*.
3	Determine the meaning of general academic and domain-specific words and phrases in a text relevant to a *grade 3 topic or subject area*.
4	Determine the meaning of general academic and domain-specific words or phrases in a text relevant to a *grade 4 topic or subject area*.
5	Determine the meaning of general academic and domain-specific words and phrases in a text relevant to a *grade 5 topic or subject area*.

Note. The standards are from *Common Core State Standards for English Language Arts and Literacy in History/Social Studies, Science, and Technical Subjects* (pp. 13 and 14), by National Governors Association Center for Best Practices and Council of Chief State School Officers, 2010, Washington, DC: Authors.

1. Meanings of unknown and multiple-meaning words and phrases (Language Standard 4)

2. Word relationships and nuances in word meanings (Language Standard 5)

3. General academic and domain-specific words and phrases (Language Standard 6)

Language Standard 4 relates to determining or clarifying the meanings of unknown and multiple-meaning words and phrases. Children are expected to identify the meanings of words and use context as a clue to determine the meanings of unfamiliar words. Students learn to use inflections, affixes, and root words to determine the meanings of unknown words. Beginning at fourth grade, students are expected to use common Greek and Latin word roots to help them determine the meanings of multisyllabic words. All students from second grade on should be able to use appropriate reference materials to help them determine precise word meanings. Table 10.3 delineates the skills and strategies needed to meet Language Standard 4.

Language Standard 5 focuses on word relationships and nuances in word meanings. In the primary grades, students concentrate on understanding categories of words and their uses. Students also begin to distinguish shades of meaning among verbs describing the same general action and among adjectives describing degrees of intensity. In grade 3, students begin to explore literal and nonliteral meanings of words and phrases. In the intermediate grades, students are expected to explore word relationships and nuances more deeply as they study figurative language such as similes and metaphors, and idioms, adages, and proverbs, and relate words to their synonyms, antonyms, and homographs. Table 10.4 delineates the skills and strategies needed to meet Language Standard 5.

Language Standard 6 requires students to acquire and use grade-appropriate words and phrases. This standard focuses on what Beck, McKeown, and Kucan (2002) call Tier 2 and Tier 3 words. Tier 1 words are those that students already know, such as *baby* and *house*. Tier 2 words are more unfamiliar words that are found across texts, such as *curious* and *location*. Tier 3 words are domain-specific words that are more often found in content area texts about a certain topic, such as *isotope* and *circumference*. The expectation of Language Standard 6 is that students will be able to use grade-appropriate vocabulary in speaking or writing. The skills and strategies needed to meet Language Standard 6 appear in Table 10.5.

How Can We Teach Reading Standard 4 So Our Students Achieve?

In this section, we discuss the Standards tasks required of students at various grade levels. For example, the fourth College and Career Readiness Anchor Standard requires students to ask and answer questions about unknown words and phrases, identify words and phrases that suggest feelings and appeal to the senses, determine the meanings of general academic and domain-specific words and phrases, and understand figurative language. We begin by describing the teaching idea, and then we discuss how it supports the standard.

Asking and Answering Questions About Words

We want students to ask and answer questions about unknown words in a text. We want them to be able to use context to determine unfamiliar words in their reading. Many unfamiliar words can be determined through the use of context, but many cannot. In the latter case, readers often use morphemic analysis to decide the meanings of the parts of a word to determine the meaning of the word. Learning the meanings of affixes and word roots helps students determine the meanings of unfamiliar words and better comprehend the text (Bear, Invernizzi, Templeton, & Johnston, 2004; Biemiller, 2004; Graves & Hammond, 1980; Nagy, 1988).

Table 10.3 Common Core State Standard 4 for Language: Meanings of Words and Phrases

Grade	Skills and Strategies

K	Determine or clarify the meanings of unknown and multiple-meaning words and phrases based on kindergarten reading and content
	   a. Identify new meanings for familiar words and apply them accurately (e.g., knowing *duck* means a bird and learning the verb *duck*)
	   b. Use the most frequently occurring inflections and affixes (e.g., *-ed, -s, re-, un-, pre-, -ful, -less*) as a clue to the meaning of an unknown word

1	Determine or clarify the meanings of unknown and multiple-meaning words and phrases based on grade 1 reading and content, choosing flexibly from an array of strategies
	   a. Use sentence-level context as a clue to the meaning of a word or phrase
	   b. Use frequently occurring affixes as a clue to the meaning of a word
	   c. Identify frequently occurring root words (e.g., *look*) and their inflectional forms (e.g., *looks, looked, looking*)

2	Determine or clarify the meanings of unknown and multiple-meaning words and phrases based on grade 2 reading and content, choosing flexibly from an array of strategies
	   a. Use sentence-level context as a clue to the meaning of a word or phrase
	   b. Determine the meaning of the new word formed when a known prefix is added to a known word (e.g., *happy/unhappy, tell/retell*)
	   c. Use a known root word as a clue to the meaning of an unknown word with the same root (e.g., *add: addition, additional*)
	   d. Use knowledge of the meanings of individual words to predict the meanings of compound words (e.g., *birdhouse, lighthouse, housefly; bookshelf, notebook, bookmark*)
	   e. Use glossaries and beginning dictionaries, both print and digital, to determine or clarify the meanings of words and phrases

3	Determine or clarify the meanings of unknown and multiple-meaning words and phrases based on grade 3 reading and content, choosing flexibly from a range of strategies
	   a. Use sentence-level context as a clue to the meaning of a word or phrase
	   b. Determine the meaning of the new word formed when a known affix is added to a known word (e.g., *agreeable/disagreeable*, comfortable, uncomfortable *care/careless, heat/preheat*)
	   c. Use a known root word as a clue to the meaning of an unknown word with the same root (e.g., *company, companion*)
	   d. Use glossaries or beginning dictionaries, both print and digital, to determine or clarify the precise meanings of key words and phrases

4	Determine or clarify the meanings of unknown and multiple-meaning words and phrases based on grade 4 reading and content, choosing flexibly from a range of strategies
	   a. Use context (e.g., definitions, examples, restatements in text) as a clue to the meaning of a word or phrase
	   b. Use common, grade-appropriate Greek and Latin affixes and word roots as clues to the meaning of a word (e.g., *telegraph, photograph, autograph*)
	   c. Consult reference materials (e.g., dictionaries, glossaries, thesauruses), both print and digital, to find the pronunciations and determine or clarify the precise meanings of key words and phrases

5	Determine or clarify the meanings of unknown and multiple-meaning words and phrases based on grade 5 reading and content, choosing flexibly from a range of strategies
	   a. Use context (e.g., cause/effect relationships, comparisons in text) as a clue to the meaning of a word or phrase
	   b. Use common, grade-appropriate Greek and Latin affixes and word roots as clues to the meaning of a word (e.g., *photograph, photosynthesis*)
	   c. Consult reference materials (e.g., dictionaries, glossaries, thesauruses), both print and digital, to find the pronunciations and determine or clarify the precise meanings of key words and phrases

Note. The skills and strategies are from *Common Core State Standards for English Language Arts and Literacy in History/Social Studies, Science, and Technical Subjects* (pp. 27 and 29), by National Governors Association Center for Best Practices and Council of Chief State School Officers, 2010, Washington, DC: Authors.

Table 10.4 Common Core State Standard 5 for Language: Word Relationships and Nuances

Grade	Skills and Strategies
K	With guidance and support from adults, explore word relationships and nuances in word meanings a. Sort common objects into categories (e.g., shapes, foods) to gain a sense of the concepts that the categories represent b. Demonstrate understanding of frequently occurring verbs and adjectives by relating them to their opposites (i.e., antonyms) c. Identify real-life connections between words and their uses (e.g., note places at school that are *colorful*) d. Distinguish shades of meaning among verbs describing the same general action (e.g., *walk, march, stroll, prance*) by acting out the meanings
1	With guidance and support from adults, demonstrate understanding of word relationships and nuances in word meanings a. Sort words into categories (e.g., colors, clothing) to gain a sense of the concepts that the categories represent b. Define words by category and by one or more key attributes (e.g., *duck* means a bird that swims; *tiger* means a large animal with stripes) c. Identify real-life connections between words and their uses (e.g., note places at home that are *cozy*) d. Distinguish shades of meaning among verbs differing in manner (e.g., *look, peek, glance, stare, glare, scowl*) and among adjectives differing in intensity (e.g., *big, larger, gigantic*) by defining or choosing them or by acting out their meanings
2	Demonstrate understanding of word relationships and nuances in word meanings a. Identify real-life connections among words and their uses (e.g., describe foods that are *spicy* or *juicy*) b. Distinguish shades of meaning among closely related verbs (e.g., *toss, throw, hurl*) and among closely related adjectives (e.g., *thin, slender, skinny, scrawny*)
3	Demonstrate understanding of word relationships and nuances in word meanings a. Distinguish the literal and nonliteral meanings of words and phrases in context (e.g., *take steps*) b. Identify real-life connections among words and their uses (e.g., describe people who are *friendly* or *helpful*) c. Distinguish shades of meaning among related words that describe states of mind or degrees of certainty (e.g., *knew, believed, suspected, heard, wondered*)
4	Demonstrate understanding of figurative language, word relationships, and nuances in word meanings a. Explain the meanings of simple similes and metaphors (e.g., as pretty as a picture) in context b. Recognize and explain the meanings of common idioms, adages, and proverbs c. Demonstrate understanding of words by relating them to their opposites (i.e., antonyms) and to words with similar but not identical meanings (i.e., synonyms)
5	Demonstrate understanding of figurative language, word relationships, and nuances in word meanings a. Interpret figurative language, including similes and metaphors, in context b. Recognize and explain the meanings of common idioms, adages, and proverbs c. Use the relationship among particular words (e.g., synonyms, antonyms, homographs) to better understand each of the words

Note. The skills and strategies are from *Common Core State Standards for English Language Arts and Literacy in History/Social Studies, Science, and Technical Subjects* (pp. 27 and 29), by National Governors Association Center for Best Practices and Council of Chief State School Officers, 2010, Washington, DC: Authors.

In the Common Core Language strand, a focus on learning the meanings of prefixes and suffixes begins in kindergarten, when students are expected to use the most frequently occurring inflections and affixes (e.g., *-ed*, *-s*, *re-*, *un-*, *pre-*, *-ful*, *-less*) as a clue to the meaning of an unknown word. By the end of fifth grade, students are expected to use common, grade-appropriate Greek and Latin affixes and word roots as clues to the meaning of a word. Students need intentional vocabulary instruction to learn how to ask and answer questions about unknown words of themselves and others (including reference materials) to learn to determine the meaning of an unfamiliar word.

Goodwin, Lipsky, and Ahn (2012) conducted a meta-analysis of the results of 30 studies involving morphological instruction, which underscores the value of teaching morphemic analysis to students. Based on their results, these researchers suggest five morphological instructional strategies that should be included in vocabulary instruction for K–8 students:

1. Segment and build with morphemes

2. Use affix and root meanings

3. Use morphemes to improve spelling

4. Segment compound words and combine words to create common compound words

5. Identify cognates to support ELs

Table 10.5 Common Core State Standard 6 for Language: Academic and Domain-Specific Words

Grade	Skills and Strategies
K	Use words and phrases acquired through conversations, reading and being read to, and responding to texts
1	Use words and phrases acquired through conversations, reading and being read to, and responding to texts, including frequently occurring conjunctions to signal simple relationships (e.g., *because*)
2	Use words and phrases acquired through conversations, reading and being read to, and responding to texts, including adjectives and adverbs to describe (e.g., When other kids are happy, that makes me happy.)
3	Acquire and accurately use grade-appropriate conversational, general academic, and domain-specific words and phrases, including those that signal spatial and temporal relationships (e.g., After dinner that night, we went looking for them.)
4	Acquire and accurately use grade-appropriate general academic and domain-specific words and phrases, including those that signal precise actions, emotions, or states of being (e.g., *quizzed*, *whined*, *stammered*) and that are basic to a particular topic (e.g., *wildlife*, *conservation*, and *endangered* when discussing animal preservation)
5	Acquire and accurately use grade-appropriate general academic and domain-specific words and phrases, including those that signal contrast, addition, and other logical relationships (e.g., *however*, *although*, *nevertheless*, *similarly*, *moreover*, *in addition*)

Note. The skills and strategies are from *Common Core State Standards for English Language Arts and Literacy in History/Social Studies, Science, and Technical Subjects* (pp. 27 and 29), by National Governors Association Center for Best Practices and Council of Chief State School Officers, 2010, Washington, DC: Authors.

Students need a variety of experiences with words containing common affixes and root words. Mountain (2005) suggests instructional techniques in which primary-grade students ask and answer questions about words in their reading that contain prefixes and suffixes. Mountain discusses teaching morphemic analysis with these students and suggests three guidelines for incorporating morphemic analysis into classroom instruction in the primary grades:

1. When you teach a word, also gradually teach its derivative forms. To the word *plant*, add (and subtract) *-s*, *-ed*, *-ing*, *-er*, and *re-*.

2. When you teach an affix, introduce it on words that carry its most common meaning; later, present other meanings. For the prefix *dis-*, start with the "not" meaning, as in *disagree*. Later introduce the "reverse" meaning, as in *disappear*.

3. When you teach a word that has meaningful parts, deconstruct and reconstruct the word with your students, pointing out the meaning of each part. For un-reach-able, show that the parts add up to the meaning "not able to be reached." (p. 747)

According to Mountain (2005), using manipulative games that involve matching prefix, suffix, and root word cards is one way for primary-grade students to practice morphemic analysis. Posting charts with affix rules, having students use Venn diagrams to compare and contrast words with affixes, and playing class games with word parts are others. In each of these activities, students learn to ask and answer questions about the parts of words to determine the meanings of the words.

Intermediate-grade students also need to focus on Greek and Latin word roots. Overturf, Montgomery, and Smith (in press) describe a learning activity called Crystal Ball Words, in which students study the meanings of affixes and Greek and Latin word roots. In this activity, students ask and answer questions about words and brainstorm words with similar prefixes, word roots, and suffixes to predict the meaning of a selected multisyllabic word.

In their description of the importance of morphological awareness for elementary students, Rasinski, Padak, Newton, and Newton (2011) suggest several classroom games that require students to ask and answer questions about words to determine their meanings. In the activity called Divide and Conquer (p. 137), students start with a list of approximately 10 words that have the same prefix (e.g., *replay*, *rewind*, *reboot*, *recycle*, etc.). Students choose one or two words from the list, identify the two basic units of each word, and speculate about what each word means. Students list each complete word, divide each word into its component parts (prefix and root), and provide a personal definition for each word. Through discussion and exploration, students come to understand that the meaning of the full word is obtained through the relationship of the base word with the prefix.

Words and Phrases That Suggest Feelings or Appeal to the Senses

For the activity Sensory Synonyms and Antonyms, students begin with a word related to their senses and then determine a synonym and antonym. For example, if students begin with the sense of sight and the word *beautiful*, the sensory synonym might be *gorgeous*, and the antonym might be *ugly*. When students begin with the sense of taste and the word *delicious*, the synonym might be *scrumptious* and the antonym might be *repulsive*. Similarly, for students starting with the sense of hearing and the word *melodic*, the synonym might be *harmonious*, and the antonym might be *discordant*. Students can add their sensory synonyms and antonyms to a class chart so students can use the words in their discussions and their writing.

General Academic and Domain-Specific Words and Phrases

Semantic Feature Analysis (Johnson & Pearson, 1984) is a graphic organizer that allows students to show which of the categories being discussed possess which of the listed characteristics. Students can use this chart before reading to make predictions and after reading to revise their thinking as necessary, based on the information revealed in the text. Figure 10.1 is a Semantic Feature Analysis about birds and bats.

Figurative Language

Authors frequently use figurative language, such as simile, metaphor, personification, hyperbole, onomatopoeia, alliteration, and idioms, in literary writing. The ability to determine the meaning of both literal and nonliteral language is a key to comprehension of poetry and expressive narrative writing and is a standard for vocabulary acquisition and use in the Language strand of the CCSS (Language Standard 5). Students will need to have numerous experiences with identifying the uses of figurative language in text and writing their own examples of figurative language.

Figure 10.1 Example of a Semantic Feature Analysis

Categories Characteristics	Birds	Bats
Have fur	–	+
Have feathers	+	–
Hatch from eggs	+	–
Live in nests	+	–
Stand up on their feet	+	–
Hang down from their feet	–	+
Fly during the day	+	–
Fly at night	+	+
Eat worms	+	–
Eat fruit	–	+
Response Key: + = Yes – = No ? = Don't know		

Before reading a selection that includes several examples of similes and metaphors, have students explore what they think a few of the similes and metaphors might mean. Each student should have a large sheet of paper (11" × 17") folded in half lengthwise. The paper should be folded top to bottom and then top to bottom again so when it is opened, the paper has eight sections. Next, we list several similes and metaphors from the text and ask students to write one of the similes or metaphors at the top of each of the eight sections. Then, in each section, the students sketch or add words that would illustrate the simile or metaphor. For example, *Owl Moon* by Jane Yolen (1987) is filled with similes and metaphors, such as "the trees stood still as giant statues" and "it was as quiet as a dream" (n.p.). When students read the text, they will be excited to hear the similes and metaphors in the story and eager to talk about how well their illustrations match the author's intended meaning. Following that, we discuss how authors use similes and metaphors to make their writing more descriptive and how readers must picture the simile or metaphor as they read in order to comprehend the text. Examples of similes and metaphors from *Owl Moon* appear in Figure 10.2.

Technology Connection

Dalton and Grisham (2011) discuss using media, including PowerPoint, as a form of creative expression as students learn about words and their relationships, and report that "recent research suggests that students may also benefit from creating multimedia representations of words" (p. 311). Dalton and Grisham have created a PowerPoint template for students that "includes a space for the word, a short definition, an explanation for why the word is important, a graphic, an audio recording or sound, and a source" (p. 311).

Another way for students to explore words and their relationships to other words using PowerPoint is for students to create PowerPoint Portrayals (Overturf et al., in press). The PowerPoint Portrayal is a series of 3 or 4 PowerPoint slides in which students introduce a word, insert a visual representation of a word (e.g., picture, photograph), add two related synonyms (or examples), and add two related antonyms (or nonexamples). Students can include sound effects or music clips and should choose colors and backgrounds that relate to the word. Students then present their slideshow to their classmates, meeting the expectations for Speaking and Listening Standards 4 and 5.

Figure 10.2 Examples of Similes and Metaphors

Integrating Other ELA Standards With Reading Literature Standard 4

When planning to teach College and Career Readiness Reading Anchor Standard 4, we can integrate several other ELA standards to design rich instructional tasks. Examples of ideas to include when creating rich instructional tasks follow.

- Reading Literature Standard 1 focuses on reading a narrative text closely. *Example:* When students engage in close reading of a narrative text, ask questions about expressive words and phrases that the author chose to use in the text.

- Reading Foundational Skills Standard 3 refers to knowing and applying grade-level phonics and word analysis skills to decode words. *Example:* Teach students to look for the meanings of root words and affixes to determine the meanings of unfamiliar words in a text.

- Writing Standard 1 lays out the expectations for writing opinions. *Example:* Teach students to use linking words and follow criteria in Writing Standard 1 when writing opinions about literary texts.

- Writing Standard 3 describes expectations for narrative writing. *Example:* Encourage students to use expressive words, phrases, and sensory details and follow criteria found in Writing Standard 3 when writing narrative text.

- Speaking and Listening Standard 1 describes students engaging effectively in a range of collaborative discussions, with specific indicators to demonstrate how to participate in an effective academic conversation. *Example:* When reading stories, dramas, and poems, engage students in both whole-group and small-group collaborative conversations related to the expressive words and phrases that the author chose to include in the text.

Integrating Other ELA Standards With Reading Informational Text Standard 4

- Reading Informational Text Standard 1 refers to closely reading an informational text. *Example:* When students read an informational text closely, encourage them to discuss the general academic and domain-specific words that the author chose to use in the text.

- Reading Foundational Skills Standard 3 refers to knowing and applying grade-level phonics and word analysis skills to decode words. *Example:* Teach students to recognize root words, affixes, onsets, and rimes to determine the meanings of unfamiliar words in a text.

- Writing Standard 1 describes the expectations for writing opinions. *Example:* Teach students to use linking words and the criteria in Writing Standard 1 when writing their opinions about informational texts.

- Writing Standard 2 describes the expectations for informative/explanatory writing. *Example:* Ask students to use precise language and domain-specific vocabulary, as well as the criteria found in Writing Standard 2, to inform about or explain a topic in informational texts.

- Speaking and Listening Standard 5 describes the expectations for students to create multimedia presentations. *Example:* Encourage students to use domain-specific words and phrases when creating audio recordings or recounting experiences to clarify ideas, enhance facts or details, or develop main ideas.

THE COMMON CORE IN ACTION

In this section, we examine one of the foundational ideas that underpins each of the Common Core Anchor Standards for Reading. For the fourth standard, "Interpret words and phrases as they are used in a text, including determining technical, connotative, and figurative meanings, and analyze how specific word choices shape meaning or tone" (NGA Center & CCSSO, 2010, p. 10), we have elected to share more detailed information about determining the meanings of general academic and domain-specific words and phrases in a text relevant to a given grade band, which is an explicit part of the Standards for Reading Informational Text in grades 3–5.

Common Core Literacy Task: Determining the Meanings of Domain-Specific Words and Phrases

Juanita is a fourth-grade teacher and is teaching a unit on life science. As one of her lessons, she plans to focus on Reading Informational Text Standard 4, which is "determine the meaning of general academic and domain-specific words or phrases in a text" (NGA Center & CCSSO, 2010, p. 14) that is appropriate for her students. She knows that this standard is correlated with Language Standard 4 for fourth grade: "determine or clarify the meaning of unknown and multiple-meaning words and phrases based on *grade 4 reading and content*, choosing flexibly from a range of strategies." The first indicator under this standard for fourth grade is to "use context (e.g., definitions, examples, or restatements in text) as a clue to the meaning of a word or phrase" (NGA Center & CCSSO, 2010, p. 29). Juanita feels strongly that being able to determine the meanings of words from the context in an informational passage is an important skill for students to possess so they can comprehend texts in all subject areas.

Although Juanita could choose any number of articles related to life science from student magazine articles or websites (e.g., *Kids Discover, National Geographic Kids*), for this lesson, she decides to use a nonfiction text called *Army Ants* by Sandra Markle (2005) to correlate with her focus on life science.

Juanita tells her students that today they will use clues to discover the meanings of words in a text. She uses the following sequence to introduce the informational book, *Army Ants*:

1. Introduce the book by showing the cover under a document camera or holding it up so all the students can see the photographs. Discuss the title of the text, the cover photograph, and the title page.

2. Point out the word *scavengers* on the cover and on the title page. Ask students if anyone knows what the word means. Briefly discuss student responses. (SL.4.1)

3. Show the rest of the photographs one by one and encourage students to briefly talk about what they see. (SL.4.1)

4. Make sure all students can see the text. Read aloud the first two sentences. Ask students to read the second sentence ("Scavengers are the cleanup crew who find and eat carrion (dead animals) in order to survive"; p. 2) and write the meaning of the word *carrion* on a sheet of paper. (RI.4.1)

5. Ask students to turn to a partner and discuss the meaning of the word *carrion* and the clues that told them the meaning of the word. (SL.4.1)

6. Explain to students that unfamiliar words in informational texts can often be found from clues located in the text. For the word *carrion*, the definition is given within the parentheses in the sentence. (L.4.1a)

7. Turn to page 7 of *Army Ants*. Show the first sentence on page 7, "For example, the biggest... ants have extra large mandibles, or toothlike mouthparts." Ask students to read the sentence and write the meaning of the word *mandibles* on their paper. (RI.4.1)

8. Ask students to turn to their partner and discuss the meaning of the word *mandibles* and the clues that told them the meaning of the word. (L. 4.4a)

9. Explain to students that for the word *mandibles*, the meaning comes after a comma in the sentence, which is another way that unfamiliar words are explained in texts. (L.4.1a)

10. Continue having students work in partners. Give students a few sentences from the text to use context clues to determine the meanings of words, such as *predator, soldiers, pheromone,* and *larvae.* (RI.4.4, L.4.1a)

11. Students fill in a three-column chart graphic organizer (see Figure 10.3). After students finish the task, Juanita will read the text aloud and ask students to confirm the definitions of the domain-specific words and phrases that they predicted from the context clues. (L.4.4a)

Figure 10.3 Example of a Domain-Specific Words Organizer

Word	Meaning	Clues in the Text That Tell the Meaning
mandibles	Parts of an ant's mouth	The text "toothlike mouthparts" comes after the comma in the sentence.

Reading Standard 4 focuses on ensuring that students can determine unfamiliar words in a text and analyze the author's word choice. It requires students to ask and answer questions about unknown words in a text, identify and evaluate words and phrases that suggest feelings or appeal to the senses, determine the meanings of general academic and domain-specific words and phrases, and understand figurative language. When students know the word, they can more deeply comprehend a text.

References

ACT. (2006). *Reading between the lines: What the ACT reveals about college readiness in reading.* Iowa City, IA: Author. Retrieved August 22, 2012, from www.act.org/research/policymakers/pdf/reading_report.pdf

Anderson, R.C., & Nagy, W.E. (1991). Word meanings. In R. Barr, M.L. Kamil, P. Mosenthal, & P.D. Pearson (Eds.), *Handbook of reading research* (Vol. 2, pp. 690–724). New York: Longman.

Bear, D.R., Invernizzi, M., Templeton, S., & Johnston, F. (2004). *Words their way: Word study for phonics, vocabulary, and spelling instruction* (3rd ed.). Upper Saddle River, NJ: Pearson.

Beck, I.L., McKeown, M.G., & Kucan, L. (2002). *Bringing words to life: Robust vocabulary instruction.* New York: Guilford.

Biemiller, A. (2004). Teaching vocabulary in the primary grades: Vocabulary instruction needed. In J.F. Baumann & E.J. Kame'enui (Eds.), *Vocabulary instruction: Research to practice* (pp. 28–40). New York: Guilford.

College Entrance Examination Board. (2002). *The AP vertical teams guide for English.* New York: Author.

Dalton, B., & Grisham, D.L. (2011). eVoc strategies: 10 ways to use technology to build vocabulary. *The Reading Teacher, 64*(5), 306–317.

Goodwin, A., Lipsky, M., & Ahn, S. (2012). Word detectives: Using units of meaning to support literacy. *The Reading Teacher, 65*(7), 461–470.

Graves, M.F., & Hammond, H.K. (1980). A validated procedure for teaching prefixes and its effect on students' ability to assign meanings to novel words. In M.L. Kamil & A.J, Moe (Eds.), *Perspectives on reading research and instruction* (pp. 184–188). Washington, DC: National Reading Conference.

Johnson, D.D., & Pearson, P.D. (1984). *Teaching reading vocabulary* (2nd ed.). New York: Holt, Rinehart and Winston.

Mountain, L. (2005). ROOTing out meaning: More morphemic analysis for primary pupils. *The Reading Teacher, 58*(8), 742–749.

Nagy, W.E. (1988). *Teaching vocabulary to improve reading comprehension.* Washington, DC: ERIC Clearinghouse on Reading and Communication Skills; Urbana, IL: National Council of Teachers of English; Newark, DE: International Reading Association.

National Governors Association Center for Best Practices & Council of Chief State School Officers. (2010). *Common Core State Standards for English language arts and literacy in history/social studies, science, and technical subjects.* Washington, DC: Authors. Retrieved August 3, 2012, from www.corestandards.org/assets/CCSSI_ELA%20 Standards.pdf

Overturf, B.J., Montgomery, L.H., & Smith, M.H. (in press). *Word nerds: Teaching all students to learn and love vocabulary.* Portland, ME: Stenhouse.

Rasinski, T.V., Padak, N., Newton, J., & Newton, E. (2011). The Latin–Greek connection: Building vocabulary through morphological study. *The Reading Teacher, 65*(2), 133–141.

Stahl, S.A., & Fairbanks, M.M. (1986). The effects of vocabulary instruction: A model-based meta-analysis. *Review of Educational Research, 56*(1), 72–110.

Children's Literature Cited

Markle, S. (2005). *Army ants.* Minneapolis, MN: Lerner.

Sandburg, C. (1970). Fog. In *The complete poems of Carl Sandburg* (p. 33). Orlando, FL: Harcourt.

Yolen, J. (1987). *Owl moon.* New York: Philomel.

CHAPTER 11

CCR Reading Anchor Standard 5: Structure of Texts

Examining How It Is Built	**College and Career Readiness Reading Standard 5** Analyze the structure of texts, including how specific sentences, paragraphs, and larger portions of the text (e.g., a section, chapter, scene, or stanza) relate to each other and the whole. (NGA Center & CCSSO, 2010, p. 10)

What Does CCR Reading Anchor Standard 5 Mean?

College and Career Readiness (CCR) Reading Anchor Standard 5 requires students to be able to read texts that are highly challenging in terms of their structure. According to ACT (2006), students should be able to "understand the function of a part of a passage when the function is subtle or complex" (p. 36). When reading, students need to be able to understand the structure of a particular complex text to comprehend it. Just as a building is constructed in a certain way, so is text. Students need to examine how it is built to understand a text, which is often written in intricate ways. Text structure is the organizational pattern that the author uses to arrange the content.

When reading literature, students may be asked not only to read complex text but also to analyze how an author's choices concerning how the structure of specific parts of the text contribute to its overall structure and meaning. Students need to be prepared not only to use text structure to comprehend but also to analyze the author's choices regarding structure. This includes how to order events within the text, the relations among the ideas in the text, and the way the author manipulates time to create effects such as mystery, tension, or surprise.

For informational text, students are expected to analyze how an author's ideas are developed and refined by particular text structures. This is the focus for Reading Informational Text Standard 5.

Reading Anchor Standard 5 focuses on two reading skills:

1. The ability to analyze the structure of texts
2. The ability to relate sentences, paragraphs, and larger portions of text to one another and the whole

Book Structures

Before we discuss text structures, we need to address the bigger picture: book structure. The structure of books typically includes their front and back covers, the title page, the table of contents, the way the text is organized, the glossary, and the index. Books are generally viewed as either literary or informational. These types of text have some characteristics in common and some that are unique.

Typically, literary books (stories) have information about the title and content on the front and back covers. Next, a title page, featuring the title, the author's name, and often the publisher, is included at the beginning of the book. The copyright information usually appears on the back of the title page. Then, depending on the length of the work, there may or may not be a table of contents that chronicles chapter titles and the page numbers on which each chapter begins. Pictures and other visual supports may or may not be included in literary books. The structure seems to be tied to the nature of the text and, oftentimes, left to the publisher. For example, Eric Carle's (2002) illustrations accompany his written message in the class picture book *The Very Hungry Caterpillar*. In *Esperanza Rising*, a young adult novel by Pam Muñoz Ryan (2000), there are chapters but no table of contents. In another of Ryan's (2004) young adult works, *Becoming Naomi León*, which is also organized by chapters, a table of contents is included.

Textbooks and other factual works typically have information on the front and back covers. They also have a title page. The copyright information usually appears on the back of the title page. This type of book usually includes a table of contents, or some sort of content listing, that chronicles chapter titles and the page numbers on which the chapters begin. If we are examining textbooks, pictures and other visual supports are usually included. If we are exploring a different type of informational text, pictures and other visuals may or may not be included. These types of books are typically organized by chapter number. Headings and subheadings are used to arrange the information within the chapters. Glossaries, or minidictionaries, are often included toward the end of textbooks. Textbooks and other informational works also often have an index, which is arranged alphabetically to help readers quickly locate a topic and the page(s) on which it appears. For example, *The Ancient Romans* by Allison Lassieur (2004) has information on both covers, a table of contents, picture supports, chapter titles, subheadings, a glossary, and an index. In addition, this volume also has a biographical dictionary, which provides information about 10 leaders of ancient Rome, and a section entitled "To Find Out More" (p. 100) that lists resources, including books, videos, and websites.

Text Structures

When discussing particular text structures, we generally begin by focusing on literary (story-based) text and informational (fact-based) text. When we examine these types of structure, we focus on how the text is organized. As Armbruster (2004) notes, the organization of the text is the arrangement of ideas and the relationships among them. Understanding and using text organization supports comprehension (Akhondi, Malayeri, & Samad, 2011). Research shows that students who are more knowledgeable about text structure recall more information than do students who are not knowledgeable and that students must be able to follow the text structure to best recall the information (Duke & Pearson, 2002).

Goldman and Rakestraw (2000) further note that experience in reading multiple genres provides students with knowledge of numerous text structures and improves their text-driven processing. Gambrell (2001) also observes that transacting with a wide variety of genres, including biography, historical fiction, legends, poetry, mythology, folk tales, and brochures, increases students' reading performance.

Narrative Text Structure. Narrative text structure is comprised of the five narrative elements: characters, setting, problem, attempts to resolve, and resolution. Instruction in story structure has shown positive results in comprehension for a wide range of students (Duke & Pearson, 2002).

Description, sequence (chronology), comparison/contrast, cause/effect, and problem/solution are the five informational text structures (McLaughlin, 2010). A brief description of each and related signal words follow.

1. *Description*—This pattern focuses on characteristics, facts, and features related to a topic, person, event, or object. Signal words for the description text pattern include *above*, *below*, *behind*, *down*, *across*, and *under*.

2. *Sequence (chronology)*—This pattern relates steps in a process or the order in which things happened. Signal words for the sequence text pattern include *first*, *second*, *third*, *then*, *next*, *during*, and *finally*.

3. *Comparison/contrast*—This pattern illuminates similarities (comparisons) and differences (contrasts). Signal words and phrases for comparison/contrast text include *although*, *but*, *compared with*, *however*, *on the one hand*, *on the other hand*, *similarly*, and *different from*.

4. *Cause/effect*—This pattern shows how events or ideas (effects) come to be because of certain other ideas, acts, or events (causes). Signal words and phrases for cause/effect text include *because*, *as a result*, *since*, *for this reason*, *in order to*, *if...then*, and *therefore*.

5. *Problem/solution*—This pattern showcases a difficulty (problem) and provides an example of how it can be resolved (solution). Signal words and phrases for the problem/solution text pattern include *because*, *since*, *therefore*, *consequently*, *as a result*, *cause*, *solve*, and *resolve*.

Informational Text Structure. Researchers suggest that we should explicitly teach the informational text structure to our students (Pressley, 2002). Research reports that if students know the text patterns and understand how to generate questions, they will improve their comprehension of text (Gambrell, 2001). Moss (2004) suggests that we should teach each text structure individually, encouraging students to master one structure before learning another.

Recognizing text structures helps students understand the type of information included in the text and predict the types of questions that may be raised about it. For example, if students are reading a biography and realize that the text pattern is sequential (chronological), questions may focus on what happened when. When reading a section of text in which the pattern is comparison/contrast, questions may focus on similarities and differences.

How Do the Common Core Standards Build to CCR Anchor Standard 5?

For Reading Literature Standard 5, early primary school students learn to recognize and tell the difference between common types of texts. By the end of grade 2, students are expected to be able to describe the structure of a story. In grades 3–5, students are expected to know more about the

Table 11.1 Common Core State Standard 5 for Reading Literature in Grades K–5

Grade	Standard
K	Recognize common types of texts (e.g., storybooks, poems).
1	Explain major differences between books that tell stories and books that give information, drawing on a wide reading of a range of text types.
2	Describe the overall structure of a story, including describing how the beginning introduces the story and the ending concludes the action.
3	Refer to parts of stories, dramas, and poems when writing or speaking about a text, using terms such as chapter, scene, and stanza; describe how each successive part builds on earlier sections.
4	Explain major differences between poems, drama, and prose, and refer to the structural elements of poems (e.g., verse, rhythm, meter) and drama (e.g., casts of characters, settings, descriptions, dialogue, stage directions) when writing or speaking about a text.
5	Explain how a series of chapters, scenes, or stanzas fits together to provide the overall structure of a particular story, drama, or poem.

Note. The standards are from *Common Core State Standards for English Language Arts and Literacy in History/Social Studies, Science, and Technical Subjects* (pp. 11 and 12), by National Governors Association Center for Best Practices and Council of Chief State School Officers, 2010, Washington, DC: Authors.

Table 11.2 Common Core State Standard 5 for Reading Informational Text in Grades K–5

Grade	Standard
K	Identify the front cover, back cover, and title page of a book.
1	Know and use various text features (e.g., headings, tables of contents, glossaries, electronic menus, icons) to locate key facts or information in a text.
2	Know and use various text features (e.g., captions, bold print, subheadings, glossaries, indexes, electronic menus, icons) to locate key facts or information in a text efficiently.
3	Use text features and search tools (e.g., key words, sidebars, hyperlinks) to locate information relevant to a given topic efficiently.
4	Describe the overall structure (e.g., chronology, comparison, cause/effect, problem/solution) of events, ideas, concepts, or information in a text or part of a text.
5	Compare and contrast the overall structure (e.g., chronology, comparison, cause/effect, problem/solution) of events, ideas, concepts, or information in two or more texts.

Note. The standards are from *Common Core State Standards for English Language Arts and Literacy in History/Social Studies, Science, and Technical Subjects* (pp. 13 and 14), by National Governors Association Center for Best Practices and Council of Chief State School Officers, 2010, Washington, DC: Authors.

parts and structures of stories, dramas, and poems. To meet this standard, students will need experiences with a variety of books, stories, dramas, and poetry. The Common Core State Standard 5 for Reading Literature in grades K–5 appears in Table 11.1.

For Reading Informational Text Standard 5, kindergartners are expected to identify the cover, back cover, and title page of a book. In grades 1–3, students learn to use various text features and search tools to locate key facts or information in a text efficiently. In grades 4 and 5, the focus is on the text structures of informational text, such as chronology, comparison, cause/effect, problem/solution, and of events, ideas, concepts, or information in texts. Students will need to engage with varied types of informational text, including nonfiction books, magazine articles, newspaper articles, and websites that provide information on various topics. The Common Core Standard 5 for Reading Informational Text is featured in Table 11.2.

There are three main skill areas to teach in Reading Standard 5 by the end of fifth grade for students to be on track for middle school and the higher expectations of the Standards in grades 6–12:

1. The ability to use text features
2. The ability to identify text structures in literary text
3. The ability to identify text structures in informational text

What Literacy Skills and Strategies Support Reading Standard 5?

Reading Standard 5 focuses on text features and structures of different types of text. Understanding how the text is constructed is a key to comprehension. "Research suggests that almost any approach to teaching the structure of informational text improves both comprehension and recall of key text information" (Duke & Pearson, 2002, p. 217).

Reading Literature Standard 5 is about story structure. For this standard, early primary school students need to know how to recognize stories, poems, fiction, and informational text. Teaching students a strong sense of story structure and how to use the appropriate terminology when discussing or writing about literary texts are focuses of Standard 5 for Reading Literature. Intermediate-grade students need to learn how to identify and explain the structures of stories, dramas, and poems. The supporting skills and strategies for Reading Literature Standard 5 are featured in Table 11.3.

For Reading Informational Text Standard 5, kindergartners need to know how to identify the different parts of a book. Our goal is to engage students in grades 1–3 in identifying and using text features to locate information and find answers to questions. In fourth and fifth grades, students need to know how to use common informational text structures to enhance their ability to find answers to questions and to be able to write solid summaries of a text. The supporting skills and strategies for Reading Informational Text Standard 5 are outlined in Table 11.4.

How Can We Teach Reading Standard 5 So Our Students Achieve?

In this section, we discuss the Standards tasks required of students at various grade levels. For example, the fifth College and Career Readiness Anchor Standard requires students to use text

Table 11.3 Common Core State Standard 5 for Reading Literature: Supporting Skills and Strategies

Grade	Skills and Strategies
K	• Recognize storybooks • Recognize poems
1	• Recognize fiction • Recognize informational text
2	• Describe how the beginning introduces the story • Describe the events in the middle of the story • Describe how the ending of a story concludes the action • Describe the story structure
3	• Refer to parts of stories using the term *chapter* • Refer to parts of dramas using the term *scene* • Refer to parts of poems using the term *stanza* • Describe how each part of the text builds on earlier sections
4	• Explain the differences between poems, drama, and prose • Refer to the structural elements of poems (e.g., verse, rhythm, meter) • Refer to the structural elements of drama (e.g., casts of characters, settings, descriptions, dialogue, stage directions)
5	• Explain how a series of chapters fits together to provide the structure of a particular story • Explain how a series of scenes fits together to provide the structure of a particular drama • Explain how a series of stanzas fits together to provide the structure of a particular poem

Table 11.4 Common Core State Standard 5 for Reading Informational Text: Supporting Skills and Strategies

Grade	Skills and Strategies
K	• Identify a front cover • Identify a back cover • Identify a title page
1	• Identify a heading • Identify a table of contents • Identify a glossary • Identify an electronic menu • Identify an icon • Use these text features to locate key facts or information
2	• Identify a caption • Identify bold print • Identify a subheading • Identify a glossary • Identify an index • Identify an electronic menu • Identify an icon • Use these text features to locate key facts or information
3	• Identify text features (e.g., keywords, sidebars) • Identify search tools (e.g., keywords, hyperlinks) • Use keywords to locate information • Use sidebars to locate information • Use hyperlinks to locate information
4	• Identify a chronology • Identify a comparison • Identify cause/effect • Identify problem/solution • Describe the overall structure (e.g., chronology, comparison, cause/effect, problem/solution) of events in a text • Describe the overall structure (e.g., chronology, comparison, cause/effect, problem/solution) of ideas or concepts in a text • Describe the overall structure (e.g., chronology, comparison, cause/effect, problem/solution) of information in a text
5	• Compare and contrast the structure (e.g., chronology, comparison, cause/effect, problem/solution) of events in two or more texts • Compare and contrast the structure (e.g., chronology, comparison, cause/effect, problem/solution) of ideas or concepts in two or more texts • Compare and contrast structure (e.g., chronology, comparison, cause/effect, problem/solution) of information in two or more texts

features and text structures to locate information efficiently. We begin by describing the teaching idea, and then we discuss how it supports the Standards.

Literary Text Structures

The Predict-o-Gram (Blachowicz, 1986) provides opportunities for students to practice using the literary text elements. When using the Predict-o-Gram, we provide students with a list of words associated with the five narrative elements: characters, setting, problem, attempts to resolve, and resolution. Students then use the words provided to make predictions concerning which words are associated with which elements. They then record their predictions on a graphic organizer. During this process, students also become familiar with vocabulary from the story. After reading and discussing the story, students revisit their Predict-o-Grams and make changes as necessary. This graphic organizer supports students' learning of literary text structures to meet College and Career Readiness Anchor Standard 5. Figure 11.1 is a completed Predict-o-Gram for *Armando and the Blue Tarp School* by Edith Hope Fine and Judith Pinkerton Josephson (2007).

Informational Text Structures

Description. When using the Semantic Map (Johnson & Pearson, 1984), students provide descriptive information about a focus word that we supply. This gives students opportunities to work with words and phrases that can be used to describe the focus word. As students offer responses, we record them in a list on the

Figure 11.1 Example of a Predict-o-Gram for a Literary Text Structure

Example Text: Fine, E.H., & Josephson, J.P. (2007). *Armando and the Blue Tarp School*. New York: Lee & Low.

Vocabulary Words:

Armando, school building, Blue Tarp School, Papa, dump, Armando's house, town, big fire, Señor David, newspaper, Isabella, photographer, reporter

Characters:
Armando, Papa, Señor David, Isabella

Setting:
The dump, in the town

Problem:
There is a big fire.

Attempts to Resolve the Problem:
The photographer and the reporter put the big fire in the newspaper.

Resolution:
There is a new school building.

chalkboard, interactive whiteboard, or computer. After each student has offered a response, we ask the students to help us determine which categories emerge from the list of responses. Next, we list the categories in the satellites on the graphic organizer. Then, we list the students' responses under the appropriate satellite. After the graphic organizer is complete, pairs of students can write descriptive paragraphs using the information from the Semantic Map and orally share them with the class. When using Semantic Maps for this purpose, it is better if students complete them after they have read the related text. This graphic organizer supports students' learning of description as an informational text structure because they provide descriptive information and then use it to write a descriptive paragraph. This directly relates to CCR Anchor Standard 5. Examples of a Semantic Map and summary paragraph about the *Tyrannosaurus rex* dinosaur appear in Figure 11.2.

Sequence (Chronology). The Sequence Chain (McLaughlin & Allen, 2009) provides students with opportunities to place items in a sequential or chronological order. This type of text structure is often used in biographies and historical accounts. Placing things in chronological order supports CCR Anchor Standard 5. An example of a completed Sequence Chain about the scientific method is featured in Figure 11.3.

Figure 11.2 Example of a Semantic Map and Summary Paragraph for _Tyrannosaurus rex_

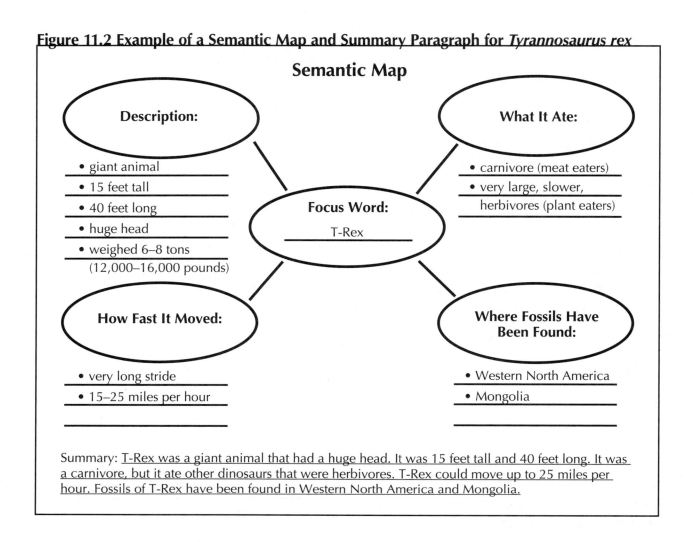

Semantic Map

Description:
- giant animal
- 15 feet tall
- 40 feet long
- huge head
- weighed 6–8 tons (12,000–16,000 pounds)

Focus Word:
T-Rex

What It Ate:
- carnivore (meat eaters)
- very large, slower, herbivores (plant eaters)

How Fast It Moved:
- very long stride
- 15–25 miles per hour

Where Fossils Have Been Found:
- Western North America
- Mongolia

Summary: T-Rex was a giant animal that had a huge head. It was 15 feet tall and 40 feet long. It was a carnivore, but it ate other dinosaurs that were herbivores. T-Rex could move up to 25 miles per hour. Fossils of T-Rex have been found in Western North America and Mongolia.

Figure 11.3 Example of a Sequence Chain

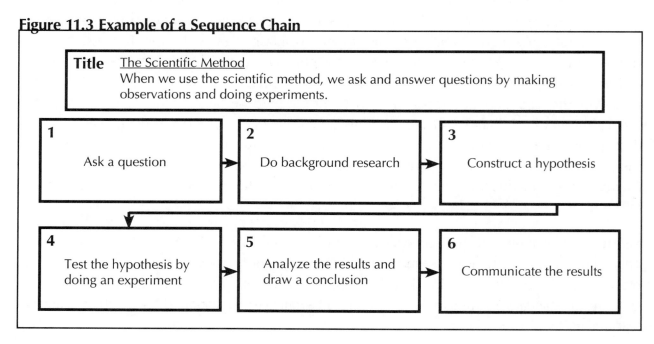

Title The Scientific Method
When we use the scientific method, we ask and answer questions by making observations and doing experiments.

1. Ask a question
2. Do background research
3. Construct a hypothesis
4. Test the hypothesis by doing an experiment
5. Analyze the results and draw a conclusion
6. Communicate the results

Comparison/Contrast. As a text structure, comparison/contrast evinces similarities and differences. When completing a Venn Diagram, students show the similarities of and differences between two topics. The similarities are recorded in the part of the circles that overlap. The differences, or what is unique about each topic, are recorded in the outer portion of each circle. This directly supports CCR Anchor Standard 5. Figure 11.4 is a Venn Diagram about sharks and dolphins. (The Comparison and Contrast Paragraph Frame, another teaching idea that requires students to think through comparison and contrast, is featured in Chapter 9.)

Cause and Effect. This text structure delineates how events or ideas (effects) come to be as the result of other ideas, acts, or events (causes). This supports CCR Anchor Standard 5. Figure 11.5 is an informational text organizer for cause and effect about the Cherokee Trail of Tears.

Problem and Solution. This informational text structure is evident when a difficulty (problem) and an example of how it can be resolved (solution) are featured in a text. This structure, which supports CCR Anchor Standard 5, is featured in Figure 11.6, which is about transportation in the United States in the 1860s.

How Can We Integrate Other ELA Standards With Reading Standard 5?

When planning to teach College and Career Readiness Reading Anchor Standard 1, we can integrate several other ELA standards to design rich instructional tasks. Examples of ideas to include when creating rich instructional tasks follow.

Figure 11.4 Example of a Venn Diagram (Comparison/Contrast)

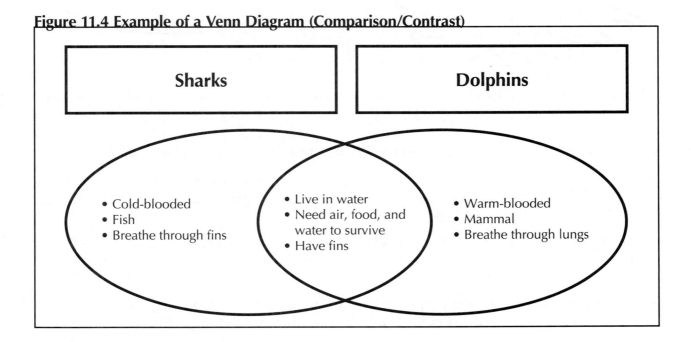

Figure 11.5 Example of an Informational Text Cause and Effect Organizer

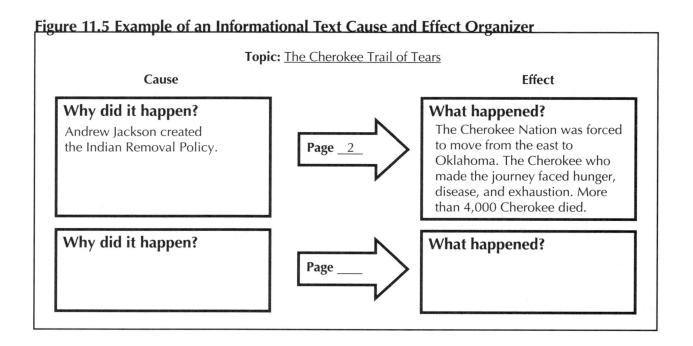

Topic: The Cherokee Trail of Tears

Cause

Effect

Why did it happen?
Andrew Jackson created the Indian Removal Policy.

Page ___2___

What happened?
The Cherokee Nation was forced to move from the east to Oklahoma. The Cherokee who made the journey faced hunger, disease, and exhaustion. More than 4,000 Cherokee died.

Why did it happen?

Page ____

What happened?

Figure 11.6 Example of an Informational Text Problem and Solution Organizer

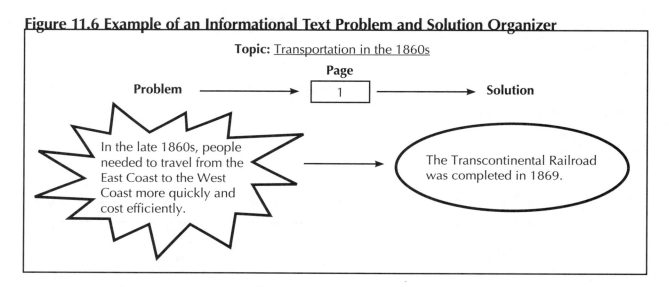

Topic: Transportation in the 1860s

Problem

Page 1

Solution

In the late 1860s, people needed to travel from the East Coast to the West Coast more quickly and cost efficiently.

The Transcontinental Railroad was completed in 1869.

Integrating Other ELA Standards With Reading Literature Standard 5

• Reading Literature Standard 1 focuses on reading a narrative text closely. *Example:* When students read a narrative text closely, encourage them to use the structure of the text to help them locate information about key details in the text.

• Reading Literature Standard 2 focuses on the ability to retell a literary text and determine the author's message or theme. *Example:* When students retell a literary text, remind them to use the narrative elements.

• Writing Standard 3 describes the expectations for narrative writing. For Writing Standard 3, young children tell stories or retell events. Students in grades 3–6 write narratives to develop real or imagined experiences or events using effective techniques, descriptive details, and clear event sequences. *Example:* Encourage students to learn literary story structures as they learn about the development of characters, settings, or events in a story.

- Speaking and Listening Standard 2 focuses on students being able to understand and discuss key details from text read aloud or from multimedia presentations. *Example:* Encourage students to discuss the narrative text structure before, during, and after read-alouds and present their ideas through a variety of media.

Integrating Other ELA Standards With Reading Informational Text Standard 5

- Reading Informational Text Standard 2 focuses on the ability to summarize the main idea and supporting details of an informational text. *Example:* Teach students to identify and discuss the main idea and supporting details when reading an informational text.

- Reading Informational Text Standard 3 focuses on describing the connections and relationships among people, events, ideas, or pieces of information in a text. *Example:* Encourage students to use various text structures, such as cause/effect and comparison/contrast, to better understand historical events, scientific ideas or concepts, or steps in technical procedures.

- Reading Informational Text Standard 8 focuses on the author's reasons and evidence in informational text. *Example:* When reading an informational text, teach students to discuss how the author supported his or her opinion with reasons and evidence by identifying cause/effect.

- Reading Informational Text Standard 9 focuses on comparing and contrasting similar texts and topics and integrating information from several texts about the same topic. *Example:* Encourage students to employ the use of text structure to be able to compare and contrast information in an informational text.

- Writing Standard 1 describes the expectations for students to write an opinion about a topic or text and support their thinking with reasons and information. *Example:* Invite students to write an opinion about a text and support their thinking with reasons and evidence using cause/effect.

- Writing Standard 2 describes the student expectations for informative/explanatory writing. Students introduce the topic; develop the topic; link words, phrases, and ideas; and provide a conclusion. *Example:* Invite students to create a piece of informative/explanatory writing in which they use a particular text structure.

THE COMMON CORE IN ACTION

In this section, we examine one of the foundational ideas that underpins each of the Common Core's Anchor Standards for Reading. For the fifth standard, "Analyze the structure of texts, including how specific sentences, paragraphs, and larger portions of the text (e.g., a section, chapter, scene, or stanza) relate to each other and the whole" (NGA Center & CCSSO, 2010, p. 10), we have elected to share more detailed information about teaching informational text structures, which is an explicit part of the Standards for grades 4 and 5.

Common Core Literacy Task: Informational Text Structures

Beginning in grade 4, students are expected to begin understanding and using the five informational text structures: description, sequence (chronology), comparison/contrast, cause/effect, and problem/solution. We know that research supports the teaching of the text structures and that using such structures supports students' comprehension of text. It is also important to note that each structure should be taught separately through explicit instruction, which includes scaffolding, or the gradual release of responsibility to students. Next, we describe how Jamal, a fifth-grade teacher, explicitly teaches his students about informational text structures.

Jamal is planning a series of reading lessons that focus on Reading Standard 5 for fifth grade. Although his primary emphasis is teaching informational text structures, he also wants to ensure that he develops rich tasks that integrate a number of other Common Core State Standards. To prepare for his teaching, Jamal knows that he will need to have not only multiple examples of interesting text written in each structure but also graphic organizers or other ideas ready to teach the structures. He also understands that writing and technology will be integrated into his plans.

After determining which text examples he will use for which text structure and how he will use the text structure–based graphic organizers, Jamal focuses on how he will explicitly teach the organizational structures. He decides to focus on the five Guided Comprehension steps of explicit instruction: explain, demonstrate, guide, practice, and reflect (McLaughlin & Allen, 2009). Jamal plans to teach the problem/solution text structure in this way:

1. *Explain*—Jamal will begin by explaining that in the problem/solution text structure, we first need to identify the problem and then ask ourselves, how was it fixed? The answer to the question is the solution to the problem. He will remind students about math problems for which they have figured out solutions and explain how, throughout history, society has encountered many problems for which solutions were created. For example, when the shortage of oil caused the price of gasoline to rise, car companies began focusing on developing electric cars, which are much cheaper to use. Students will listen and be prepared to summarize. (SL.5.2)

2. *Demonstrate*—Jamal will distribute the graphic organizer for this text structure. He will introduce the text (an article on great American inventions) and demonstrate by reading sections of the article aloud. After reading the first segment, he will think aloud about when people used to use notes and letters to communicate and wonder how that problem was solved. Then, Jamal will read another segment and pose similar questions. He will note the structure-associated signal words in each segment and record his responses on the Informational Text Problem and Solution Organizer, which he provided to the students at the start of the lesson. Again, students will be prepared to summarize the information. (SL.5.2)

3. *Guide*—Jamal will explain that he will read another segment and ask the students to work in partners to determine the solution. They will then verify the solution in the text. Jamal will encourage the students to record their thoughts on the Informational Text Problem and Solution Organizer. Next, he will invite the partners to read a short segment, discuss it, and identify the problem and solution. Again, they will record their thinking on the graphic organizer. He will also ask them to discuss the signal words used in that segment.

He will guide the students through this process, offering support as needed. Then, they will repeat this process. Afterward, the class will generate and respond to questions about the problem/solution text structure and the signal words that are used in it. They will also make connections to the Text Structure Signal Words Chart, where the signal words for informational text structures are posted. Finally, he will guide the partners to brainstorm problems and select one to write a short paragraph about, using the problem/solution text structure. Jamal will guide students through this process and provide paragraph frames to students who may need them. (SL.5.1, W.5.2, W.5.4, W.5.8)

4. *Practice*—Students will practice by working on their own to read text containing the problem/solution text structure. They will record their thinking on the graphic organizer and discuss the passages with their partner. Then, students will work on their own to write an example of the problem/solution text structure. (RI.5.5, W.5.8, SL.5.1)

5. *Reflect*—Students will reflect on this text structure and how it differs from others that they have learned. The class will discuss the subject areas in which students might expect to see this pattern and how knowing text structures can help them understand what they read. (RI.5.5)

Reading Standard 5 focuses on ensuring that students are able to read texts that have a variety of organizational structures. It requires students to analyze the structure and relate portions of a text to each other and the whole. Students use text structures to build understanding of a text, just as architects use blueprints to build homes. When they understand text structures, students examine how it is built—they use the blueprints—to understand the texts that they read.

References

ACT. (2006). *Reading between the lines: What the ACT reveals about college readiness in reading.* Iowa City, IA: Author. Retrieved August 22, 2012, from www.act.org/research/policymakers/pdf/reading_report.pdf

Akhondi, M., Malayeri, F., & Samad, A.A. (2011). How to teach expository text structure to facilitate reading comprehension. *The Reading Teacher, 64*(5), 368–372.

Armbruster, B.B. (2004). Considerate texts. In D. Lapp, J. Flood, & N. Farnan (Eds.), *Content area reading and learning: Instructional strategies* (2nd ed., pp. 47–57). Mahwah, NJ: Erlbaum.

Blachowicz, C.L.Z. (1986). Making connections: Alternatives to the vocabulary notebook. *Journal of Reading, 29*(7), 643–649.

Duke, N.K., & Pearson, P.D. (2002). Effective practices for developing reading comprehension. In A.E. Farstrup & S.J. Samuels (Eds.), *What research has to say about reading instruction* (3rd ed., pp. 205–242). Newark, DE: International Reading Association.

Gambrell, L.B. (2001). *It's not either/or but more: Balancing narrative and informational text to improve reading comprehension.* Paper presented at the 46th annual convention of the International Reading Association, New Orleans, LA.

Goldman, S.R., & Rakestraw, J.A. (2000). Structural aspects of constructing meaning from text. In M.L. Kamil, P.B. Mosenthal, P.D. Pearson, & R. Barr (Eds.), *Handbook of reading research* (Vol. 3, pp. 311–335). Mahwah, NJ: Erlbaum.

Johnson, D.D., & Pearson, P.D. (1984). *Teaching reading vocabulary* (2nd ed.). New York: Holt, Rinehart and Winston.

McLaughlin, M. (2010). *Content area reading: Teaching and learning in an age of multiple literacies.* Boston: Allyn & Bacon.

McLaughlin, M., & Allen, M.B. (2009). *Guided Comprehension in grades 3–8* (Combined 2nd ed.). Newark, DE: International Reading Association.

Moss, B. (2004). Teaching expository text structures through information trade book retellings. *The Reading Teacher*, 57(8), 710–719.

National Governors Association Center for Best Practices & Council of Chief State School Officers. (2010). *Common Core State Standards for English language arts and literacy in history/social studies, science, and technical subjects.* Washington, DC: Authors. Retrieved August 3, 2012, from www.corestandards.org/assets/CCSSI_ELA%20 Standards.pdf

Pressley, M. (2002). *Reading instruction that works: The case for balanced teaching* (2nd ed.). New York: Guilford.

Children's Literature Cited

Carle, E. (2002). *The very hungry caterpillar.* New York: Puffin.

Fine, E.H., & Josephson, J.P. (2007). *Armando and the Blue Tarp School.* New York: Lee & Low.

Lassieur, A. (2004). *The ancient Romans.* New York: Scholastic.

Ryan, P.M. (2000). *Esperanza rising.* New York: Scholastic.

Ryan, P.M. (2004). *Becoming Naomi León.* New York: Scholastic.

CHAPTER 12

CCR Reading Anchor Standard 6: Point of View

	College and Career Readiness Reading Standard 6
Seeing in Different Ways	Assess how point of view or purpose shapes content and style of a text. (NGA Center & CCSSO, 2010, p. 10)

What Does CCR Reading Anchor Standard 6 Mean?

In College and Career Readiness (CCR) Reading Anchor Standard 6, the emphasis is on point of view and author's purpose. Whether the text is literary or informational, the author writes from a certain point of view so the reader feels a certain way or is persuaded to a certain belief. The goal is for students to understand that stories may be told and text may be written in different ways depending on who is doing the telling or writing. Students are asked to explain how various narrators see in different ways.

Understanding the point of view from which a text is written helps the reader comprehend the text in a deeper way. In English or literature courses, students may be asked to write a Point of View Analysis, which is an essay describing the point of view of the narrator in a literary text and describing how that point of view is used in a text to communicate the author's message. A Point of View Analysis requires students to consider nuances in the text that they might not see otherwise. According to high school Common Core Standard 6 for Reading Literature, by the end of high school, students are expected to know how to analyze points of view or cultural experiences in literary works from around the world and to demonstrate knowledge of literary elements, such as satire, sarcasm, irony, and understatement, based on a sophisticated analysis of a narrator's point of view.

When reading informational text, being able to analyze the author's or narrator's point of view means being able to determine the credibility of the text. The more credible the author, the more credible the information is. Not only are students required to determine the author's point of view or purpose for writing the text, but they are also required to analyze how an author uses rhetoric (in this case, style and content) to advance that point of view or purpose. The high school Common Core Standard 6 for Reading Informational Text states that by the end of grade 12, students should be able to "determine an author's point of view or purpose in a text in which the rhetoric is particularly effective, analyzing how style and content contribute to the power, persuasiveness, or beauty of the text" (NGA Center & CCSSO, 2010, p. 40).

Reading Anchor Standard 6 focuses on two reading skills:

1. The ability to assess how point of view shapes the content and style of a text
2. The ability to assess how purpose shapes the content and style of a text

Point of View

A text may be written from one point of view or from a variety of perspectives. A text may be analyzed to determine point of view as a literary device or to determine the author's point of view about a topic. The text may also be analyzed to determine the effectiveness of the author's use of argument in a speech, essay, editorial, or article stating an opinion.

As a literary device, one point of view may be that of a first-person narrator. In first-person narration, the author writes as if he or she were a character in the story who is telling the story. This narrator uses pronouns such as *I* and *my*. Another type of point of view as a literary device, and one that is not used often, is second-person narration. In second-person narration, the author writes as if the reader were in the story. This narrator uses pronouns such as *you* and *your*.

A third type of point of view, and one that is used extensively as a literary device, is that of a third-person narrator. In third-person narration, the author writes the story as an outside voice looking in on the events of the story. In third-person omniscient narration, the author can see inside the minds of all the characters and describe their thoughts. In third-person limited narration, the author only tells the story from one character's point of view. These narrators use pronouns such as *he* and *she*.

Purpose

The author's purpose is the reason the text was written. Literary texts are written to entertain. Even when a text is written to entertain, the author wants the reader to think or feel a certain way and writes from a particular point of view. Informational texts may be written to answer a question, describe, or explain an event, situation, person, or procedure. Students who can determine an author's reasons for writing an informational text are more aware of the text's intended message.

How Do the Common Core Standards Build to CCR Anchor Standard 6?

For Reading Literature Standard 6, students are expected to understand and determine the point of view from which the text is written. Whether it is a story, poem, or drama, either the narrator or the characters tell the story from a certain point of view. In kindergarten, students name the author and illustrators of stories, and first graders identify who is telling the story at different points in the text. Second grade has an emphasis on point of view of characters, while third graders are expected to be able to distinguish their own point of view from that of the author's. At the intermediate grades, students learn to compare and contrast points of view and should be able to describe the ways in which traits of the narrator or speaker inform how they describe events. Table 12.1 shows Common Core State Standard 6 for Reading Literature.

In Reading Informational Text Standard 6, kindergartners name the author and illustrator of informational texts and tell what each one does. First-grade students learn to tell the difference between getting information from images and getting information from words, while second graders identify why the author wrote the text. Third graders learn to tell the difference between their own point of view and the author's. In the intermediate grades, students read firsthand and secondhand accounts of the same event or topic, describe the similarities and differences in points of view, and then learn to analyze different ways that writers or speakers describe their own point of view of the same event or topic. Common Core Standard 6 for Reading Informational Text is delineated in Table 12.2.

There are three main skill areas to teach in Reading Standard 6 by the end of fifth grade for students to be on track for middle school and the higher expectations of the Standards in grades 6–12:

- Point of view

- Determining an author's main purpose for a text

- Comparing and contrasting points of view

Table 12.1 Common Core State Standard 6 for Reading Literature in Grades K–5

Grade	Standard
K	With prompting and support, name the author and illustrator of a story and define the role of each in telling the story.
1	Identify who is telling the story at various points in a text.
2	Acknowledge differences in the points of view of characters, including by speaking in a different voice for each character when reading dialogue aloud.
3	Distinguish their own point of view from that of the narrator or those of the characters.
4	Compare and contrast the point of view from which different stories are narrated, including the difference between first- and third-person narrations.
5	Describe how a narrator's or speaker's point of view influences how events are described.

Note. The standards are from *Common Core State Standards for English Language Arts and Literacy in History/Social Studies, Science, and Technical Subjects* (pp. 11 and 12), by National Governors Association Center for Best Practices and Council of Chief State School Officers, 2010, Washington, DC: Authors.

Table 12.2 Common Core State Standard 6 for Reading Informational Text in Grades K–5

Grade	Standard
K	Name the author and illustrator of a text and define the role of each in presenting the ideas or information in a text.
1	Distinguish between information provided by pictures or other illustrations and information provided by the words in a text.
2	Identify the main purpose of a text, including what the author wants to answer, explain, or describe.
3	Distinguish their own point of view from that of the author of a text.
4	Compare and contrast a firsthand and secondhand account of the same event or topic; describe the differences in focus and the information provided.
5	Analyze multiple accounts of the same event or topic, noting important similarities and differences in the point of view they represent.

Note. The standards are from *Common Core State Standards for English Language Arts and Literacy in History/Social Studies, Science, and Technical Subjects* (pp. 13 and 14), by National Governors Association Center for Best Practices and Council of Chief State School Officers, 2010, Washington, DC: Authors.

What Literacy Skills and Strategies Support Reading Standard 6?

Every piece of text was written from a particular point of view. To teach Reading Standard 6, we need to teach about point of view in different types of text.

For Reading Literature Standard 6, we need to give students opportunities to determine point of view in a wide variety of stories, dramas, and poetry. Literary texts that have different points of view work best to provide our students with such broad experiences. The supporting skills and strategies for Reading Literature Standard 6 are listed in Table 12.3.

For Reading Informational Text Standard 6, we provide consistent opportunities for students to read well-written informational text with images. Beginning in grade 2, we need to ask, "Why do you think the author wrote this text?" when reading an informational text to help students think about the author's purpose for writing it. In grade 3, we should teach the difference between the students' own point of view and that of the author and ask questions such as, "What do you think?" and "What does the author think?" In the intermediate grades, students need opportunities to compare and contrast firsthand and secondhand accounts and different points of view of the same event or topic. This means selecting materials that represent primary and secondary sources or varied texts about the same topic. Table 12.4 features the supporting skills and strategies for Reading Informational Text Standard 6.

Table 12.3 Common Core State Standard 6 for Reading Literature: Supporting Skills and Strategies

Grade	Standard
K	• Name the author of a story • Name the illustrator of a story • Define the roles of the author and illustrator in telling a story
1	• Recognize when a narrator is telling the story • Recognize when a character is telling the story • Identify who is telling the story at various points
2	• Identify characters • Identify the point of view of the characters • Decide what type of voice to use for each character • Read the dialogue using appropriate voices for different characters
3	• Recognize one's own point of view • Identify the narrator's point of view • Identify a character's point of view • Distinguish among one's own, the narrator's, and characters' points of view
4	• Define *compare/contrast* • Define point of view • Define *first-person narration* • Define *third-person narration* • Compare and contrast points of view
5	• Identify the narrator's or speaker's point of view • Describe the narrator's or speaker's point of view • Determine traits or knowledge that a narrator or speaker may have that might influence the description of events • Describe how the narrator's point of view influences the description of an event • Describe how the speaker's point of view influences the description of an event

Table 12.4 Common Core State Standard 6 for Reading Informational Text: Supporting Skills and Strategies

Grade	Standard
K	• Name the author of an informational text • Name the illustrator of an informational text • Define the roles of the author and illustrator in presenting information
1	• Identify whether information is provided in the images • Distinguish between information provided by images and information provided by words
2	• Identify the author's purpose • Identify the main idea • Identify what the author wants to answer, explain, or describe
3	• Recognize one's own point of view • Recognize the author's point of view • Explain the difference between one's own and the author's point of view
4	• Define *compare/contrast* • Define *firsthand account* • Define *secondhand account* • Compare accounts of the same event or topic • Contrast accounts of the same event or topic • Describe how the focus and information is different in each account
5	• Determine the point of view in each account of the same event or topic • Compare points of view in each account of the same event or topic • Contrast points of view in each account of the same event or topic

How Can We Teach Reading Standard 6 So Our Students Achieve?

In this section, we discuss the Standards tasks required of students at various grade levels. For example, the sixth College and Career Readiness Anchor Standard requires students to distinguish between their own and a narrator's point of view, determine the author's purpose for writing a text, and compare and contrast points of view about the same events or topics. We begin by describing the teaching idea, and then we discuss how it supports the Standards.

Point of View

A major emphasis of Reading Standard 6 for both literature and informational text is point of view. The teaching idea that we selected for point of view is the Open-Mind Portrait (Tompkins, 2010). The purpose of this activity is to understand a character's perspective or point of view. This teaching idea can be used with stories, biographies, or informational text with descriptions of individuals.

Invite students to draw and color a portrait of a character from a story or a famous person from a biography. Ask students to cut out the portrait and use it to trace one or more blank head shapes onto one or several sheets of paper. On the blank pages, students draw or write about the person's thoughts or feelings throughout the story to observe how the character's point of view develops over the course of the text.

An alternative is for students to fold a large sheet of paper in half. On one half, they draw a portrait of a character from the book. On the other half, they draw the same shape as the portrait but do not fill in the facial features. Instead, they fill the head with words and images to represent the character's point of view. An example of an Open-Mind Portrait based on Kevin Henkes's (1991) book *Crysanthemum* appears in Figure 12.1.

Figure 12.1 Example of an Open-Mind Portrait

Example Text: Henkes, K. (1991). *Chrysanthemum*. New York: Greenwillow.

Comparing and Contrasting Points of View

Reading Standard 6 for both literature and informational text has a major emphasis on helping students understand point of view. We can encourage students to compare and contrast different viewpoints in a story by using a teaching idea called Thinking Hats (de Bono, 1985). First, we introduce a story by building students' background knowledge. Then, we divide students into small groups to discuss the concept of perspective, or point of view. We read the text aloud or provide multiple copies of the text so students can read and discuss the text with a partner.

We use Jigsaw II (Slavin, 1995), a cooperative learning technique, for students to think about the different perspectives of characters in the story. Students work in small groups to brainstorm a list of the character's possible points of view in the story. Next, students regroup into "expert" Thinking Hats groups. The students in each group discuss the story from the viewpoint of one character. After the group discussion, students return to their original small groups as an expert on the point of view of one character. The original small group discusses the story, including the points of view of all the characters. After the discussion, the group records the characters' thoughts on the Thinking Hats chart. Then, they compare and contrast the characters' points of view by discussing the similarities and differences. Figure 12.2 features McLaughlin and DeVoogd's (2004) use of Thinking Hats with Jane Yolen's (1992) book *Encounter*. After building their background knowledge using informational text about Christopher Columbus, the students read *Encounter* and discussed the story from the points of view of Columbus, the Tainos people, the sailors, and Queen Isabella.

Figure 12.2 Example of a Thinking Hats Organizer

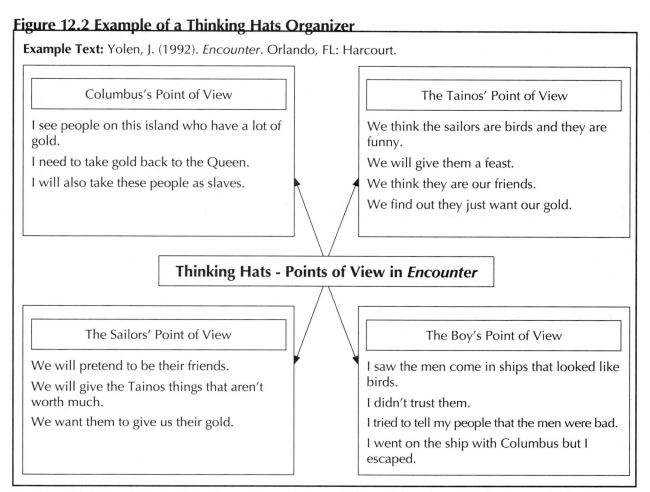

Example Text: Yolen, J. (1992). *Encounter*. Orlando, FL: Harcourt.

Columbus's Point of View

I see people on this island who have a lot of gold.

I need to take gold back to the Queen.

I will also take these people as slaves.

The Tainos' Point of View

We think the sailors are birds and they are funny.

We will give them a feast.

We think they are our friends.

We find out they just want our gold.

Thinking Hats - Points of View in *Encounter*

The Sailors' Point of View

We will pretend to be their friends.

We will give the Tainos things that aren't worth much.

We want them to give us their gold.

The Boy's Point of View

I saw the men come in ships that looked like birds.

I didn't trust them.

I tried to tell my people that the men were bad.

I went on the ship with Columbus but I escaped.

Note. From *Critical Literacy: Enhancing Students' Comprehension of Text* (p. 131), by M. McLaughlin and G. DeVoogd, 2004, New York: Scholastic. Copyright 2004 by Maureen McLaughlin and Glenn L. DeVoogd. Reprinted with permission.

Thinking Hats can be used to consider different perspectives of characters in almost any literary text. For example, when reading *Charlotte's Web* by E.B. White (1952/2006), Thinking Hats can be used to determine the points of view of Fern, Charlotte, Wilbur, and Templeton.

Thinking Hats can also be used to compare and contrast varied perspectives about informational text, such as different accounts of historical events or descriptions of the same scientific concepts written by different authors. For example, this activity could be used to discuss a variety of perspectives in *Remember Pearl Harbor: American and Japanese Survivors Tell Their Stories* by Thomas B. Allen (2001). When students participate in Thinking Hats, they think critically about diverse points of view.

Technology Connection

One way to teach students about point of view is to encourage them to create comic strips in which the characters describe their perspectives on a situation. Students can create their own stories or use the cartoon figures in a comic strip creator to represent a character from a published story or poem. When students create a series of comic panels to represent a story and include speech and thought bubbles, they decide what the character might think, say, and do. With the teacher's guidance, students can use comic strips to think critically.

There are several free comic strip creators available online. One we like is called Make Beliefs Comix (www.makebeliefscomix.com), which is an educational comic strip creator students can use to create comics in one of seven languages: English, Spanish, French, German, Italian, Portuguese, or Latin. On this website, there is also a page with suggestions for using comics with students across a range of physical and learning disabilities.

How Can We Integrate Other ELA Standards With Reading Standard 6?

When planning to teach CCR Anchor Standard 6, we can integrate several other ELA standards to design rich instructional tasks. Examples of ideas to include when creating rich instructional tasks follow.

Integrating Other ELA Standards With Reading Literature Standard 6

- Reading Literature Standard 1 focuses on reading a narrative text closely. *Example:* When students engage in close reading of a text, encourage them to determine the point of view of the author or one or more characters.

- Reading Literature Standard 2 focuses on the ability to retell a literary text and determine the author's message or theme. *Example:* When students read closely, invite them to infer the theme of a literary text and/or author's purpose by examining the author's or characters' points of view when exploring actions, dialogue, and thoughts and feelings.

- Reading Literature Standard 3 focuses on being able to describe characters, settings, or events in a story or drama, drawing on specific details in the text. *Example:* Ask students to describe the points of view of various characters.

- Reading Literature Standard 7 focuses on how the images in a text or multimedia version of a text can help establish mood, tone, and meaning. *Example:* When reading a literary text, teach students to analyze images for clues and key details about the author's point of view in a story.

- Writing Standard 1 describes the expectations for students to write an opinion about a topic or text and support their point of view with reasons and information. *Example:* When students read a literary text, encourage them to state an opinion about the text and provide a rationale for their thinking.

- Speaking and Listening Standard 1 describes the expectation for students to engage effectively in a range of collaborative discussions, with specific indicators to demonstrate how to participate in an effective academic conversation. *Example:* When reading stories, dramas, and poems, engage students in whole-group, small-group, and paired collaborative conversations.

Integrating Other ELA Standards With Reading Informational Text Standard 6

- Reading Informational Text Standard 1 refers to engaging in close reading of an informational text. *Example:* When students read an informational text closely, encourage them to determine the author's point of view and purpose for writing the text.

- Reading Informational Text Standard 2 focuses on the ability to summarize the main idea and supporting details of an informational text. *Example:* When students read an informational text, ask them to identify the main idea and supporting details. Use their findings to encourage discussion of the author's purpose for writing the text.

- Reading Informational Text Standard 7 focuses on how the images in a text or multimedia version of the text can help establish the key ideas. *Example:* Encourage students to use the images in a text to determine characters' points of view.

- Reading Informational Text Standard 8 focuses on the author's reasons and evidence in informational text. *Example:* After students read a text in which the author has stated an opinion, have them discuss the author's opinion and point of view.

- Reading Informational Text Standard 9 focuses on comparing and contrasting important points and key details in two or more texts or integrating information from several texts on the same topic. *Example:* Encourage students to compare and contrast authors' points of view when reading multiple perspectives on the same topic.

- Reading Informational Text Standard 10 refers to the expectation that students be able to read more challenging texts. *Example:* When students engage in reading a more complex text, encourage them to determine and discuss point of view and the author's purpose for writing the text.

- Writing Standard 1 describes the expectation of students writing opinions about a topic or text and supporting their points of view with reasons and information. *Example:* Encourage students to create text from multiple perspectives.

- Speaking and Listening Standard 1 addresses students engaging effectively in a range of collaborative discussions, with specific indicators that demonstrate how to participate in an effective academic conversation. *Example:* Encourage students to engage in a number of collaborative academic conversations about informational text after determining the author's point of view and purpose for writing the text.

THE COMMON CORE IN ACTION

In this section, we examine one of the foundational ideas that underpins each of the Common Core's Anchor Standards for Reading. For the sixth standard, "Assess how point of view or purpose shapes the content and style of a text" (NGA Center & CCSSO, 2010, p. 10), we have elected to share more detailed information about the purpose of an informational text, which is an explicit part of the Standards for grade 2.

Common Core Literacy Task: Identifying the Main Purpose of a Text

Sarah, a second-grade teacher, is planning a social studies themed unit called Kids Around the World. Of course, she plans to include a lot of informational text. As she teaches the unit, she will integrate Reading Informational Text Standard 6 into her social studies lessons. This standard's expectation for second grade is to "identify the main purpose of a text, including what the author wants to answer, explain, or describe" (NGA Center & CCSSO, 2010, p. 13).

Sarah talks with her library media specialist and checks out a number of children's books that she can use for her Kids Around the World theme. The following are a few of the books that she chose:

- *Wake Up, World! A Day in the Life of Children Around the World* by Beatrice Hollyer (1999)
- *It's Back to School We Go! First Day Stories From Around the World* by Ellen Jackson (2003)
- *Children From Australia to Zimbabwe: A Photographic Journey Around the World* by Maya Ajmera and Anna Rhesa Versola (2001)
- *Hello World! Greetings in 42 Languages Around the Globe!* by Manya Stojic (2002)
- *My Granny Went to Market: A Round-the-World Counting Rhyme* by Stella Blackstone (2006)
- *On the Same Day in March: A Tour of the World's Weather* by Marilyn Singer (2000)
- *Let's Eat: What Children Eat Around the World* by Beatrice Hollyer (2004)
- *Come to the Great World: Poems From Around the Globe* selected by Wendy Cooling (2004)
- *Throw Your Tooth on the Roof: Tooth Traditions From Around the World* by Selby B. Beeler (1998)
- *Tooth Tales From Around the World* by Marlene Targ Brill (1998)

Sarah plans to read selected books aloud as part of her social studies theme. The following is her planned routine for each book:

1. Gather the students on the carpet where they can see the book and a map of the world.
2. Introduce the book by doing a picture walk. Point out text features such as the table of contents, maps, photographs, and charts. (RI.2.5)
3. Read the book aloud to the students, modeling expression and fluent reading.
4. Stop periodically throughout the book and encourage the students to ask and answer questions such as who, what, where, when, why, and how to demonstrate understanding of key details in the book. (RI.2.1, SL.2.2) Place pins or stickers on the map as students point out key facts for different countries and cultures described in the book.
5. Help the students identify the main topic of the book. (RI.2.2)
6. Discuss any unfamiliar words in the text that are important for students to know. (RI.2.4)
7. For each book, ask, "Why did the author write this book?" Facilitate a student discussion of the main purpose of the text. (RI.2.6, SL.2.1)
8. In their Kids Around the World journals, the students list the author's purpose for writing the text. (RI.2.6)
9. In their Kids Around the World journals, the students write the title of the book and explain something new that they learned from the text. (W.2.8) Then, they illustrate their journal entry.
10. Later in the unit, Sarah will ask her students to revisit the books and use their journal entries to participate in shared research about aspects of life in other countries. (W.2.7) She will also ask the students to compare and contrast the most important points presented in two of the books. (RI.2.9) (See Chapter 15 for teaching ideas on comparing and contrasting texts.)

Reading Standard 6 focuses on ensuring that students can determine point of view and the author's main purpose for a text. It requires students to determine point of view, decide the author's main purpose for writing the text, and compare and contrast points of view from a character's perspective or from firsthand and secondhand accounts of events. When students see in different ways, they can more deeply comprehend a text.

References

de Bono, E. (1985). *Six thinking hats.* Boston: Little, Brown.

McLaughlin, M., & DeVoogd, G. (2004). *Critical literacy: Enhancing students' comprehension of text.* New York: Scholastic.

National Governors Association Center for Best Practices & Council of Chief State School Officers. (2010). *Common Core State Standards for English language arts and literacy in history/social studies, science, and technical subjects.* Washington, DC: Authors. Retrieved August 3, 2012, from www.corestandards.org/assets/CCSSI_ELA%20 Standards.pdf

Slavin, R.E. (1995). *Cooperative learning: Theory, research and practice* (2nd ed.). Boston: Allyn & Bacon.

Tompkins, G.E. (2010). *Literacy for the 21st century: A balanced approach* (5th ed.). Boston: Allyn & Bacon.

Children's Literature Cited

Ajmera, M., & Versola, A.R. (2001). *Children from Australia to Zimbabwe: A photographic journey around the world* (Rev. ed.). Watertown, MA: Charlesbridge.

Allen, T.B. (2001). *Remember Pearl Harbor: American and Japanese survivors tell their stories.* Washington, DC: National Geographic Society.

Beeler, S.B. (1998). *Throw your tooth on the roof: Tooth traditions from around the world.* New York: Houghton Mifflin.

Blackstone, S. (2006). *My granny went to market: A round-the-world counting rhyme.* Cambridge, MA: Barefoot.

Brill, M.T. (1998). *Tooth tales from around the world.* Watertown, MA: Charlesbridge.

Cooling, W. (Ed.). (2004). *Come to the great world: Poems from around the globe.* New York: Holiday House.

Henkes, K. (1991). *Chrysanthemum.* New York: Greenwillow.

Hollyer, B. (1999). *Wake up, world! A day in the life of children around the world.* New York: Henry Holt.

Hollyer, B. (2004). *Let's eat! What children eat around the world.* New York: Henry Holt.

Jackson, E. (2003). *It's back to school we go! First day stories from around the world.* Minneapolis, MN: Millbrook.

Singer, M. (2000). *On the same day in March: A tour of the world's weather.* New York: HarperTrophy.

Stojic, M. (2002). *Hello world! Greetings in 42 languages around the globe!* New York: Scholastic.

White, E.B. (2006). *Charlotte's web.* New York: HarperFestival. (Original work published 1952)

Yolen, J. (1992). *Encounter.* Orlando, FL: Harcourt.

CHAPTER 13

CCR Reading Anchor Standard 7: Diverse Media and Formats

 Putting It Together	**College and Career Readiness Reading Standard 7** Integrate and evaluate content presented in diverse media and formats, including visually and quantitatively, as well as in words. (NGA Center & CCSSO, 2010, p. 10)

What Does CCR Reading Standard 7 Mean?

College and Career Readiness (CCR) Reading Anchor Standard 7 focuses on the ability to draw on information from multiple sources to address a question or solve a problem. Students need to be able to select appropriate material and evaluate their sources to conduct authentic, credible research and present that research in writing or speaking. They need to be able to integrate information from diverse media (e.g., audio, video, multimedia presentations) and in varied formats (e.g., textbooks, charts, graphs, magazine articles, newspapers) and then put it together to find answers and solve problems.

Reading Anchor Standard 7 focuses on two reading skills:

1. The ability to integrate content presented in diverse media and formats as well as in print

2. The ability to evaluate content presented in diverse media and formats as well as in print

When reading literature, students need to analyze multiple interpretations of a story, drama, or poem, such as a recorded or live production of a play or a recorded novel or poem. They may be asked to evaluate how an artist has represented a key scene from literature or evaluate the choices made by a director about how a novel is depicted in film. Technology will play a key role as students search for, review, and analyze online depictions of literary text compared with the written word.

In the disciplines, students need to be able to integrate and analyze sources to develop a coherent understanding of a topic or issue. Students are expected to compare and contrast a written text with an audio, video, or multimedia version of it. An example of this might be a written speech and the recorded version. Students are expected to use a variety of media to present a particular topic or idea, and they need to be able to evaluate the advantages and disadvantages of using diverse media and formats to present their ideas. Students also need to develop an efficient sense of how to review a number of resources on the same topic or issue, evaluate the sources and information, and choose the resources that are most credible before creating a written or oral presentation.

How Do the Common Core Standards Build to CCR Anchor Standard 7?

The aim of Common Core Reading Standard 7 is to build the skills necessary to be able to integrate and evaluate content presented in diverse media and formats by the end of high school.

For literature, kindergartners learn to describe the relationship between images and the story or text in which they appear. In grades 2 and 3, students focus on learning to use the images and details in a story to comprehend it. In fourth grade, students look for connections between a written version of the story and an individual or oral presentation of the same story. Fifth graders begin to analyze the effectiveness of visual and multimedia elements in literary text or multimedia productions of the same literary work. Common Core State Standard 7 for Reading Literature appears in Table 13.1.

For informational text, kindergartners learn to describe the relationship between images and the text. Students in grades 2 and 3 learn to use images and details in a text to describe its key ideas and to clarify the information in the text. Fourth graders learn to interpret the kind of information

Table 13.1 Common Core State Standard 7 for Reading Literature in Grades K–5

Grade	Standard
K	With prompting and support, describe the relationship between illustrations and the story in which they appear (e.g., what moment in a story an illustration depicts).
1	Use illustrations and details in a story to describe its characters, setting, or events.
2	Use information gained from the illustrations and words in a print or digital text to demonstrate understanding of its characters, setting, or plot.
3	Explain how specific aspects of a text's illustrations contribute to what is conveyed by the words in a story (e.g., create mood, emphasize aspects of a character or setting).
4	Make connections between the text of a story or drama and a visual or oral presentation of the text, identifying where each version reflects specific descriptions and directions in the text.
5	Analyze how visual and multimedia elements contribute to the meaning, tone, or beauty of a text (e.g., graphic novel, multimedia presentation of fiction, folktale, myth, poem).

Note. The standards are from *Common Core State Standards for English Language Arts and Literacy in History/Social Studies, Science, and Technical Subjects* (pp. 11 and 12), by National Governors Association Center for Best Practices and Council of Chief State School Officers, 2010, Washington, DC: Authors.

Table 13.2 Common Core State Standard 7 for Reading Informational Text in Grades K–5

Grade	Standard
K	With prompting and support, describe the relationship between illustrations and the text in which they appear (e.g., what person, place, thing, or idea in the text an illustration depicts).
1	Use the illustrations and details in a text to describe its key ideas.
2	Explain how specific images (e.g., a diagram showing how a machine works) contribute to and clarify a text.
3	Use information gained from illustrations (e.g., maps, photographs) and the words in a text to demonstrate understanding of the text (e.g., where, when, why, and how key events occur).
4	Interpret information presented visually, orally, or quantitatively (e.g., in charts, graphs, diagrams, time lines, animations, or interactive elements on Web pages) and explain how the information contributes to an understanding of the text in which it appears.
5	Draw on information from multiple print or digital sources, demonstrating the ability to locate an answer to a question quickly or to solve a problem efficiently.

Note. The standards are from *Common Core State Standards for English Language Arts and Literacy in History/Social Studies, Science, and Technical Subjects* (pp. 13 and 14), by National Governors Association Center for Best Practices and Council of Chief State School Officers, 2010, Washington, DC: Authors.

they see in charts, graphs, diagrams, timelines, animations, and interactive elements on webpages. In fifth grade, students draw on information from multiple sources to locate an answer to a question or solve a problem. Table 13.2 features Reading Informational Text Standard 7.

There are three main skill areas to teach in Reading Standard 7 by the end of fifth grade for students to be on track for middle school and the higher expectations of the Standards in grades 6–12:

1. Interpret illustrations and details in a story
2. Analyze visual and multimedia elements in a text
3. Use print and digital sources to find information

What Literacy Skills and Strategies Support Reading Standard 7?

Reading Standard 7 describes the expectation for students to interpret illustrations and visual elements of text and to compare and contrast text versions with versions of the text that rely on auditory, visual, or multimedia modes of presentation. For Reading Standard 7, students also learn to use multiple sources, both print and digital, to find information.

There is an expanding body of research supporting multimedia in the classroom as a way to improve learning. It may be that using appropriate videos embedded into content lessons can affect comprehension and vocabulary skills. Hall and Stahl (2012) state that "there is growing evidence suggesting that comprehension skills can transfer across different types of media" (p. 404). These authors synthesize research showing positive effects of instruction that includes multimedia on the comprehension of at-risk students and those who are not at risk, students with learning disabilities, and English learners. Ikpeze and Boyd (2007) describe a study of the use of WebQuests (Web-based inquiry learning), including the use of multiple tasks, collaboration, making thoughtful connections, critical reading, and learning in a Web-based environment. The researchers found that using WebQuests with intermediate-grade students has the result of promoting thoughtful and critical literacy.

Zhang, Duke, and Jimenez (2011) conducted a study of an approach with intermediate-grade students for critically evaluating websites, which they called the WWWDOT Framework:

1. **W**ho wrote this and what credentials do they have?
2. **W**hy was it written?
3. **W**hen was it written?
4. **D**oes it help meet my needs?
5. **O**rganization of the site?
6. **T**o-do list for the future. (p. 152)

The researchers found that intermediate-grade students who have been engaged in instruction using the WWWDOT Framework are more aware of the need to evaluate a website for credibility.

For Reading Standard 7, we need to plan for lessons that focus on interpreting pictures, graphics, and multimedia elements. We also need the tools for students to be able to conduct simple research. Our classrooms should be rich in images and opportunities to engage in multimedia for students to meet the expectations of this standard.

For Reading Literature Standard 7, in all grades, we need to plan for numerous lessons that focus on interpreting illustrations in picture books as well as other texts that illustrate stories, dramas, or poetry. In the intermediate grades, we need to provide multimedia versions of the same texts that students have read so they have opportunities to connect written and performed versions of the story. In order for fifth graders to analyze visual and multimedia elements of literary text, they must have many opportunities to view and listen to multimedia presentations. The supporting skills and strategies for Reading Literature Standard 7 appear in Table 13.3.

Table 13.3 Common Core State Standard 7 for Reading Literature: Supporting Skills and Strategies

Grade	Standard
K	• Identify images in a story • Understand what a story is • Describe what part of the story an image depicts
1	• Identify the characters in a story • Identify the settings in a story • Identify the events in a story • Use story images to identify the characters, settings, and events • Use story details to identify the characters, settings, and events • Understand description in a text • Use images and details in a story to describe the characters, settings, and events
2	• Identify the characters in a story • Identify the settings in a story • Identify the plot of a story • Recognize digital text • Obtain information from images and printed and digital text • Know how to explain to demonstrate understanding • Explain a story's characters from information in the images and printed words • Explain a story's setting from information in the images and printed words • Explain a story's plot from information in the images and printed words
3	• Explain the images in a story • Recognize the mood of a story • Explain how the images contribute to the mood of a story • Explain how the images emphasize aspects of a character in a story • Explain how the images emphasize aspects of a setting in a story • Explain what parts of a text's images contribute to what is conveyed by the printed words
4	• Understand how to make connections • Recognize description in a text • Make connections between descriptions in the text of a story and a visual or oral presentation of it • Recognize stage directions in a drama • Make connections between descriptions and stage directions in the text of a drama and a visual or oral presentation of it
5	• Define *analyze* • Identify visual elements of texts, such as graphic novels • Identify multimedia elements in multimedia presentations of fiction, folk tales, myths, and poems • Recognize meaning in visual and multimedia elements of a text • Recognize tone in visual and multimedia elements of a text • Recognize beauty in visual and multimedia elements of a text • Analyze visual and multimedia elements of a text for meaning • Analyze visual and multimedia elements of a text for tone • Analyze visual and multimedia elements of a text for beauty • Analyze how visual and multimedia elements contribute to the meaning, tone, or beauty of a text, such as a graphic novel and multimedia presentations of fiction, folk tales, myths, and poems

Table 13.4 Common Core State Standard 7 for Reading Informational Text: Supporting Skills and Strategies

Grade	Standard
K	• Identify images in a text • Understand what informational text is • Identify what person, place, thing, or idea in a text an image depicts
1	• Identify details in a text • Identify key ideas in a text • Understand description in a text • Use images in a text to describe key ideas in the text • Use details in a text to describe key ideas in the text
2	• Identify images (e.g., diagram) in an informational text • Know how to explain to demonstrate understanding • Define *contribute* • Define *clarify* • Explain how an image contributes to and clarifies a text
3	• Recognize key events in a text • Gain information from a text's images, such as maps and photographs • Use information from a text to explain where, when, why, and how key events in the text occur • Use information from the images to explain where, when, why, and how events occur in the text • Demonstrate understanding of the text using information gained from images and printed words
4	• Define *interpret* • Recognize the text features of nonfiction (e.g., charts, graphs, diagrams, timelines, animations, interactive elements on webpages) • Interpret information in text features presented visually • Interpret information in text features presented orally • Interpret information in text features presented quantitatively • Explain how information presented visually, orally, and quantitatively adds to a better understanding of printed and digital text
5	• Obtain information from print sources • Obtain information from digital sources • Demonstrate how to answer a text-based question • Locate the answer to a question quickly, drawing on information from multiple print or digital sources • Identify problem-solving steps • Solve a problem efficiently, drawing on information from multiple print or digital sources

Reading Informational Text Standard 7 outlines the expectation for students to interact with rich visual, auditory, and multimedia elements in content area materials. Students need access to high-quality content area texts and materials that include such elements. Examples of these are 21st-century student magazines and newspapers that include colorful, detailed, and accurate depictions of content area concepts and/or procedures. Students are also expected to use online and digital media to find answers and solve problems. This means that students should be engaged in learning experiences that involve appropriate technology and technological tools to help them learn more about a topic or issue. Table 13.4 features the supporting skills and strategies for Reading Informational Text Standard 7.

How Can We Teach Reading Standard 7 So Our Students Achieve?

In this section, we discuss the Standards tasks required of students at various grade levels. For example, the seventh College and Career Readiness Anchor Standard requires students to interpret images and details in a story, use and analyze visual and multimedia elements in varied texts, and use print and digital sources to find information. We begin by describing the teaching idea, and then we discuss how it supports the Standards.

Interpreting Images and Details in a Story

To demonstrate their interpretation of images, students can write out the story that they see in wordless picture books. The author-illustrators of such works are careful to focus on the five narrative elements: characters, setting, problem, attempts to resolve, and resolution. Students interpret the elements through the author-illustrator's vision of the story. Using wordless picture books is a motivational and effective way to help students understand that illustrations can tell a story. An alternative writing activity occurs in a small-group setting. This time, the small groups use the same wordless picture book to write a group story. Then, they share their stories orally with the class. It is interesting to note that even though all the groups work with the same text, the stories will be quite distinctive. Two of our favorite wordless picture book author-illustrators are David Wiesner and Alexandra Day.

Using Visual and Multimedia Elements in Varied Texts

Bookmark Technique (McLaughlin, 2010) is a strategy application that focuses on students' understanding of what they are reading. It is comprised of four bookmarks. On the first bookmark, students write about what they thought was most interesting in the text. On the second bookmark, they write about something they found confusing. The third bookmark provides students with opportunities to write about a word they think the whole class needs to discuss. The fourth component of Bookmark Technique focuses on students' ability to use visuals while reading a text. When completing this graphic organizer, students note a chart, map, graph, or illustration that helped them understand what they read. Students record their choice of image and explain how it helped them understand the text. Figure 13.1 is Bookmark #4 for *Oil* by John Farndon (2007).

Using Print and Digital Sources to Find Information

When students engage in Internet Inquiry (Leu & Leu, 1999), a discovery-based process, they use digital sources to research a topic. During Internet Inquiry, students identify important questions and then gather information as they seek responses. This is a student-centered activity in which students choose issues to explore and take responsibility for completing the research. Students can work individually or in groups organized by interest. Internet Inquiry has five phases of student participation:

1. Generate research questions about a theme or topic being studied

2. Search for responses to the research questions on the Internet

3. Analyze the information found online

4. Choose a mode to present the findings

5. Share the results with the whole class

Figure 13.1 Example for the Bookmark Technique

Example Text: Farndon, J. (2007). *Oil*. New York: Dorling Kindersley.

Bookmark #4

Choose a chart, map, graph, or illustration that helped you understand the text.

What did you choose?
I chose the offshore oil rig that shows what the rig looks like below the ocean and above it.

Why did you choose it?
It helped me picture what a rig looks like, how big it is, the parts it has, how it is built, and how it works.

Pages 32–33

For example, if we were planning to engage our students in Internet Inquiry about major historical figures, such as Dr. Martin Luther King Jr. or Winston Churchill, we might follow these guidelines:

1. Create an Internet Inquiry about biographies of famous historical figures.
2. Invite students to select a person to research from a list of possibilities.
3. Provide and explain the rubric that will be used to evaluate Internet Inquiries to the students.
4. Encourage students to choose how they will present the biographical information that they locate about the person they chose.
5. Encourage students to generate questions to direct their research. For example, the following are possible questions for a student who chooses to investigate Dr. Martin Luther King Jr.:
   - Who were some of the people who influenced Dr. King?
   - What was the message in his "I Have a Dream" speech?
   - What contribution did Dr. King make to society?
6. Monitor students' progress as they gather and analyze information.
7. Invite students to participate in periodic conferencing or workshops to ask questions, engage in peer review, and share ideas about the projects they are developing.
8. Use the rubric to evaluate students' Internet Inquiries.

Technology Connection

The Fact Fragment Frenzy interactive tool (grades 1–6) on ReadWriteThink's website (www .readwritethink.org/classroom-resources/student-interactives/fact-fragment-frenzy-30013 .html#overview) can be used to help students understand how to find facts in a nonfiction text. In this activity, students drag words from a page of a virtual book to make a list of keywords in a virtual notebook. Then, students print the notebook page and rewrite the notes in their own words. This helps students understand how to take notes and write about information without plagiarizing.

How Can We Integrate Other ELA Standards With Reading Standard 7?

When planning to teach CCR Anchor Standard 7, we can integrate several other ELA standards to design rich instructional tasks. Examples of ideas to include when creating rich instructional tasks follow.

Integrating Other ELA Standards With Reading Literature Standard 7

- Reading Literature Standard 1 focuses on reading a narrative text closely. *Example:* When reading an illustrated text, encourage students to closely examine and discuss the illustrations for information about the characters, setting, or plot.
- Reading Literature Standard 2 focuses on the ability to retell a literary text and determine the author's message or theme. *Example:* Encourage intermediate-grade students to examine written texts and elements in multimedia presentations to determine themes.

- Reading Literature Standard 3 focuses on being able to describe characters, settings, or events in a story or drama, drawing on specific details in the text. *Example:* Teach students to examine illustrations and multimedia elements to describe characters, settings, or events in a story or drama.

- Reading Literature Standard 9 focuses on comparing and contrasting the adventures and experiences of characters; two or more versions of the same story; themes, settings, and plots in books by the same author; treatment of similar themes and topics; and stories in the same genre on their approach to similar themes and topics. *Example:* Ask students to compare and contrast a text and its multimedia version.

- Writing Standard 1 describes students writing an opinion about a topic or text and supporting their point of view with reasons and information from the text. *Example:* When students read, view, or listen to a literary text, ask them to write an opinion about the text, including opinions about the visual or multimedia elements of the text, and justify their thinking by providing supporting information.

- Speaking and Listening Standard 1 describes students engaging effectively in a range of collaborative discussions, with specific indicators to demonstrate how to participate in an effective academic conversation. *Example:* When reading stories, dramas, and poems, engage students in both whole-group and small-group collaborative conversations about the text that includes discussing the illustrations or multimedia elements of the text.

- Language Standard 5 is the vocabulary standard that refers to the descriptive use of language. *Example:* When students describe visual or multimedia elements of a literary text, encourage them to use descriptive adjectives, shades of word meaning, and figurative language.

Integrating Other ELA Standards With Reading Informational Text Standard 7

- Reading Informational Text Standard 1 refers to closely reading an informational text. *Example:* When students read informational texts closely to understand historical, scientific, or technical concepts, encourage discussion about the information found in visual or multimedia elements of the text.

- Reading Informational Text Standard 2 focuses on the ability to summarize the main idea and supporting details of an informational text. *Example:* When students read an informational text, ask them to use the visual and multimedia elements of the text to help determine the main idea and supporting details.

- Reading Informational Text Standard 5 refers to the use of text features (e.g., headings, captions, tables of contents) and text structures (e.g., chronology, comparison, cause/effect). *Example:* Explicitly teach students to use text features and structures to describe the individuals or concepts in a historical, scientific, or technical text.

- Reading Informational Text Standard 6 is about point of view. *Example:* Encourage students to examine the visual and multimedia elements of an informational text in addition to the printed words to help them identify or analyze the author's point of view.

- Writing Standard 7 refers to participating in brief shared or individual research projects that build background knowledge about a topic. *Example:* When students are engaged in shared or individual research projects, teach them to use a variety of sources and integrate the information to build knowledge about the topic.

- Writing Standard 8 focuses on recalling information from experiences or gathering information from sources to answer questions about a topic. *Example:* When searching for answers to questions about a topic, encourage students to explore a variety of informational texts, both print and digital, to answer questions and solve problems related to a specific topic.

- Speaking and Listening Standard 1 describes the expectation for students to engage effectively in a range of collaborative discussions, with specific indicators to demonstrate how to participate in an effective academic conversation. *Example:* When engaging in collaborative academic conversations about informational texts, encourage students to discuss the contributions made by the visual and multimedia elements.

- Language Standard 6 is the vocabulary standard that refers to general academic and domain-specific words and phrases. *Example:* When students are describing visual and multimedia elements of a text, teach them to use vocabulary that is specific to the discipline.

THE COMMON CORE IN ACTION

In this section, we examine one of the foundational ideas that underpins each of the Common Core's Anchor Standards for Reading. For the seventh standard, "Integrate and evaluate content presented in diverse media and formats, including visually and quantitatively, as well as in words" (NGA Center & CCSSO, 2010, p. 10), we have elected to share more detailed information about using digital sources to search for information, which is an explicit part of the standard for grades 4 and 5.

Common Core Literacy Task: Internet Workshop

Phyllis is a fifth-grade teacher. She knows that technology should be interwoven in instruction to meet the CCSS. She is planning to engage her students in a social studies project about Plymouth Colony that includes Reading Standard 7 as part of her instruction. She decides to use Internet Workshop (Leu, 2002). When engaging in Internet Workshop, students expand their understandings of the topic being studied. Phyllis has planned an Internet Workshop before and knows it is especially useful for introducing students to websites for an upcoming unit and for developing their background knowledge. For example, she knows that if she is beginning to teach a unit or topic about which her students have little or no background knowledge, she can use Internet Workshop to help increase their knowledge before reading text chapters or engaging in more formal projects. She can also use Internet Workshop when students are creating projects or after learning to extend their thinking. This activity provides students with regular opportunities for sharing and peer feedback.

Phyllis develops a number of essential questions that she wants her students to answer about Plymouth Colony. During Internet Workshop, her students can work individually, in collaboration with classmates, or in conjunction with international peers (Speaking and Listening Standard 1). For this activity, she plans to divide students into partners and give each partner a different set of questions. Each pair will explore a different aspect of the Plymouth Colony and report their findings to the class. When engaged in Internet Workshop, her students will search the Internet and draw on multiple sources of information to research the answers to these questions and to build knowledge about the topic (Writing Standard 7).

Phyllis understands that the workshop format is flexible, but it usually involves the following steps:

1. Locate a central site, or several sites, on the Internet with content related to a classroom unit of instruction and set a bookmark for the location(s). This limits random surfing on the Internet and helps ensure student safety online.

2. Develop an activity related to class learning goals that requires students to use the selected website(s). Internet Workshop is especially beneficial when used before learning to help students build background knowledge and during learning to enrich individual and class knowledge of the topic.

3. Encourage students to record information in an electronic journal. While students are online, teachers should monitor their work.

4. Hold periodic workshop sessions so students can share their work, raise questions, reveal new insights, and discuss the skills needed to function effectively online.

As the students participate in the Internet Workshop project, Phyllis plans for the students to do the following:

- Work with a partner to conduct a short research project that uses several sources to build knowledge (SL.5.1, W.5.7)

- Read the website information closely and take notes, using quotation marks for direct quotes (RI.5.1)

- Determine the main ideas of different sections of the website and summarize those ideas (RI.5.2)

- Determine the meaning of the social studies words found in the different sections of the website and use them in their notes (RI.5.4, L.5.4)

- Read different accounts of Plymouth Colony and take note of the similarities and differences in the point of view of the writers (RI.5.6)

- Integrate information from several websites about Plymouth Colony (RI.5.9)

- Using their notes from their electronic journals, write an answer to each question that is a summary of the information found (W.5.2, W.5.8)

- Use appropriate content area words in the summaries (W.5.2b, L.5.6)

- Use correct standard English grammar, usage, capitalization, punctuation, and spelling in completed summaries (L.5.1, L.5.2)

- Use their summaries to report on their topic for the rest of the class (SL.5.4)

Phyllis's students are motivated by the use of technology in social studies and love working on these projects together, and she knows they are working to meet the expectations of several ELA standards as they learn about Plymouth Colony by using Internet Workshop. She shares with the primary-grade teachers down the hall that this activity can just as easily be used for whole-group projects in the primary grades.

Reading Standard 7 focuses on ensuring that students can analyze and integrate information. It requires students to use and analyze visual and multimedia elements in text and use multiple sources to find information. When students put it together, they can evaluate texts and sources and successfully engage in research projects.

References

Hall, M., & Stahl, K.A.D. (2012). Devillainizing video in support of comprehension and vocabulary instruction. *The Reading Teacher, 65*(6), 403–406.

Ikpeze, C.H., & Boyd, F.B. (2007). Web-based inquiry learning: Facilitating thoughtful literacy with WebQuests. *The Reading Teacher, 60*(7), 644–654.

Leu, D.J., Jr. (2002). Internet Workshop: Making time for literacy. *The Reading Teacher, 55*(5), 466–472.

Leu, D.J., Jr., & Leu, D.D. (1999). *Teaching with the Internet: Lessons from the classroom* (Rev. ed.). Norwood MA: Christopher-Gordon.

McLaughlin, M. (2010). *Guided Comprehension in the primary grades* (2nd ed.). Newark, DE: International Reading Association.

National Governors Association Center for Best Practices & Council of Chief State School Officers. (2010). *Common Core State Standards for English language arts and literacy in history/social studies, science, and technical subjects.* Washington, DC: Authors. Retrieved August 3, 2012, from www.corestandards.org/assets/CCSSI_ELA%20 Standards.pdf

Zhang, S., Duke, N.K., & Jimenez, L.M. (2011). The WWWDOT approach to improving students' critical evaluation of websites. *The Reading Teacher, 65*(2), 150–158.

Children's Literature Cited

Farndon, J. (2007). *Oil.* New York: Dorling Kindersley.

CHAPTER 14

CCR Reading Anchor Standard 8: Opinions, Reasons, and Evidence

Hearing the Argument

College and Career Readiness Reading Anchor Standard 8
Delineate and evaluate the argument and specific claims in a text, including the validity of the reasoning as well as the relevance and sufficiency of the evidence. (NGA Center & CCSSO, 2010a, p. 10)

What Does CCR Reading Anchor Standard 8 Mean?

College and Career Readiness (CCR) Reading Anchor Standard 8 focuses on argumentation, a concept that is often misunderstood. When we discuss argumentation in the CCR Anchor Standards, we are referring to formal argumentation, sometimes called rhetoric. Rhetoric, which is typically associated with the teachings of the ancient Greek philosopher Aristotle, is the ability to write or speak in order to inform, persuade, or motivate an audience to support one side of an issue.

Reading Anchor Standard 8 focuses on three reading skills:

1. The ability to delineate and evaluate specific claims

2. The ability to delineate and evaluate the validity of the reasoning of the claim

3. The ability to delineate and evaluate the sufficiency of the evidence for the reasoning

The Difference Between Persuasion and Argument

Although many may believe that *argument* and *persuasion* are synonymous, there is a significant difference between these two terms. In persuasion, a writer or speaker attempts to change the reader's or listener's mind, often by trying to convince the reader to feel a certain way about an issue. In argument, the author attempts to reveal a truth, using facts and/or research to support the author's position.

Persuasive writers and speakers often use techniques that have been developed to affect a reader's or listener's emotions. Such techniques are the foundation of highly expensive advertising campaigns in print and digital media. Common persuasive techniques that may be familiar are bandwagon, slogan, repetition, testimony, expert opinion, and emotional appeal. Writers and speakers often use persuasive techniques when attempting to convince readers or listeners to believe in their position on a political or policy issue or an idea that might affect a certain community.

By contrast, argumentation uses reasons and evidence to convince the reader of one side of an issue regardless of how the writer or speaker actually feels about the issue. In an argument, a writer can argue a position for either side because he or she can prepare to support either side with reasons (facts) and evidence. Emotion is the basis of persuasion, whereas logic is the basis of argumentation. Argumentation can be described as "the facts are on my side." This is the type of reading and writing required in CCR Anchor Standard 8.

What Makes a Strong Argument?

A speaker or writer who is developing an argument uses different persuasive strategies to bolster that argument. The basic persuasive strategies in a formal argument are called logos, ethos, and pathos. Logos is the logic that the author uses to develop the text and the facts that the author uses to support the argument. A strong argument is bolstered by a logical organization that outlines what the audience is supposed to believe, the reasons they are supposed to believe it, and the evidence the author presents. An argument includes a claim (the speaker's or author's opinion), grounds for the claim (reasons why the speaker or author believes the opinion is valid), and evidence for the reasons.

Ethos has to do with the source's credibility or the author's authority. For example, an audience tends to trust an author or speaker who has strong credentials and is consistent. A person reading a text about how to take care of a pet is more likely to be convinced by a veterinarian than a person with few or no qualifications.

Pathos is the emotional appeal that some authors and speakers use to prove their point. When an author uses pathos, he or she uses powerful language and facts that relate to the emotions of the audience. For example, if an author is writing against drunk driving, vivid descriptions of people who have been injured or killed in drunk driving accidents will appeal to the emotions of the reader and make them more likely to side with the author's proposition. An example of a familiar speech using ethos, logos, and pathos is Dr. Martin Luther King, Jr.'s "I Have a Dream."

Students will be expected to recognize logical, valid arguments in a text. Students will also be expected to argue a point by making a claim in writing or a speech and supporting the claim with logical, valid evidence. Students should be able to recognize plausible data, evaluate whether the author has supported the data, and draw logical conclusions from the data. In the workplace, employees may need to outline an argument for one idea over another and provide valid reasons for their decision. Reading and analyzing an argument means being able to recognize whether an author has actually proved his or her point with sound reasons that are believable and convincing.

How Do the Common Core Standards Build to CCR Anchor Standard 8?

Common Core Reading Standard 8 is only applicable to informational text in grades K–5. At the elementary level, students learn to identify, describe, and explain the way an author supports the points in a text. This is the foundation for more formal argumentative reading and writing, which begins in grade 6.

In grades K–2, students focus on how an author supports points in the text. In third grade, students learn text structures and transitions that authors frequently use to write a position, such as comparison, cause/effect, and sequence. In fourth and fifth grades, students learn to explain an author's use of reasons and information in a deeper way. By the end of grade 5, students are expected to read and analyze the way a writer constructed an informational text that informs the reader about a topic or portrays an author's opinion. Table 14.1 delineates Common Core State Standard 8 for Reading Informational Text.

There are three main skill areas to teach in Reading Standard 8 by the end of fifth grade for students to be on track for middle school and the higher expectations of the Standards in grades 6–12:

1. Support points in a text with reasons

2. Make connections between sentences and paragraphs

3. Identify information (facts) that supports reasons

What Literacy Skills and Strategies Support Reading Standard 8?

Informational picture books, magazine articles, and digital texts that contain strong main ideas, facts, and supporting details can be used to meet Reading Standard 8. To learn the foundations of argument, students need to read examples of informational texts in which the author has stated an opinion and provided reasons and evidence that supports that opinion. Opinion-based articles can often be found in magazines and newspapers written for elementary students, such as *TIME For Kids*. See Table 14.2 for a list of supporting skills and strategies for Reading Informational Text Standard 8.

Table 14.1 Common Core State Standard 8 for Reading Informational Text in Grades K–5

Grade	Standard
K	With prompting and support, identify the reasons an author gives to support points in a text.
1	Identify the reasons an author gives to support points in a text.
2	Describe how reasons support specific points the author makes in a text.
3	Describe the logical connection between particular sentences and paragraphs in a text (e.g., comparison, cause/effect, first/second/third in a sequence).
4	Explain how an author uses reasons and evidence to support particular points in a text.
5	Explain how an author uses reasons and evidence to support particular points in a text, identifying which reasons and evidence support which point(s).

Note. The standards are from *Common Core State Standards for English Language Arts and Literacy in History/Social Studies, Science, and Technical Subjects* (pp. 13 and 14), by National Governors Association Center for Best Practices and Council of Chief State School Officers, 2010, Washington, DC: Authors.

Table 14.2 Common Core State Standard 8 for Reading Informational Text: Supporting Skills and Strategies

Grade	Skills and Strategies
K	• Understand the term *reason* • Identify the author's reasons in a text
1	• Identify the author's reasons in a text
2	• Describe how reasons support what the author says
3	• Define *sentence* • Define *paragraph* • Know the structure of a paragraph • Recognize text structures
4	• Differentiate fact from opinion • Identify how authors use reasons • Identify how authors use evidence
5	• Identify how authors use reasons and evidence to support specific points

How Can We Teach Reading Standard 8 So Our Students Achieve?

In this section, we discuss the Standards tasks required of students at various grade levels. For example, Reading Standard 8 requires students to support points in a text with reasons, understand the connections between sentences and paragraphs, and provide information that supports the author's reasons. We begin by describing the teaching idea, and then we discuss how it supports the Standards.

Supporting Points in a Text With Reasons

Although Standard 8 only focuses on informational text, literary picture books can be used as an engaging way to introduce the concept of providing reasons for an opinion with early primary-grade students. These books can be used as mentor texts to teach students how to support points in a text with facts. The following are a few examples of texts that might be used as mentor texts for opinion and reasons with K–2 students:

- *Don't Let the Pigeon Drive the Bus!* by Mo Willems (2003)
- *Earrings!* by Judith Viorst (1993)
- *Click, Clack, Moo: Cows That Type* by Doreen Cronin (2000)
- *Dear Mrs. LaRue: Letters From Obedience School* by Mark Teague (2002)
- *I Wanna Iguana* by Karen Kaufman Orloff (2004)
- *My Brother Dan's Delicious* by Steven L. Layne (2003)
- *I Want a Dog!* By Helga Bansch (2009)

We can use the prompts in Figure 14.1 to guide students' learning. The following teaching suggestions support this aspect of the CCSS:

1. With students on the carpet, read aloud a picture book in which a main character tries to persuade another character.

2. Ask the students, "What does _____ (the character's name) want?" Write the character's name on a chart. Responding to the student discussion, write what the character wants under his or her name.

3. Ask, "How does _____ (the character's name) try to persuade someone else to get what they want?" Add the ways the character tries to persuade someone else to the chart. Leave space so you can add to the chart during the discussion.

4. Ask, "What does _____ (the character's name) say to try to get what he/she wants?" Add any quotes from the text that support the character's opinion.

5. Ask, "What could _____ (the character's name) have said instead?" Guide students to think about how the character could have possibly strengthened his or her opinion by stating facts to support the opinion.

Figure 14.1 Example of a Graphic Organizer for Supporting Opinions in a Text

Example Text: Bansch, H. (2009). *I want a dog!* New York: North-South.

Text: *I Want a Dog!*

Character: Lisa

Wants: A dog

How does the character try to persuade?
Lisa says the dog could travel with the family
- "Dogs love the mountains"
- "Dogs love the beach"

Lisa says she will be good.
- "I will be as good as gold."

Lisa says she will be bad.
- "Then I will be truly terrible."

Maybe instead?
- A dog would be a friend.
- A dog would be protection.
- I could train a dog to help do things.

By engaging in rich discussions of stories in which the author or narrator is attempting to convince the reader, we can guide students to think about the power of supporting a logical opinion with logical reasons. We can then transition to teaching students how authors use reasons to support points in an informational text, which is the focus of Reading Standard 8 for the early primary grades. A persuasive mentor text can be a springboard to writing opinions, as K–2 students are expected to write their opinions about topics or books and support their opinions with reasons (Writing Standard 1).

Connections Between Sentences and Paragraphs

The expectation for Reading Informational Text Standard 8 for grade 3 is that students will "describe the logical connection between particular sentences and paragraphs in a text (e.g., comparison, cause/effect, first/second/third in a sequence)" (NGA Center & CCSSO, 2010a, p. 14). Montelongo and Hernandez (2007) discuss research findings that suggest elementary students have difficulty in dealing with expository structures and paragraphs. In fact, Garner et al. (1986) suggest that elementary students view a paragraph as a graphic (the paragraph is where the sentences indent) and often do not realize that a paragraph is a connected set of sentences in a logical order. In Chapter 11, we discussed text structures in detail and included teaching ideas for each text structure. The teaching idea for this chapter is adapted from an activity described by Montelongo and Hernandez.

To help students understand the connection among sentences in a paragraph, we can give them a list of sentences to organize. The list should be a mixture of related (about the same topic) and unrelated (about random topics) sentences. The related sentences should actually be an embedded paragraph. The sentences of the embedded paragraph should be out of order and mixed up with the unrelated sentences.

Students cut the sentences apart and put them into two categories: related sentences and unrelated sentences. Students then take the related sentences and arrange them into a logical order to form a paragraph. The sentence that is the main idea should be first. The rest of the sentences should be arranged according to a logical organization, with each sentence building the paragraph. Signal words, such as *first*, *then*, and *finally*, will help students understand the organization of the paragraph. A concluding sentence should be at the end. Finally, students glue or tape the sentences onto a sheet of paper.

Practice with arranging paragraphs with different expository text structures, such as comparison, cause/effect, and sequence, will help students learn to recognize the different ways that expository paragraphs are written. When students have to make decisions about which sentences do or do not belong in the paragraph and then determine a logical order for the sentences, they learn about the nature and structure of paragraphs (Montelongo & Hernandez, 2007). This will not only help them better comprehend text but also help them understand how to write paragraphs. To further comprehension of paragraphs that state an opinion, the activity can be extended to include embedded opinion paragraphs.

Identifying Evidence That Supports Reasons

Fifth-grade students will need to "explain how an author uses reasons and evidence to support particular points in a text, identifying which reasons and evidence support which point(s)" (NGA

Center & CCSSO, 2010a, p. 14). Students can use the What–Why–How? graphic organizer to analyze an opinion text (see Figure 14.2). The What–Why–How? activity requires students to ask questions about the text and summarize the key ideas to determine the author's opinion. Students also record how the author supports his or her opinion with reasons and information. This organizer can help students comprehend the author's message and understand the way authors organize a text that discusses an opinion.

When reading a text that discusses an opinion, ask these questions:

- "What does the author think? In the first column of the What–Why–How? graphic organizer, write one sentence that tells the author's opinion."

- "Why does the author think this way? In the second column, write reasons the author includes in the text for his or her opinion."

- "How do facts in the text support the author's thinking? In the third column, write some facts that the author included to support each reason."

Writing Standard 1 describes the expectations for students to be able to write an opinion and support it. Appendix C of the Common Core State Standards (NGA Center & CCSSO, 2010b) provides

Figure 14.2 Example of a What–Why–How? Graphic Organizer

Example Text: Knight, M.J. (2009). *Why should I walk more often?* Mankato, MN: Black Rabbit.

What does the author think?	Why does the author think this way?	How do facts in the text support the author's thinking?
People should walk more often.	**?** 1. Walking is fun and free and helps us stay fit.	1. In the United States, less than half of all children walk or bike to school. 2. Walking to school helps you get to know your neighborhood. 3. Walking one mile in 20 minutes uses as much energy as playing soccer for 12 minutes.
	? 2. Traffic fumes make carbon dioxide, which hurts the Earth.	1. There are more than 600 million cars, vans, and trucks in the world today. 2. Vehicles make so many fumes that they are changing the gases in the air and harming the Earth. 3. One car making a short trip to school and back gives off enough carbon dioxide to fill 60 balloons.
	? 3. There are ways to go to school that don't use gas.	1. Children in many other countries walk to school in a group instead of riding in a car. 2. Bicycling is the least polluting way of traveling besides walking. 3. One bus holds the same number of people as 10 cars.

examples of student writing that meets Writing Standard 1 for each grade level. Use the student examples for opinion writing (argument) and the What–Why–How? graphic organizer to analyze how the writer supported his or her opinion with reasons and information and to provide student models of writing opinions.

Technology Connections

The Persuasion Map interactive tool on ReadWriteThink's website (www.readwritethink.org/files/ resources/interactives/persuasion_map) can help students plan a persuasive essay or debate. It can also be adapted to analyze a persuasive text. Students use a step-by-step procedure to fill in the boxes on an interactive template that introduce the author's opinion in an introduction and provide main reasons for the opinion, facts or examples for each reason, and a conclusion. The finished product is a completed graphic organizer that can be used to guide a debate or the writing of a persuasive essay.

Persuasion often comes in the form of a letter (e.g., a letter to the editor, the principal, or city council regarding an issue). Students can use the Letter Generator interactive tool on ReadWriteThink's website (www.readwritethink.org/files/resources/interactives/letter_generator) to learn to write a friendly letter and a business letter in the correct formats.

How Can We Integrate Other ELA Standards With Reading Standard 8?

When planning to teach CCR Anchor Standard 8, we can integrate several other ELA standards to design rich instructional tasks. The following are examples of ideas to include when creating rich instructional tasks for reading informational texts.

- Reading Informational Text Standard 1 refers to closely reading an informational text. *Example:* When doing a close reading of an informational text that includes an opinion, teach students to carefully consider the author's opinion, as well as the supporting reasons and information.

- Reading Informational Text Standard 3 focuses on describing the connections and relationships among people, events, ideas, or pieces of information in a text. *Example:* When students are reading a text that contains an author's opinion, invite them to use a graphic organizer to record ways the author uses reasons and information to support his or her opinion.

- Reading Informational Text Standard 6 refers to point of view. *Example:* Engage students in discussing the author's point of view when reading an informational text.

- Writing Standard 1 lays out the expectations for writing opinions. *Example:* Using the criteria in Writing Standard 1, teach students to write their opinions with supporting reasons and evidence.

- Speaking and Listening Standard 3 refers to listening to a speaker. *Example:* When listening to a speaker give an opinion, teach students to ask and answer questions about the reasons and evidence the speaker uses to justify his or her opinion.

- Speaking and Listening Standard 4 refers to reporting on a topic. *Example:* Teach students how to give an oral presentation in which they present an opinion, using reasons, evidence, and appropriate speaking skills.

- Language Standard 6 is about the use of grade-appropriate general academic and domain-specific words and phrases. *Example:* Teach students to use appropriate words and phrases, such as *opinion, reasons, evidence, information,* and *facts,* when speaking and writing about opinions.

THE COMMON CORE IN ACTION

In this section, we examine one of the foundational ideas that underpins each of the Common Core's Anchor Standards for Reading. For the eighth Standard, "Delineate and evaluate the argument and specific claims in a text, including the validity of the reasoning as well as the relevance and sufficiency of the evidence" (NGA Center & CCSSO, 2010a, p. 10), we have elected to share more detailed information about reading and writing opinion pieces, which is an explicit part of the Standards.

Common Core Literacy Task: Reading and Writing Opinions

Michelle needs to teach her fourth-grade students how to read and write opinions. She has reviewed the ELA Common Core Standards with her colleagues, and they have worked together to plan some lessons based on the CCSS. Michelle knows that in fourth grade, students are expected to "explain how an author uses reasons and evidence to support particular points in a text" (NGA Center & CCSSO, 2010a, p. 14). She also knows that according to the Standards, her students should be able to write opinion pieces and support their opinion with reasons and information (Writing Standard 1).

While planning the first part of her lesson sequence on reading and writing opinions, Michelle reads Writing Standard 1 for fourth grade again:

> Write opinion pieces on topics or texts, supporting a point of view with reasons and information.
>
> a. Introduce a topic or text clearly, state an opinion, and create an organizational structure in which related ideas are grouped to support the writer's purpose.
>
> b. Provide reasons that are supported by facts and details.
>
> c. Link opinion and reasons using words and phrases (e.g., *for instance, in order to, in addition*).
>
> d. Provide a concluding sentence or section related to the opinion presented.

Michelle and her team have already engaged the students in activities that explore opinions, reasons, and evidence. The students know that authors of opinion articles often discuss both sides of an issue. Michelle decides to begin this lesson with an article that discusses both sides of an opinion. She searches magazines that are specifically written for school use and finds an article focused on an opinion that she thinks will engage the students. The article she decides to use for this lesson is titled "Debate! Should Dodge Ball be Banned in Schools?" (TIME For Kids Staff, 2011), from the online version of *TIME For Kids* magazine.

Michelle plans to use the following lesson sequence with this article to teach her students how to read opinions, reasons, and evidence :

1. Review what the students know about opinions, reasons, and evidence (facts that explain reasons).

2. Tell the students that they will be reading an article called "Debate! Should Dodge Ball Be Banned in Schools?" Briefly discuss student experiences with dodgeball (about two minutes

or less). This discussion will ensure that all the students have an idea of the nature of dodgeball before reading the article and will motivate them to find out more. (SL.4.1)

3. Introduce For and Against, the graphic organizer (see Figure 14.3). Using an interactive whiteboard, document camera, or overhead projector, Michelle will model for her students by writing the issue of the article (Should dodgeball be banned in schools?) on the top line of her copy. She will also think aloud as she writes. The students will write on their own copies of the organizer as she models. (R.4.8, W.4.8, W.4.9b) Students will then read the article.

4. In the first box, Michelle will ask students to write one sentence for the issue (dodgeball should be banned in schools) that was discussed in the article. In the opposite box, they will write one sentence against the issue (dodgeball should not be banned in schools). Again, Michelle will model on her copy so everyone can see. (R.4.8, W.4.8, W.4.9b)

Figure 14.3 Example of a For and Against Graphic Organizer

Example Text: TIME For Kids Staff. (2011, December 13). Debate! Should dodge ball be banned in schools? *TIME For Kids*. Retrieved July 23, 2012, from www.timeforkids.com/news/debate/23691

Issue: <u>Should dodgeball be banned in schools?</u>

For		Against	
Write <u>one</u> sentence <u>for</u> the issue. Dodgeball should be banned in schools.		**Write <u>one</u> sentence <u>against</u> the issue.** Dodgeball should not be banned in schools.	
List reasons to be for the issue.	**List at least two facts (evidence) for each reason.**	**List reasons to be against the issue.**	**List at least two facts (evidence) for each reason.**
Reason: It is too violent.	**Fact:** Kids become human targets.	**Reason:** It teaches important skills.	**Fact:** Quick decision-making
	Fact: It can lead to bullying.		**Fact:** Hand–eye coordination
Reason: Nell Williams, PE professor at Eastern Connecticut State University, is against it.	**Fact:** "PE Hall of Shame"	**Reason:** Rick Hanetho, founder of the National Amateur Dodgeball Association, defends it.	**Fact:** It allows kids who are not athletes to participate.
	Fact: It allows stronger kids to pick on weaker kids.		**Fact:** It teaches important skills.
Reason: Kids who get hit by the ball sit on the bench.	**Fact:** They just watch those who play.	**Reason:** Kids have fun if supervised.	**Fact:** They don't try to hurt anyone.
	Fact:		**Fact:** They use a soft, squishy ball.

5. Michelle will continue to model for the students as she guides them to look for the first reasons to ban dodgeball that the author discussed in the article (e.g., "too violent"; para. 1). Students should list the reasons to ban dodgeball in the boxes on the "For" side of the organizer. They should also write down any facts that the author included in the article in support of each reason. (R.4.8, W.4.8, W.4.9b)

6. Michelle will guide her students to look for reasons not to ban dodgeball and write them on the "Against" side of the organizer (e.g., "teaches...quick decision-making"; para. 1). Because this is the students' first encounter with this skill, she will continue to think aloud and write on her own graphic organizer to help them understand what they are required to do on their organizers. (R.4.8, W.4.8, W.4.9b)

7. After completing the organizer together, Michelle will facilitate a class discussion about how the author presented the issue. She will focus on opinions, reasons, and evidence about banning dodgeball in schools that are explained in the article. (W.4.9b, SL.4.1)

Over the next few days, Michelle will provide her students with the opportunity to analyze several opinion texts and will scaffold her students to be able to complete the For and Against organizer independently.

After the students have read and discussed several articles in which authors supported opinions with reasons and evidence, Michelle will ask the students to choose an issue or topic that they feel strongly about, and teach them how to write a persuasive essay that expresses a reasoned opinion about that issue or topic. First, Michelle will introduce her students to the Persuasion Map interactive tool on ReadWriteThink's website for students to plan their essays (see the Technology Connections section of this chapter). This tool allows students to enter an opinion or statement, reasons, and facts to support the reasons. Students can print, save, or e-mail their persuasion map. Using the printed map as a prewriting organizer and engaging in the writing process (Writing Standards 4–6), Michelle's students will write an organized opinion piece that supports a point of view with reasons and information (Writing Standard 1).

Reading Standard 8 focuses on ensuring that students can analyze the way an author supports an opinion with reasons and evidence. This standard requires students to recognize how an author supports points in a text with evidence, understand the connections among sentences and paragraphs in a text, and explain how an author supports an opinion with reasons and information. When students hear the argument, they can explain how authors support what they think.

References

Garner, R., Alexander, P., Slater, W., Hare, V.C., Smith, T., & Reis, R. (1986). Children's knowledge of structural properties of expository text. *Journal of Educational Psychology, 78*(6), 411–416.

Montelongo, J.A., & Hernandez, A.C. (2007). Reinforcing expository reading and writing skills: A more versatile sentence completion task. *The Reading Teacher, 60*(6), 538–546.

National Governors Association Center for Best Practices & Council of Chief State School Officers. (2010a). *Common Core State Standards for English language arts and literacy in history/social studies, science, and technical subjects.* Washington, DC: Authors. Retrieved August 3, 2012, from www.corestandards.org/assets/CCSSI_ELA%20Standards.pdf

National Governors Association Center for Best Practices & Council of Chief State School Officers. (2010b). *Common Core State Standards for English language arts and literacy in history/social studies, science, and technical* subjects: *Appendix C: Samples of student writing.* Washington, DC: Authors. Retrieved August 3, 2012, from www.corestandards.org/assets/Appendix_C.pdf

TIME For Kids Staff. (2011, December 13). Debate! Should dodge ball be banned in schools? *TIME For Kids.* Retrieved July 23, 2012, from www.timeforkids.com/news/debate/23691

Children's Literature Cited

Bansch, H. (2009). *I want a dog!* New York: North-South.

Cronin, D. (2000). *Click, clack, moo: Cows that type.* New York: Simon & Schuster Books for Young Readers.

Knight, M.J. (2009). *Why should I walk more often?* Mankato, MN: Black Rabbit.

Layne, S.L. (2003). *My brother Dan's delicious.* Gretna, LA: Pelican.

Orloff, K.K. (2004). *I wanna iguana.* New York: G.P. Putnam's Sons.

Teague, M. (2002). *Dear Mrs. LaRue: Letters from obedience school.* New York: Scholastic.

Viorst, J. (1993). *Earrings!* New York: Aladdin.

Willems, M. (2003). *Don't let the pigeon drive the bus!* New York: Hyperion Books for Children.

CHAPTER 15

CCR Reading Anchor Standard 9: Compare/Contrast Themes and Topics

Weighing the Works

College and Career Readiness Reading Anchor Standard 9
Analyze how two or more texts address similar themes or topics to build knowledge or to compare the approaches the authors take. (NGA Center & CCSSO, 2010, p. 10)

What Does CCR Reading Standard 9 Mean?

Comparing and contrasting texts, themes, and topics means being able to understand them in deeper ways. The aim of College and Career Readiness (CCR) Reading Anchor Standard 9 is for students to compare and contrast similar themes or topics from a variety of sources. For example, students may be asked to compare and contrast how authors approach issues in texts about similar subjects. Students need to weigh the works to determine and analyze similarities and differences.

Reading Anchor Standard 9 focuses on two reading skills:

1. The ability to analyze how two or more texts address similar themes or topics to build knowledge

2. The ability to analyze how two or more texts address similar themes or topics to compare the authors' approaches

A frequent assignment in the upper grades is to write a comparative analysis in which students compare and contrast two or more objects, ideas, or concepts. The students may be asked to read about and then compare and contrast issues, historical figures, poems, processes, themes in literature and so forth, in classes across the curriculum. In a comparative analysis, the students may discuss two similar things that have significant differences or two things that have obvious differences but also some interesting commonalities. In a comparative analysis, the students observe similarities and differences and then take the raw data and make them into a coherent argument (Walk, 1998).

Comparing and Contrasting in Literature

In English or literature classes, students may be asked to compare and contrast characters, settings, themes, or poetic styles. They may be asked to write a comparative analysis of two works by the same author or two stories with the same basic plot. In this case, students need to understand how to compare and contrast works of literature for similarities and differences and then write a comparison that proves a point or makes an argument. The Common Core expectations for high school require students to analyze how an author draws on and transforms source material in a specific work. An example is how Shakespeare treats a theme or topic from the Bible and how a later author draws on a play by Shakespeare. Students are also expected to demonstrate knowledge of 18th-, 19th-, and early 20th-century foundational works of American literature, including how two or more texts of the same theme treat similar themes or topics.

Comparing and Contrasting in the Disciplines

In the disciplines, students may be asked to write a comparative analysis of issues, topics of information, historical figures, historical documents, or scientific procedures. In this case, students need to understand how to compare and contrast topics and themes in informational texts for similarities and differences and write a coherent argument. The expectations of CCR Anchor Standard 9 stretch across high school grades and subject areas (e.g., literary text in history/social studies, informational text in science and technical subjects). In the upper grades, students are expected to compare and contrast important documents in U.S. history; integrate information from diverse sources, both primary and secondary, into a coherent understanding of an idea or event; and synthesize information from a range of sources about scientific processes, concepts, or phenomena.

Ways to Compare and Contrast

When authors compare and contrast, there are two basic organizational text structures that they choose from: text-by-text (sometimes called whole-to-whole or block) and point-by-point (Walk, 1998). In the text-by-text structure, the author describes all of one thing (A) and then all of the other thing (B). In the point-by-point structure, the author writes about one point for both A and B, then moves to a second point about both A and B, and so on. Another type of organizational structure is similarities and differences. In this text structure, the author writes about the similarities between A and B and then about the differences between A and B. Students will choose one of these organizational structures to organize comparative essays.

How Do the Common Core Standards Build to CCR Anchor Standard 9?

Common Core Reading Standard 9 focuses on the comparison of texts and the integration of information from more than one source. For literature, kindergartners and first graders learn to compare and contrast the adventures and experiences of characters in stories. In grade 2, students compare and contrast versions of the same story, while in grade 3, students compare and contrast themes, settings, and plots by the same author about similar characters. In fourth grade, students compare and contrast the treatment of similar themes, topics, and patterns of events in stories, myths, and traditional literature. Fifth graders compare and contrast stories in the same genre. Table 15.1 contains Common Core State Standard 9 for Reading Literature.

For Reading Informational Text Standard 9, kindergartners and first graders identify similarities and differences between two texts on the same topic. In grades 2 and 3, students compare and contrast the most important points from texts on the same topic. In grades 4 and 5, students

Table 15.1 Common Core State Standard 9 for Reading Literature in Grades K–5

Grade	Standard
K	With prompting and support, compare and contrast the adventures and experiences of characters in familiar stories.
1	Compare and contrast the adventures and experiences of characters in stories.
2	Compare and contrast two or more versions of the same story (e.g., Cinderella stories) by different authors or from different cultures.
3	Compare and contrast the themes, settings, and plots of stories written by the same author about the same or similar characters (e.g., in books from a series).
4	Compare and contrast the treatment of similar themes and topics (e.g., opposition of good and evil) and patterns of events (e.g., the quest) in stories, myths, and traditional literature from different cultures.
5	Compare and contrast stories in the same genre (e.g., mysteries and adventure stories) on their approaches to similar themes and topics.

Note. The standards are from *Common Core State Standards for English Language Arts and Literacy in History/Social Studies, Science, and Technical Subjects* (pp. 11 and 12), by National Governors Association Center for Best Practices and Council of Chief State School Officers, 2010, Washington, DC: Authors.

Table 15.2 Common Core State Standard 9 for Reading Informational Text in Grades K–5

Grade	Standard
K	With prompting and support, identify basic similarities in and differences between two texts on the same topic (e.g., in illustrations, descriptions, or procedures).
1	Identify basic similarities in and differences between two texts on the same topic (e.g., in illustrations, descriptions, or procedures).
2	Compare and contrast the most important points presented by two texts on the same topic.
3	Compare and contrast the most important points and key details presented in two texts on the same topic.
4	Integrate information from two texts on the same topic in order to write or speak about the subject knowledgeably.
5	Integrate information from several texts on the same topic in order to write or speak about the subject knowledgeably.

Note. The standards are from *Common Core State Standards for English Language Arts and Literacy in History/Social Studies, Science, and Technical Subjects* (pp. 13 and 14), by National Governors Association Center for Best Practices and Council of Chief State School Officers, 2010, Washington, DC: Authors.

integrate information from multiple texts on the same topic to be able to write or speak about a subject. Table 15.2 features Common Core State Standard 9 for Reading Informational Text.

There are two main skill areas to teach in Reading Standard 9 by the end of fifth grade for students to be on track for middle school and the higher expectations of the Standards in grades 6–12:

1. The ability to compare and contrast texts

2. The ability to integrate information from multiple texts

What Literacy Skills and Strategies Support Reading Standard 9?

The focus of Reading Standard 9 is on comparing texts, ideas, characters, events in history, and so forth. For students to meet Reading Standard 9, we need to deliberately focus on teaching them how to compare and contrast to prove a point (argument).

For Reading Literature Standard 9, we need to give students plenty of opportunities to discuss and write about similarities (comparisons) and differences (contrasts) between characters in stories and the adventures and experiences that the characters have. For second graders to be able to identify two or more versions of the same story, we should have stories from different cultures available in the classroom. For grade 3, the standard specifically states that students should be able to compare and contrast works written by the same author on a similar topic, such as books in a series. In grade 4, students are expected to be able to compare and contrast similar themes and topics in stories, myths, and traditional literature from different cultures. In fifth grade, students compare and contrast literature in different genres, and the standards specifically mention mysteries and adventure stories as examples. Classrooms need to be flooded with high-quality literature for students to address the expectations of Reading Literature Standard 9. In Table 15.3, we list the supporting skills and strategies necessary to achieve Common Core Reading Literature Standard 9.

In grades 1–3, the focus of Reading Informational Text Standard 9 is to compare and contrast informational texts or the information found in them. To compare and contrast in informational texts, students need access to a wide variety of nonfiction materials, such as books about science or social studies topics, literary nonfiction, magazines, newspapers, and websites. In grades 4 and 5, the focus is on applying comparison skills as students obtain and integrate knowledge from informational texts to be able to write or speak about a topic to demonstrate their knowledge.

Table 15.3 Common Core State Standard 9 for Reading Literature: Supporting Skills and Strategies

Grade	Skills and Strategies
K	• Identify stories that are familiar • Recognize characters in familiar stories • Recognize adventures and experiences in familiar stories • Compare (determine similarities in) the adventures and experiences of the characters in familiar stories • Contrast (determine differences in) the adventures and experiences of the characters in familiar stories
1	• Identify the characters in a story • Recognize the adventures and experiences in a story • Compare the adventures and experiences of the characters in stories • Contrast the adventures and experiences of the characters in stories
2	• Identify two or more versions of the same story by different authors • Identify two or more versions of the same story from different cultures • Compare two or more versions of the same story by different authors • Contrast two or more versions of the same story by different authors • Compare two or more versions of the same story from different cultures • Contrast two or more versions of the same story from different cultures
3	• Identify the theme of a story • Identify the settings in a story • Identify the plot of a story • Compare the themes, settings, and plots of stories written by the same author about the same or similar characters • Contrast the themes, settings, and plots of stories written by the same author about the same or similar characters
4	• Identify themes and topics (e.g., good vs. evil) in stories, myths, or traditional literature from different cultures • Identify patterns of events (e.g., a quest) in stories, myths, or traditional literature from different cultures • Compare the treatment of similar themes, topics, and patterns of events in two or more stories, myths, and traditional literary texts from different cultures • Contrast the treatment of similar themes, topics, and patterns of events in two or more stories, myths, and traditional literary texts from different cultures
5	• Identify the main topic in a story • Identify the genre (e.g., mystery, adventure) of a story • Compare stories in the same genre on their approaches to similar themes and topics • Contrast stories in the same genre on their approaches to similar themes and topics

Table 15.4 Common Core State Standard 9 for Reading Informational Text: Supporting Skills and Strategies

Grade	Skills and Strategies
K	• Identify how two texts on the same topic are similar (e.g., illustrations, descriptions, procedures) • Identify how two texts on the same topic differ (e.g., illustrations, descriptions, procedures)
1	• Identify how two texts on the same topic are similar (e.g., illustrations, descriptions, procedures) • Identify how two texts on the same topic differ (e.g., illustrations, descriptions, procedures)
2	• Identify the most important points in a text • Compare the most important points in two texts on the same topic • Contrast the most important points in two texts on the same topic
3	• Identify the most important points in a text • Identify the key details in a text • Identify the most important points in two separate texts • Identify the key details in two separate texts • Compare the most important points and key details in two texts on the same topic • Contrast the most important points and key details in two texts on the same topic
4	• Obtain information from a text to write or speak about the subject to demonstrate knowledge • Obtain information from two texts on the same topic to write or speak about the subject to demonstrate knowledge • Integrate information from two texts on the same topic to write or speak about the subject to demonstrate knowledge
5	• Obtain information from a text to write or speak about the subject to demonstrate knowledge • Obtain information from two or more texts on the same topic to write or speak about the subject to demonstrate knowledge • Integrate information from two or more texts on the same topic to write or speak about the subject to demonstrate knowledge

Intermediate-grade students also need access to varied texts to do research from multiple texts for a writing or speaking project. Table 15.4 features supporting skills and strategies for Reading Informational Text Standard 9.

How Can We Teach Reading Standard 9 So Our Students Achieve?

In this section, we discuss the Standards tasks required of students at various grade levels. For example, the ninth College and Career Readiness Anchor Standard requires students to compare and contrast texts and integrate information from texts. We begin by describing the teaching idea, and then we discuss how it supports the Standards.

Compare and Contrast Texts

Questions Into Paragraphs (E.M. McLaughlin, 1987) is a graphic organizer that provides students with an efficient way to record topic-related ideas from multiple sources. In the organizer featured in Figure 15.1, the topic of hurricanes is explored through two sources: a textbook and a website. After students respond to each question from both sources, they write a paragraph based on their responses. Students are especially motivated to use Questions Into Paragraphs because they generate the research questions.

Integrate Information From Texts

Press Conference (M. McLaughlin, 2010) is an inquiry-based activity that promotes oral communication. This activity is based on student interest in a particular content-related topic. Students peruse newspapers, magazines, or the Internet to find articles of interest to themselves

Figure 15.1 Example of a Questions Into Paragraphs Activity

Example Texts: Tarbuck, E.J., & Lutgens, F.K. (1997). *Earth science*. Upper Saddle River, NJ: Prentice-Hall.
National Hurricane Center: www.nhc.noaa.gov

Topic: Hurricanes

Questions	Answers	
	Source A: *Earth Science* by Tarbuck & Lutgens	**Source B:** www.nhc.noaa.gov
1. What are hurricanes?	Hurricanes are whirling tropical cyclones that produce winds of at least 74 miles per hour.	A hurricane is an intense tropical weather system with a well defined circulation and *sustained* winds of 74 mph (64 knots) or higher.
2. How do hurricanes develop?	A hurricane is a heat engine that is fueled by the energy given off when huge quantities of water vapor condense.	Hurricanes are products of a tropical ocean and a warm, moist atmosphere. They are powered by heat from the sea.
3. How are hurricanes classified?	The intensity of a hurricane is determined according to the Saffir-Simpson Hurricane Scale. It ranges from category 1 (least powerful) to category 5 (most powerful).	The Saffir-Simpson Hurricane Scale is a 1 to 5 rating based on the hurricane's sustained wind speed. This scale estimates potential property damage. Category 3 and higher are considered major. Katrina was a category 3.

Hurricanes are severe tropical weather systems that are usually described as whirling cyclones having sustained winds of 74 miles per hour or more. Hurricanes are powered by heat given off when massive quantities of water vapor condense. They often develop over tropical seas. The power of hurricanes is determined according to the Saffir–Simpson Hurricane Scale. The scale estimates property damage by designating hurricanes in categories from 1 (least powerful) to 5 (most powerful). Hurricanes in category 3 or higher are considered most dangerous. Katrina is an example of a category 3 hurricane.

and their peers. When they find a topic in which they have interest, they discuss it with us. Then, they begin their research. Because the resulting Press Conference presentation lasts only a few minutes, it is the type of inquiry-based activity that each student might present once each marking period.

When preparing for Press Conference, students usually use three websites as sources. After reading the information that they have researched, focusing on its essential points, synthesizing it, raising additional questions, and reflecting on personal insights, the students share the information through an informal presentation to the class. Members of the audience then raise questions, just as if they were participating in an actual press conference. If the presenter cannot answer the question, he or she joins the questioner in researching a response and reporting back to the class.

Technology Connections

The Comparison and Contrast Guide interactive tool (grades 3–12) on ReadWriteThink's website (www.readwritethink.org/classroom-resources/student-interactives/comparison-contrast-guide-30033.html) provides a tutorial on how to compare and contrast and how to write to compare and contrast. The interactive guide explains the parts of a comparison paragraph and essay, detailing the widely accepted ways to write a comparative analysis: whole-to-whole (block), point-by-point, and similarities and differences organizational text structures. Students can use this guide to understand how to write their own comparison or to analyze how an author has compared and contrasted texts or ideas.

The Compare and Contrast Map interactive tool (grades 3–12) on ReadWriteThink's website (www.readwritethink.org/classroom-resources/student-interactives/compare-contrast-30066.html) can be used to help students generate a comparative essay or can be adapted to analyze an author's comparative writing. The interactive includes a template for students to complete, with the components of what the student is comparing organized by the student's choice of whole-to-whole (block), point-by-point, or similarities and differences organizational text structures. The finished product is a graphic organizer that students can use to write a comparative essay.

How Can We Integrate Other ELA Standards With Reading Standard 9?

When planning to teach CCR Anchor Standard 9, we can integrate several other ELA standards to design rich instructional tasks. Examples of ideas to include when creating rich instructional tasks follow.

Integrating Other ELA Standards With Reading Literature Standard 9

- Reading Literature Standard 1 focuses on reading a narrative text closely. *Example:* Encourage students to read narrative text closely to compare and contrast texts and ideas and to obtain and integrate information.

- Reading Literature Standard 2 focuses on the ability to retell a literary text and determine the author's message or theme. *Example:* Teach students to compare and contrast themes in literature.

- Reading Literature Standard 3 addresses being able to describe characters, settings, or events in a story or drama, drawing on specific details in the text. *Example:* Explicitly teach students to use specific information in a story or drama to compare and contrast characters, settings, or events in the text.

- Reading Literature Standard 4 refers to the author's choice and use of words in a literary text. *Example:* When students compare and contrast characters, settings, ideas, or literary texts, encourage them to include the author's use of language, including examples of figurative language.

- Reading Literature Standard 5 refers to terms that are germane to literary texts. *Example:* Teach students to use specific vocabulary, such as *chapter*, *scene*, and *stanza*, when discussing or writing about various literary texts.

- Reading Literature Standard 6 refers to point of view. *Example:* Explicitly teach students to compare and contrast the points of view of the characters in or the authors of literary texts.

- Reading Literature Standard 7 focuses on how the illustrations in a text or a multimedia version of a text can help establish mood, tone, and meaning. *Example:* Ask students to compare and contrast the mood or tone of illustrations when discussing or writing about literary texts.

- Writing Standard 1 lays out the expectations for writing opinions. *Example:* Following the criteria in Writing Standard 1, teach students to compare and contrast characters, settings, ideas, or texts and write their opinions about which ones they prefer, including supportive reasons and evidence.

- Writing Standard 2 lays out the expectations for informative/explanatory writing. *Example:* Following the criteria in Writing Standard 2, teach students to compare and contrast sources in an informative/explanatory paragraph.

- Speaking and Listening Standard 1 describes students' effective engagement in a range of collaborative discussions, with specific indicators to demonstrate how to participate in an effective academic conversation. *Example:* When engaged in whole-group and small-group collaborative conversations, encourage students to compare and contrast characters, settings, themes, or texts.

Integrating Other ELA Standards With Reading Informational Text Standard 9

- Reading Informational Text Standard 1 refers to closely reading an informational text. *Example:* When engaging in a close reading of an informational text, teach students to compare and contrast information in the text.

- Reading Informational Text Standard 2 focuses on the ability to summarize the main idea and supporting details of an informational text. *Example:* Teach students to compare and contrast information in a text to identify the main idea and supporting details.

- Reading Informational Text Standard 3 focuses on describing the connections and relationships among people, events, ideas, or pieces of information in a text. *Example:* When students are reading, encourage them to use information gleaned from connections and relationships to compare and contrast texts and ideas.

- Reading Informational Text Standard 4 focuses on students determining the meanings of unfamiliar words in a text. *Example:* When comparing and contrasting informational texts or integrating information from several texts, teach students to use domain-specific words and phrases found in the texts in their speaking or writing.

- Reading Informational Text Standard 7 focuses on how the illustrations in a text or a multimedia version of a text can help establish the key ideas. *Example:* Explicitly teach students to refer to the illustrations or multimedia elements when comparing and contrasting texts or integrating information from multiple texts.

- Writing Standard 1 delineates the expectations for writing opinions. *Example:* Following the criteria in Writing Standard 1, encourage students to write an opinion and include supporting ideas from the texts.

- Writing Standard 7 refers to participating in a brief shared or individual research project that builds knowledge about a topic. *Example:* When participating in a research project, encourage students to use a variety of sources to integrate information about the topic.

- Writing Standard 8 focuses on recalling information from experiences or gathering information from sources to answer questions about a topic. *Example:* Teach students to integrate information from a variety of sources, both print and digital, to answer questions and solve problems about a topic.

- Speaking and Listening Standard 1 describes students engaging effectively in a range of collaborative discussions, with specific indicators to demonstrate how to participate in an effective academic conversation. *Example:* Following the criteria outlined in Speaking and Listening Standard 1, teach students how to participate in an academic conversation about the ideas found in disciplinary texts.

- Speaking and Listening Standard 2 focuses on students understanding and discussing key details from a text read aloud or from a multimedia presentation of a text. *Example:* Teach students to be active listeners who write down key information when listening to a text read aloud or engaging in a multimedia presentation.

- Language Standard 6 is the vocabulary standard that refers to general academic and domain-specific words and phrases. *Example:* When students write or discuss ideas from an informational text, encourage them to use vocabulary specific to the concepts found in the text.

THE COMMON CORE IN ACTION

In this section, we examine one of the foundational ideas that underpins each of the Common Core's Anchor Standards for Reading. For the ninth standard, "Analyze how two or more texts address similar themes or topics in order to build knowledge or to compare the approaches the authors take" (NGA Center & CCSSO, 2010, p. 10), we have elected to share more detailed information about comparing and contrasting two or more versions of the same story by different authors or from different cultures, which is an explicit part of the Standards for grade 2.

Common Core Literacy Task: Comparing Different Versions of the Same Story

Liana is a second-grade teacher who is planning to teach lessons to meet Reading Literature Standard 9, "Compare and contrast two or more versions of the same story (e.g., Cinderella stories) by different authors or from different cultures" (NGA Center & CCSSO, 2010, p. 11). She decides to use different versions of a fairy tale to teach this standard. She knows that fairy tales are stories that have magical elements and usually have a happy ending. She also knows that fairy tales were passed down through oral tradition before being recorded in written forms, and different versions of the same tale are sometimes found in countries all over the world.

Liana decides to begin with the story of Cinderella. Liana first searches online sources to see what she can find about different versions of Cinderella on the Internet. She finds several websites that discuss fairy tales and have links to versions of Cinderella that have been written in a number of countries. To her astonishment, Liana finds that there are at least 345 versions of Cinderella that are part of different cultures. She thinks it would be interesting for her students to compare and contrast a few different versions of this story.

Liana decides that reading aloud and discussing picture book versions of Cinderella is appropriate for her second-grade students. She is careful to consider the heritage of the students in her classroom and tries to choose materials that they would find culturally relevant. She checks out the following books from the school library:

- *Cinderella* by Charles Perrault (1999)
- *Adelita: A Mexican Cinderella Story* by Tomie dePaola (2002)
- *The Golden Sandal: A Middle Eastern Cinderella Story* by Rebecca Hickox (1998)
- *Glass Slipper, Gold Sandal: A Worldwide Cinderella* by Paul Fleischman (2007)

She plans to use the first three books in lessons on comparing and contrasting different versions of the same story from different authors or from different cultures. She will then use the last book as part of her culminating activity.

To prepare to teach these lessons to meet Reading Literature Standard 9 with read-alouds of the picture books, Liana reads the books carefully, noting the language pattern, sentence structure, and the story line of each. She practices reading each story aloud with expression so she can model fluent and expressive reading, including speaking in a different voice for each character when reading the dialogue to acknowledge points of view for the characters (Reading Literature Standard 6, Reading Foundational Skills Standard 4b). Liana makes sure that she can pronounce any unfamiliar words (e.g., words from another language) correctly. She studies the illustrations and decides what she wants to emphasize as she reads the stories. She then puts sticky notes on certain pages to remind herself of concepts that might be unfamiliar to her students and to focus the discussion on the Standards.

Liana gathers the students on the carpet. First, she tells them that they are going to read several different versions of a fairy tale this week. Liana and the students discuss the meaning of *fairy tale* and talk about why people told these kinds of stories. She shares with the students that sometimes the same stories are told in different countries, but the characters and settings are written like the people of each country would tell the story to match their culture. For example, in one book that they will read, Cinderella is named Adelita, and in another, she is named Maha. Liana tells the students that they will be listening to stories from different countries that have a character like Cinderella.

As Liana reads the first book aloud, she will follow her preplanned lesson format:

1. On the carpet, engage the students in a whole-group discussion about the book, *Cinderella* by Charles Perrault. (SL.2.1)

2. During the discussion, guide the students to ask and answer such questions as who, what, where, when, why, and how to demonstrate understanding of key details in the story. (RL.2.1, SL 2.3) The students should ask and answer questions about the beginning of the story, the characters, the setting, the problem, the events, and how the problem was solved in the end. They should ask and answer questions about key details in the illustrations as well as in the text. (RL.2.7)

3. Discuss the words *beginning, setting, character, problem, event*, and *ending*. Make a list of the words on a chart and show how each pertains to the sequence in the story. (L.2.6)

4. After reading the entire book aloud, divide her students into partners. Hand out cards that have one of the following words on each: *Beginning, Setting, Characters, Problem, Events*, or *Ending*. After a few minutes to prepare, each partner should be ready to talk about their card. (RL.2.5, SL.2.4) Choose one student for each card and help them line up in the order they would appear in the story.

The next day, Liana repeats steps 1–4 with another Cinderella book, *Adelita: A Mexican Cinderella Story* by Tomie dePaola, and adds the following step. She does the same on the third day with *The Golden Sandal: A Middle Eastern Cinderella Story* by Rebecca Hickox.

5. Create a Venn diagram on a chart or the interactive whiteboard and give each student a copy of their own blank Venn diagram. Lead students in a discussion in which they compare (list similarities) and contrast (list differences) the versions of Cinderella (RL.2.9) that were read aloud so far. For example, *Adelita* takes place in Mexico, while *The Golden Sandal* takes place in the Middle East; in *Adelita*, the maid helps Adelita go to the party, whereas in *The Golden Sandal*, a red fish helps Maha.

On the fourth day, after Liana has led her students to compare and contrast at least three versions of Cinderella from different countries and cultures, she reads aloud *Glass Slipper, Gold Sandal: A Worldwide Cinderella* by Paul Fleischman. This book is a compilation of Cinderella stories from around the world. As Liana reads aloud, she stops often so students can compare and contrast Fleischman's story with the familiar story of Cinderella (Reading Literature Standard 9). Liana has also projected a map of the world on the interactive whiteboard so she can help students locate where some of the stories take place.

For a formative assessment, students write an explanatory paragraph (Writing Standard 2), comparing and contrasting two different Cinderella stories. Students can use their Venn diagrams and the list of vocabulary words on the chart generated during the week to help them plan their paragraphs. Students will follow these instructions:

1. Write an introductory sentence stating which Cinderella story you chose.
2. Write at least one sentence in which you explain how this Cinderella story is like another one (compare).
3. Write at least one sentence in which you explain how this Cinderella story is different from another one (contrast).
4. Write a concluding sentence.

To expand this lesson, Liana may show selected clips from movie versions of Disney's *Cinderella* (easily found on YouTube.com) and ask students to compare and contrast the picture book story versions of Cinderella with the movie versions.

Reading Standard 9 focuses on ensuring that students can compare and contrast texts and text elements. It requires students to compare and contrast texts, individuals, ideas, events, and concepts and integrate information from multiple texts. When students weigh the works, they are better able to decide on not only what information to use but also how to use it.

References

McLaughlin, E.M. (1987). QuIP: A writing strategy to improve comprehension of expository structure. *The Reading Teacher, 40*(7), 650–654.

McLaughlin, M. (2010). *Content area reading: Teaching and learning in an age of multiple literacies.* Boston: Allyn & Bacon.

National Governors Association Center for Best Practices & Council of Chief State School Officers. (2010). *Common Core State Standards for English language arts and literacy in history/social studies, science, and technical subjects.* Washington, DC: Authors. Retrieved August 3, 2012, from www.corestandards.org/assets/CCSSI_ELA%20 Standards.pdf

Tarbuck, E.J., & Lutgens, F.K. (1997). *Earth science.* Upper Saddle River, NJ: Prentice-Hall.

Walk, K. (1998). *How to write a comparative analysis.* Cambridge, MA: Writing Center, Harvard University. Retrieved July 17, 2012, from www.fas.harvard.edu/~wricntr/documents/CompAnalysis.html

Children's Literature Cited

dePaola, T. (2002). *Adelita: A Mexican Cinderella story.* New York: G.P. Putnam's Sons.

Fleischman, P. (2007). *Glass slipper, gold sandal: A worldwide Cinderella.* New York: Henry Holt.

Hickox, R. (1998). *The golden sandal: A Middle Eastern Cinderella story.* New York: Holiday House.

Perrault, C. (1999). *Cinderella.* Zurich, Switzerland: North-South.

CHAPTER 16

CCR Reading Anchor Standard 10: Text Complexity

Stepping Higher	**College and Career Readiness Reading Anchor Standard 10** Read and comprehend complex literary and informational texts independently and proficiently. (NGA Center & CCSSO, 2010a, p. 10)

What Does CCR Reading Standard 10 Mean?

Our students should be able to read, comprehend, and discuss complex text. College and Career Readiness (CCR) Reading Anchor Standard 10 states the expectation that students should be able to read on grade level and be able to read and comprehend complex literary narratives and informational texts by the end of high school. Students are expected to read and comprehend such texts on their own in classes across the curriculum.

Reading Anchor Standard 10 focuses on two reading skills:

1. The ability to read and comprehend complex literary texts independently and proficiently

2. The ability to read and comprehend complex informational texts independently and proficiently

Complex literary narratives have been defined as essays, short stories, and novels that display a number of characteristics: use of ambiguous language in literary devices, complex and subtle interactions among characters, challenging context-dependent vocabulary, and usually messages and or meanings that are not explicit in the text (ACT, 2006). In English and other arts and humanities classes, students will read, analyze, discuss, and write about complex essays, short stories, and novels.

Complex informational texts have been defined as materials that include a sizable amount of data, present difficult concepts that are not explicit in the text, use demanding words and phrases whose meanings must be determined from context, and are likely to include intricate explanations of processes or events (ACT, 2006). Students encounter complex informational texts in every subject area and should be able to read and comprehend such texts independently in every class.

How Do the Common Core Standards Build to CCR Anchor Standard 10?

The Common Core State Standards are designed with the expectation that students build to understanding more complex texts. For students to read and comprehend these texts, they must begin a staircase of complexity starting with the ability to read grade-appropriate complex texts by the end of first grade. Beginning in grade 2, the Standards are divided into grade bands. In the text complexity band for grades 2 and 3, second graders will need scaffolding to read and comprehend materials for these two grades, while third graders should be able to read these materials independently and proficiently by the end of grade 3. In the text complexity band for grades 4 and 5, fourth graders will need scaffolding to read and comprehend materials for these two grades, and fifth graders should be able to read these materials independently and proficiently by the end of grade 5.

Dimensions of Text Complexity

Appendix A of the CCSS (NGA Center & CCSSO, 2010b) includes a section about text complexity (pp. 2–9). It also contains a discussion of a research base that provides a rationale for increasing text complexity. Appendix A states that text complexity is based on three types of dimensions:

1. Qualitative dimensions of text complexity can only be measured by an attentive human reader and include concepts such as levels of meaning or purpose, the way the text is structured, how clear the language is, and the types of knowledge demands the text makes on the reader. The qualitative dimension refers to the kinds of background knowledge of text structure, vocabulary, and language any reader must have to be able to comprehend the text.

2. Quantitative dimensions of text complexity are typically measured by computer software and include components such as word length or frequency, sentence length, and text cohesion. The quantitative dimension refers to the measured reading level of a text. The Common Core Standards specifically mention text levels as measured by Lexiles.

3. Reader and task considerations must be evaluated by a teacher employing his or her professional judgment, experience, and knowledge of the students and the subject. Reader and task considerations refer to knowing students' abilities, experiences, interests, and possible motivation for reading a particular text before making a determination that the text is appropriate for that group of students.

All three components of determining text complexity are important in the classroom, and all three should be considered when choosing appropriate materials for a particular group of students.

Exemplar Texts

Appendix B of the CCSS (NGA Center & CCSSO, 2010c) includes exemplar texts for each text complexity band. These texts are not required, nor are they the only texts that teachers should use in the classroom. The suggested texts in Appendix B are provided so teachers can compare texts that they plan to use with the types of texts that represent appropriate complexity in the Standards. Literature for grades K–5 includes stories, poetry, chapter books, and plays. Informational text for these grades includes literary nonfiction (informational text told in a narrative way) and texts in history/social studies, science, and technical subjects (e.g., how-to texts).

Supporting Students Reading Below the Text Complexity Expectation

While there is an expectation in the Standards for students to read complex text, there is also a caveat in point 4 of the section headed "What Is Not Covered by the Standards":

> The Standards set grade-specific standards but do not define the intervention methods or materials necessary to support students who are well below or well above grade-level expectations. No set of grade-specific standards can fully reflect the great variety in abilities, needs, learning rates, and achievement levels of students in any given classroom. (NGA Center & CCSSO, 2010a, p. 6)

In the "Readers and Tasks" section of Appendix A (NGA Center & CCSSO, 2010b), three related considerations are discussed:

1. "*Students' ability to read complex text does not always develop in a linear fashion.*" This statement indicates that individual students need opportunities to read complex texts but also should be allowed "to experience the satisfaction and pleasure of easy, fluent reading." Teachers can continue to plan instruction using "particular texts that are easier than those required for a given grade band" as long as students are moving toward texts of higher levels of complexity (p. 9).

2. "*Students reading well above and well below grade-band level need additional support.*" This point focuses on the needs of students who are reading above grade level and gifted readers (see Chapter 5). It states that "students who struggle greatly to read texts within (or even below) their text complexity grade band must be given the support needed to enable them to read at a grade-appropriate level of complexity" (p. 9).

3. "*Even many students on course for college and career readiness are likely to need scaffolding as they master higher levels of text complexity.*" This point addresses the fact that most students need scaffolded instruction—the gradual release of responsibility to students—as they learn to tackle complex text. It states that "although such support is educationally necessary and desirable, instruction must move generally toward *decreasing scaffolding* and *increasing independence*" (p. 9). Students need to be taught how to comprehend texts of all types as they learn how to approach more complex texts.

When considering text complexity, we need to think about the needs of our students. Then, we need to collaborate to provide materials that are appropriate to help them build to the text complexity that ensures they can be successful in college and their future careers.

According to the Standards (NGA Center & CCSSO, 2010a, p. 5), literature should comprise 50% of instructional text at the elementary level. Students read stories, dramas, and poetry in the appropriate text complexity bands. Reading Standard 10 for Literature appears in Table 16.1.

The Standards (NGA Center & CCSSO, 2010a, p. 5) also note that informational text should comprise 50% of instructional text in grades K–5. These texts include history/social studies, science, and technical texts, such as nonfiction books, magazine articles, newspaper articles, documents, technical procedures, and webpages. Reading Informational Text Standard 10 is featured in Table 16.2.

Table 16.1 Common Core State Standard 10 for Reading Literature in Grades K–5

Grade	Standard
K	Actively engage in group reading activities with purpose and understanding.
1	With prompting and support, read prose and poetry of appropriate complexity for grade 1.
2	By the end of the year, read and comprehend literature, including stories and poetry, in the grades 2–3 text complexity band proficiently, with scaffolding as needed at the high end of the range.
3	By the end of the year, read and comprehend literature, including stories, dramas, and poetry, at the high end of the grades 2–3 text complexity band independently and proficiently.
4	By the end of the year, read and comprehend literature, including stories, dramas, and poetry, in the grades 4–5 text complexity band proficiently, with scaffolding as needed at the high end of the range.
5	By the end of the year, read and comprehend literature, including stories, dramas, and poetry, at the high end of the grades 4–5 text complexity band independently and proficiently.

Note. The standards are from *Common Core State Standards for English Language Arts and Literacy in History/Social Studies, Science, and Technical Subjects* (pp. 11 and 12), by National Governors Association Center for Best Practices and Council of Chief State School Officers, 2010, Washington, DC: Authors.

Table 16.2 Common Core State Standard 10 for Reading Informational Text in Grades K–5

Grade	Standard
K	Actively engage in group reading activities with purpose and understanding.
1	With prompting and support, read informational texts appropriately complex for grade 1.
2	By the end of the year, read and comprehend informational texts, including history/social studies, science, and technical texts, in the grades 2–3 text complexity band proficiently, with scaffolding as needed at the high end of the range.
3	By the end of the year, read and comprehend informational texts, including history/social studies, science, and technical texts, at the high end of the grades 2–3 text complexity band independently and proficiently.
4	By the end of the year, read and comprehend informational texts, including history/social studies, science, and technical texts, in the grades 4–5 text complexity band proficiently, with scaffolding as needed at the high end of the range.
5	By the end of the year, read and comprehend informational texts, including history/social studies, science, and technical texts, at the high end of the grades 4–5 text complexity band independently and proficiently.

Note. The standards are from *Common Core State Standards for English Language Arts and Literacy in History/Social Studies, Science, and Technical Subjects* (pp. 13 and 14), by National Governors Association Center for Best Practices and Council of Chief State School Officers, 2010, Washington, DC: Authors.

There are two main skill areas to teach in Reading Standard 10 by the end of fifth grade for students to be on track for middle school and the higher expectations of the Standards in grades 6–12:

1. Read and comprehend literary texts at the suggested text complexity bands

2. Read and comprehend informational texts at the suggested text complexity bands

What Literacy Skills and Strategies Support Reading Standard 10?

To read and comprehend complex literary text, all the skills and strategies from Reading Literature Standards 1–9 must be taught and integrated. Supporting skills and strategies for Reading Literature Standard 10 are broken down in Table 16.3.

Table 16.3 Common Core State Standard 10 for Reading Literature: Supporting Skills and Strategies

Grade	Skills and Strategies
K	Skills and strategies from Reading Literature Standards 1–9 with prompting and support
1	Skills and strategies from Reading Literature Standards 1–9 with prompting and support
2	Skills and strategies from Reading Literature Standards 1–9
3	Skills and strategies from Reading Literature Standards 1–9
4	Skills and strategies from Reading Literature Standards 1–9
5	Skills and strategies from Reading Literature Standards 1–9

Table 16.4 Common Core State Standard 10 for Reading Informational Text: Supporting Skills and Strategies

Grade	Skills and Strategies
K	Skills and strategies from Reading Informational Text Standards 1–9 with prompting and support
1	Skills and strategies from Reading Informational Text Standards 1–9 with prompting and support
2	Skills and strategies from Reading Informational Text Standards 1–9
3	Skills and strategies from Reading Informational Text Standards 1–9
4	Skills and strategies from Reading Informational Text Standards 1–9
5	Skills and strategies from Reading Informational Text Standards 1–9

To read and comprehend complex informational text, all the skills and strategies in Reading Informational Text Standards 1–9 must be taught and integrated. See Table 16.4 regarding the supporting skills and strategies for Reading Informational Text Standard 10.

How Can We Teach Reading Standard 10 So Our Students Achieve?

To be able to read complex literary and informational text at the recommended text complexity band, we need to teach the concepts in Standards 1–9. Students demonstrate their ability to read complex text when engaged in the type of close reading described in Reading Standard 1. Standards 1–9 all come into play when reading complex text.

How Can We Integrate Other ELA Standards With Reading Standard 10?

When planning to teach CCR Anchor Standard 10, we can integrate several other ELA standards to design rich instructional tasks. Examples of ideas to include when creating rich instructional tasks follow.

Integrating Other ELA Standards With Reading Literature Standard 10

- Reading Literature Standard 1 focuses on reading a narrative text closely. *Example:* When engaging in close reading of a complex text, invite students to ask and answer questions about key details while referring to the text to determine the central idea or theme and supporting details in the text.

- Reading Literature Standard 2 focuses on the ability to retell a literary text and determine the author's message or theme. *Example:* When students read a complex text, encourage them to infer the theme of a literary text by exploring the characters' actions, dialogue, and thoughts and feelings.

- Reading Literature Standard 3 focuses on being able to describe characters, settings, and events in a story or drama, drawing on specific details in the text. *Example:* When students read a complex literary text, encourage them to carefully describe the traits of the characters, the significance of the setting, and the manner in which the events take place.

- Reading Literature Standard 4 refers to the author's choice and use of words in a literary text. *Example:* When students read a complex literary text, invite them to discuss the author's use of particular words and phrases, including examples of figurative language.

- Reading Literature Standard 5 refers to terms that are germane to literary texts, such as *chapter*, *scene*, and stanza. *Example:* When reading a complex literary text, encourage students to refer to the structural elements of stories, dramas, and poems.

- Reading Literature Standard 6 refers to point of view. *Example:* When reading complex text, invite students to distinguish and explain an author's or character's point of view.

- Reading Literature Standard 7 focuses on how the illustrations in a complex text or a multimedia version of the text can help establish mood, tone, and meaning. *Example*: When reading a complex literary text, encourage students to carefully study and analyze illustrations in the text for clues and key details about the author's intent.

- Reading Literature Standard 9 focuses on comparing and contrasting aspects of a literary text, such as the adventures of characters, two or more versions of the same story, and similar themes and topics. *Example:* Encourage students to compare and contrast two or more complex literary texts.

- Writing Standard 1 describes the expectations for students to write an opinion about a topic or text and support their point of view with reasons and information. *Example:* When students read a complex literary text, encourage them to write and discuss their opinions about the text.

- Speaking and Listening Standard 1 describes the expectation for students to engage effectively in a range of collaborative discussions, with specific indicators to demonstrate how to participate in an effective academic conversation. *Example:* When reading complex stories, dramas, and poems, engage students in both whole-group and small-group collaborative conversations.

- Speaking and Listening Standard 2 focuses on listening to a text read aloud or a multimedia presentation of the text. *Example:* Depending on the grade level, invite students to ask and answer questions about a complex literary text, determine the main ideas and supporting details, describe the key ideas and details, paraphrase, or summarize.

- Language Standard 4 refers to determining or clarifying the meanings of unknown and multiple-meaning words and phrases. *Example:* When students read a complex literary text, ask them to determine the meanings of unknown words and phrases using context, word roots, affixes, and reference materials.

- Language Standard 5 is the vocabulary standard that refers to the descriptive use of language. *Example:* When students read a complex literary text, encourage them to analyze the way the author used descriptive adjectives, shades of word meaning, and figurative language.

Integrating Other ELA Standards With Reading Informational Text Standard 10

- Reading Informational Text Standard 1 refers to closely reading an informational text. *Example:* When engaging in close reading of a complex informational text, students need to ask and answer questions about key details, refer to the text, and draw inferences to determine the central idea and supporting details in the text.

- Reading Informational Text Standard 2 focuses on the ability to summarize the main idea and supporting details of an informational text. *Example:* When students read a complex informational text, invite them to discuss the main idea and supporting facts.

- Reading Informational Text Standard 3 focuses on describing the connections and relationships among people, events, ideas, and pieces of information in a text. *Example:* When students read a complex informational text, encourage them to use the clues about connections and relationships that they find in the text to increase their understanding of historical events, scientific ideas or concepts, or steps in a technical procedure.

- Reading Informational Text Standard 4 focuses on the use of words and phrases in an informational text. *Example:* When reading a complex informational text, ask students to identify and discuss the domain-specific words and phrases that the author uses.

- Reading Informational Text Standard 5 refers to the use of text features (e.g., headings, captions, tables of contents) and text structures (e.g., chronology, comparison, cause/effect). *Example:* When students read a complex informational text, whether in printed or digital form, teach them to use text features and structures to increase their understanding of the text.

- Reading Informational Text Standard 6 addresses point of view. *Example:* When reading a complex informational text, have students identify or analyze the author's point of view.

- Reading Informational Text Standard 7 focuses on how the images in a text or multimedia version of it can help establish the key ideas. *Example:* When reading a complex informational text, encourage students to refer to the images in the text when attempting to clarify the main idea and key details.

- Reading Informational Text Standard 8 addresses the author's reasons and evidence in informational text. *Example:* When students read a complex text in which the author has stated an opinion, teach them to determine how the author supported his or her opinion with reasons and evidence.

- Reading Informational Text Standard 9 focuses on comparing and contrasting two informational texts on the same topic or integrating information from several texts on the same topic. *Example:* Teach students to compare and contrast two complex informational texts.

- Writing Standard 1 focuses on students writing opinions and supporting their point of view with reasons and information. *Example:* As students read a complex informational text, encourage them to write and discuss their opinions about the text.

- Speaking and Listening Standard 1 describes the expectation for students to engage effectively in a range of collaborative discussions, with specific indicators to demonstrate how to participate in an effective academic conversation. *Example:* Engage students in a variety of collaborative academic conversations about complex informational texts.

- Speaking and Listening Standard 2 focuses on listening to a text read aloud or viewing a multimedia presentation of a text. *Example:* Depending on grade level, encourage students to ask and answer questions about a complex informational text, describe the key ideas and details, paraphrase, or summarize.

- Language Standard 4 refers to determining or clarifying the meanings of unknown and multiple-meaning words and phrases. *Example:* When students read a complex informational text, invite them to determine the meanings of unknown words and phrases using context, affixes, word roots, and reference materials.

- Language Standard 6 is the vocabulary standard that refers to knowledge of general academic and domain-specific words and phrases. *Example:* When students read a complex informational text, teach them specific concept words and phrases that affect their comprehension of the text.

THE COMMON CORE IN ACTION

In this section, we examine one of the foundational ideas that underpins each of the Common Core Reading Anchor Standards. For the tenth Standard, "Read and comprehend complex literary and informational texts independently and proficiently" (NGA Center & CCSSO, 2010, p. 10), we have elected to share more detailed information about the process of reading and interpreting a classic poem in grades 2 and 3.

Common Core Teaching Task: Interpreting Poetry

Anthony is a third-grade teacher who is implementing the Common Core Standards. In his classroom, he teaches comprehension lessons and conducts small guided reading groups in which students are learning to read with instructional-level texts. He periodically plans a close reading lesson in which he follows the steps for a close reading (see Chapter 7). However, Anthony also periodically plans a lesson to teach students the skills they need to be able to approach a complex text. He wants his students to be confident when they attempt to read a text that may be considered challenging.

Planning for the use of complex text in the classroom means that Anthony needs to integrate a number of ELA standards in his teaching. In fact, when students read a complex text, they are often integrating most, if not all, of the Reading Standards. He also knows that it may be necessary to scaffold instruction—gradually release responsibility to students—for some of his students reading more complex text. To do this, he plans to integrate standards found in a previous grade level. For example, asking and answering questions about unknown words in a text is a Common Core Standard for kindergarten. Third graders should already know the skill, but Anthony plans to explicitly include asking and answering questions about unknown words in this lesson.

Anthony reviews Appendix B of the Common Core State Standards (NGA Center & CCSSO, 2010c) to select a text either from the provided exemplar text list or at a corresponding level of complexity. He decides to use an exemplar text found in the CCSS for grades 2 and 3. For this lesson, he will use the poem "Afternoon on a Hill" by Edna St. Vincent Millay to teach his students how to think about a complex text. He writes the poem on a chart to post in the classroom.

Afternoon on a Hill

I will be the gladdest thing
    Under the sun!
I will touch a hundred flowers
    And not pick one.

I will look at cliffs and clouds
    With quiet eyes,
Watch the wind bow down the grass,
    And the grass rise.

And when lights begin to show
   Up from the town,
I will mark which must be mine,
   And then start down!

—Edna St. Vincent Millay

Here are the components of Anthony's lessons for this poem:

1. The students listen to Anthony expressively read the poem aloud several times. Then, he asks them to read aloud with him. (SL.2.2, SL.3.2)

2. Anthony guides his students to ask and answer questions about unknown words in the poem. (RL.K.4, RL.1.4, RL.2.1, RL.3.1)

3. The students examine the rhyme pattern by reading the poem with emphasis on the rhyming words and listen to the beats in the poem by clapping the rhythm. (RL.2.4)

4. Anthony encourages the students to ask questions about key details in the poem. (RL.2.1, RL.3.1, SL.2.1, SL.2.2, SL.3.1, SL.3.2)

5. The students choose lines or phrases of the poem and illustrate that part to visualize the meaning. They explain their artwork to the class and participate in collaborative discussions about what they think the poem means. (SL.2.1, SL.2.4, SL.3.1, SL.3.4)

By integrating a number of the ELA Standards, Anthony teaches his third graders some of the skills that they may need to approach more complex text.

Students need a great deal of instruction to be able to meet the increased demands of Reading Standard 10. Stepping higher up the staircase of text complexity means analyzing text selections for grade-level expectations and planning lessons that integrate the ELA Standards. It also means providing instruction in reading comprehension strategies so students have the competencies they need to be able to comprehend more complex text. By combining different types of reading instruction, we can ensure that our students are truly on their way to becoming college and career ready.

References

ACT. (2006). *Reading between the lines: What the ACT reveals about college readiness in reading.* Iowa City, IA: Author. Retrieved August 22, 2012, from www.act.org/research/policymakers/pdf/reading_report.pdf

National Governors Association Center for Best Practices & Council of Chief State School Officers. (2010a). *Common Core State Standards for English language arts and literacy in history/social studies, science, and technical subjects.* Washington, DC: Authors. Retrieved August 3, 2012, from www.corestandards.org/assets/CCSSI_ELA%20Standards.pdf

National Governors Association Center for Best Practices & Council of Chief State School Officers. (2010b). *Common Core State Standards for English language arts and literacy in history/social studies, science, and technical subjects: Appendix A: Research supporting key elements of the Standards and glossary of key terms.* Washington, DC: Authors. Retrieved August 3, 2012, from www.corestandards.org/assets/Appendix_A.pdf

National Governors Association Center for Best Practices & Council of Chief State School Officers. (2010c). *Common Core State Standards for English language arts and literacy in history/social studies, science, and technical subjects: Appendix B: Text exemplars and sample performance tasks.* Washington, DC: Authors. Retrieved August 3, 2012, from www.corestandards.org/assets/Appendix_B.pdf

Future Directions

As the Common Core State Standards Initiative unfolds, as teachers, we continue to engage in interpreting the Standards and developing plans that are most appropriate for our students. States are constructing systems for Standards implementation. Districts are designing professional development and district resources. Teachers and administrators are reading the Standards closely, working collaboratively with colleagues to think about the best instructional methods, skills, and strategies that will help their students meet the Standards.

Implementation of the ELA Standards requires us to think in a new way. Phrases such as "staircase of text complexity," "close reading," "text-based evidence," and "writing to sources" are becoming part of our daily speech, and we find ourselves searching for resources and texts to incorporate into our teaching. Designing student-centered lessons based on the Common Core State Standards and constructing Standards-based classrooms takes energy, dedication, and hard work. We know we are up to the task.

Amid all this Standards activity, we have come to a vital realization: We are not alone! There are thousands of teachers across the United States working to determine the best instructional methods and assessment plans for implementing the ELA Standards. As the Common Core Initiative develops, we will share successful plans for helping students meet the Standards, and we will see new teaching ideas and resources emerge. With so many dedicated professionals working together, the goal of all students being college and career ready is far more likely to become a reality.

Index

Note. Page numbers followed by *f* and *t* indicate figures and tables, respectively.